Published by Ockley Books Ltd

First published 2016

ISBN 978-1910906026

Front cover, layout & design by Michael Kinlan

Printed & bound in Scotland by:
Bell & Bain,
Glasgow,

www.bell-bain.com

PETER LEGEND

My Story by Peter Legend

with Graham Fowles

OCKLEY BOOKS
.com

PETER LEGEND

England's Peter Legend was a mainstay
of the highly regarded Wessex side
during the eighties and early nineties.
International selectors and ordinary
fans alike appreciated his classical seam
bowling skills and his hard-hitting
batting style. Twice winner of the
Wessex CC Player of the Season Award,
Peter enjoyed a highly decorated career.
After retiring from the professional
game, he turned his attention
to the world of business.
In addition to founding Legend Estate
Services – Wessex's leading chain of
independent estate agents – Peter has
also enjoyed significant success as
a property developer.

He now lives with his wife
Bethan in Casterbridge.

GRAHAM FOWLES

Graham Fowles had the fortune to meet Peter when working for an advertising agency that pitched unsuccessfully for the Legend Estate Services account. His previously published cricket writing amounts to a pair of contributions within the *Guardian*'s Over-By-Over coverage: one offering a theory of the *heavy ball*, the other in defence of Michael Vaughan's hair.

He lives in London.

LEGEND
ESTATE SERVICES

A successful business demands
strong leadership: my clients, my
customers and my staff deserve
that leadership.

AUTHOR'S NOTE

Before I started working on this book, I asked myself who'd want to read about Peter Legend after all these years? But then I thought to myself not everyone has played first-class cricket at the highest level. And not everyone can say that they were Wessex CC player of the season. Twice. And even fewer can say that they made it to the very pinnacle of the sport and represented their country. And *nobody* else can say that they saved the blushes of a nation at the Carisbrook in 1993. And so I thought to myself, this *is* a story worth telling.

When my typist first came down from London he brought with him this huge bag of books. He had everything in there from way back like your Brian Close and Dennis Amiss; he'd got the people you'd expect like Botham and Gower; and then he'd got all the recent titles like the ones from Strauss, Vaughan, Trescothick and so on. He hadn't just stuck to cricket – there was even stuff like the Tony Adams one. There were more books in that bag than I could count – I'd literally never seen so many in the same place at the same time before. And I hadn't read any of them.

He'd even got the one by Ronnie Irani, which he said was very *instructive*. I said to him, "Ronnie fucking Irani" (no offence Ronnie mate if you're reading this), "but I think what this demonstrates is that I'm going to do the talking and you're going to stick to the typing."

I'd be surprised, for example, if Kevin Pietersen's book doesn't reveal a thoroughly decent, likeable guy behind the public persona. He should be getting better advice if it doesn't. But once again, I haven't read it. If I was going to tell my story, I was going to do it my way. So I made a point of never so much as opening the cover of one of those other books. I didn't want to know how they'd gone about telling their stories, because this book was going to be about me – my story.

I'm going to go right back to the beginning, starting before I'd made a name for myself, when I was growing up as a kid in and around Whetstock. I'm going to tell you about my family and my time at school. I'm going to tell you how I developed my game at Emminster Cricket Club. And from there, how my journey took me to Canberra Park at Budmouth, and then on to the England team. But more than anything this book is going to lift the lid on what the professional game was really like in the eighties and early nineties. I'm going to tell the story warts and all, and I'm not going to be pulling any punches, especially when it comes to the way I was eventually treated by the England set-up.

Looking back, I think it's fair to say that my time in the game was one hell of a ride. Sadly, for many top sportsmen it's all over when they retire. But not me. Actually, I think it was my experience in the world of first-class professional sport that helped me to go on and become the successful businessman I am today.

I would like to thank Pitch Prose for allowing me to reproduce passages from *One Summer on the South Coast*, by Justin Bridges. Although, to be honest, I'm rather less thankful to the author for writing the book in the first place.

Just when *My Story* was about to go to press, the recent incident concerning Dougie Barrett became breaking news across Wessex. Obviously I was both shocked and saddened by the accusations. My publisher and I discussed, at some length, whether in the light of these developments we should consider revising the entire manuscript, but eventually we decided to simply add a final chapter in order to bring readers right up to date.

Hindsight affords us the luxury of amending our opinions to fit the facts as we now see them. I didn't have that luxury when I wrote the first draft, and I certainly didn't have that luxury as I lived my life. It would be dishonest to pretend otherwise. And equally, I didn't have the time to rewrite the whole book. A successful business demands strong leadership: my clients, my customers and my staff deserve that leadership.

There are too many people to thank here. You all know who you are, and you all know that you will always have a place in my heart. But I do have to give a special mention to my wife Bethan, who's been an almost permanent presence in my life for more than 30 years. And a big shout-out to the guys at Legend Estate Services, Knollsea – our latest branch. I know you guys are really offering a brilliant service out there on the east coast!

I've enjoyed writing this book. I hope you enjoy reading it. My name is Peter Legend and this is my story.

Peter Legend
Durnover Green, Casterbridge

We'd get on our bikes and
scour the local area for
cast-off sports equipment.

I. IN AND AROUND WHETSTOCK

Sometimes, when I think about my story, it seems as though it was almost inevitable. It seems as though I was always destined to become a successful professional sportsman and represent my county. After all, that's exactly what happened. And in a way, everything that had happened in my life before I stepped out onto the field for England was simply leading up to that moment. I *am* Peter Legend. I *have* played Test cricket. And I *did* save a match and a series for my country.

But other times I think about it, my story seems quite improbable. How could a lad from Whetstock possibly go on to play for England? How could he make the jump from the lower levels of league cricket to play for Wessex itself? And how could he do it without all the advantages of a professional club's development programme? And then, how could he go even further to become the first ever Wessex cricketer to play the international game? Put like that it seems unbelievable. But still, it's true.

I don't know if I've ever believed in destiny. But I did know that when I walked across that white line for England – the line that separates the coaches, the spectators and the commentators from the players – that I was joining an elite group of men. And I know now, as I knew then, that it would be the defining moment of my career. Looking back, it seems that the very course of the rest of my life would be determined by my performance in that crucible of destiny on the far side of the world; so very far away from the place of my birth in Wessex some three decades before.

I was born at 8:37pm on Friday 1st November 1963 in Casterbridge General Hospital. As a child, on my occasional trips to Casterbridge, I remember the hospital as a grime-encrusted, forbidding-looking Victorian building – an ideal setting for a horror movie. The hospital was closed at the end of the 1990s and moved to a new purpose-built site on the western side of the town centre. More recently the original hospital building has been – very successfully, in my opinion – converted into a number of one- and two-bedroom flats. The building has lost none of its imposing presence over the years, but an exterior cleaning programme has revealed an almost regal aspect to the design. At Legend Estate Services we usually have one on our books at any given time. With a great location only a short walk from the town centre and with fully fitted Neff kitchens, I think they're an ideal first-time buy for young professionals. Don't hesitate to put a call into our Casterbridge office if you're interested – we're ready to take your call until 7pm every weekday. (Except Fridays when our people head off for a well-earned pint at 6.)

My father, Jimmy Legend, used to tell this hilarious story about the night I was born. Apparently the weather was dreadful that Friday, with a gusting wind driving sheets of dense rain across Casterbridge. My father arrived at the hospital some time around 8 o'clock. Pretty much soaked to the bone, he made his way from the main entrance, where he'd parked his Mark 1 Ford Consul, to the maternity ward. He found the midwife. "Terrible night isn't it?" she said to him by way of a greeting. "You're not wrong there, love," he replied; "I've gone and lost my wallet and locked myself out of the house."

The midwife consoled him by saying, "Well at least you're here in time for the birth, Mr Legend." "Here for the birth?" he replied. "No. If you'd been listening, love, you'd have understood that I'm here to pick up some cash and a set of keys to the house."

Having found my mother's things and then grabbed what he needed, he left and drove home to Whetstock, and spent the rest of the evening in the Red Lion.

My father was what I'd call a traditional dad. Parenting has changed so much since I was born. These days I see fathers-to-be going to all the antenatal classes, attending the birth, changing the baby, rushing home from work to read bed-time stories, spending most of the weekend driving them to all those activities and generally treating the whole area of fatherhood as something like a second full-time job. Well, things were a bit different when I was born.

It's easy to forget just how much has changed over the last fifty years. Take work, for example. These days at Legend Estate Services when we get an instruction, we're around on the same day to take the photos and measure the property. (We'll get in a professional photographer if the asking price is over £500k, but otherwise we'll take a branch camera and one of those Bosch optical devices to get the measurements.) Ten minutes, and we're in and out. We'll then write the description, drop in the photos and upload it to our website. This is then linked to the property aggregators such as rightmove.co.uk and we'll also immediately Tweet our followers to say that the new property is available. We think that's just the level of exceptional service that clients should expect of us at Legend Estate Services. But three years ago we weren't using Twitter. Ten years ago we weren't working with the aggregators. Fifteen years ago we didn't have a website. And twenty years ago we didn't have a digital camera.

But fifty years ago, that's a whole lifetime away. I was born before President Kennedy was shot. I was born before the Beatles had appeared on the Ed Sullivan Show. I was born before steam trains had been replaced on the London to Budmouth line. And, perhaps more importantly, I was born long before an indoor toilet was installed at our house in Whetstock.

Whetstock is a small West Wessex village; Port Bredy is a few miles to the south and Casterbridge is a little further away to the east. It's perfect for professionals who want to avoid the bustle of the major Wessex conurbations. Whetstock has changed a little since I grew up there – the crafts village is a more recent development and now there's a second general store – but the overall character of the place remains much the same.

There isn't that much to Whetstock. When I was born, apart from the general store that doubled as a Post Office, Whetstock boasted a church, a village hall and the Red Lion. And within this traditional village, I grew up in an equally traditional family environment. We didn't have much money, so my elder brother Danny and me had to make our own entertainment. But I think this is part of the reason why we both went on to represent Wessex Cricket Club.

Like me, Dad was born in Casterbridge. His father had been a local farm labourer. Dad was bright enough to get into the local grammar school there, and he was probably the first member of our family who could read and write properly. After his national service he got a job as an encyclopaedia salesman, going door-to-door across Wessex. Some time in 1960 he knocked at Oxford Cottage, in the very heart of Whetstock. Valerie Pickles answered the door and the rest, as they say, is history. Her parents had been smallholders in the village. Valerie's mother had recently passed away, her father having died a few years earlier. She had consequently inherited Oxford Cottage, but was otherwise reliant on part-time jobs around the village and the surrounding farms for income.

Though Dad didn't make an encyclopaedia sale that day, in many ways he closed a rather bigger deal. Within six months James and Valerie were married in Whetstock church and Dad moved into Oxford Cottage. Daniel was born in as short a time-frame as was considered decent, and I arrived a couple of years after that.

While we could be thankful that Mum had inherited a house, it has to be said that it wasn't a very good one. Oxford Cottage was both small and dilapidated. It was a two-up two-down and you entered the living room straight from the street. The living room was separated from the kitchen by stairs that ran across the width of the property. There was a small yard at the back with the outside toilet in it and just enough space to hang the laundry. Upstairs were the two bedrooms; my parents had chosen the room at the back. They said it was because there was less street noise away from the road. I'm inclined to think it was Mum's way of saving Dad from the temptations of the tell-tale signs of a lock-in at the Red Lion.

I spent the first sixteen years of my life sharing a space ten feet four inches by ten feet seven inches with my brother. Every day was a battle for territory. With two single beds in the room, there was only a narrow corridor of space between them. Behind the door as you entered the room was a slightly musty sideboard that doubled as both a desk and storage. We had one wooden chair that was usually covered in discarded clothes. The spaces under the beds were rammed with various belongings. Finding anything was a nightmare. Privacy wasn't a word that meant anything to me at all. From memory, even today I could still produce an anatomically accurate drawing of Danny's adolescent cock in any conceivable state if required: normal, early morning swollen but un-tampered with, seriously tampered with, or post-tampered with. It's not that I held any particular fascination for his cock, you understand, it's just that it was a physically unavoidable part of my life in those days.

I guess that without actually ever sitting down to discuss it, we had decided that despite the initial embarrassment, it was better to just get on with the essential teenage occupation of wanking yourself raw. And it was better to do it freely, openly and with gusto, rather than timidly, furtively and badly. Whatever visual stimulation we acquired was shared as a community resource.

We didn't have a television, so our living room wasn't a particularly entertaining place to be when I was a child. There were two old sofas in there, which I'm guessing used to belong to Mum's parents. We had an old valve sideboard radio, which stood on legs. And on top of that we had a record player; one of those suitcase designs that allowed you to stack records on the spindle. The arm was automated so that it would give the records a sharp tap on the edge, making the bottom one fall down onto the platter and begin to play. This was all very well if you had some records you wanted to line up in the first place but my parents had a record collection that was composed of a few marching band recordings, a Count Basie album and a copy of *A Hard Day's Night*. When I was about seven I quite liked the Beatles. I really liked it when Count Basie's horn section would come in with those huge stabs, "Bah! Baaah!!" But nothing gave me greater pleasure than singing along to the theme from the *Dam Busters*, "Dah Dah dur dur da da Dah Dah Dah." I only got to do this when my dad was out though, because he seemed to have some sort of allergic reaction to music. All of it. He even seemed to get a bit agitated during the intro music to *The Archers*.

Dad was an accomplished league cricketer. I didn't get to see him play until I was seven or eight. Up until then he'd been competing at a pretty high standard for Emminster, but he never took either Danny or me over to the ground to watch him. He'd just arrive home on Saturday night after the game and I'd have to prepare a bowl of warm water with a drop of Fairy Liquid and a glass of white wine vinegar. And he'd sit there in the living room, reading the *Emminster News* while this curious chemical smell wafted around the room. I think for most players of my generation, the first smell you associate with cricket is linseed oil: as you rub the oil into a bat you become familiar with its deep and distinctive aromatic notes, and then the way in which the oil somehow unleashes the wood scents from within the blade. The white wine vinegar and Fairy, on the other hand, was really piercing – you experienced it directly between your eyes – and then somehow it would unleash the even less appetising scents of my father's feet.

These days, whenever Bethan prepares a salad dressing, it's invariably a vinaigrette with a good slug of white wine vinegar in it. Perhaps the aroma takes her back to happy student days sampling rustic meals in beautiful locations overlooking the Mediterranean. But for me, the smell of the stuff just triggers a vision of my painfully slow journey from the sink in the kitchen, through to the living room: I'm holding the plastic bowl, trying not to spill the contents and hoping that I've got the temperature right this time.

To be fair, when he came back from cricket, Dad's feet were always in a complete state: red, angry and blistered. It wasn't really surprising if you looked at his bowling boots. I'd guess they dated from the late fifties and the leather had gone as hard as mahogany. The uppers were as solid as a kettle, and the soles had no flex in them whatsoever. I can only assume that he thought they were his lucky boots or something like that. He'd rarely talk about the game itself, just bark out instructions from behind his paper. "More hot water. Not that much! Jesus Christ! More cold Pete. That's more like it." At the end of this weekly ritual, he'd just say, "Fetch me my shoes; I'm going over the road." By which he meant that he was going to spend the rest of the night in the Red Lion.

Dad was an all-rounder. He was a very elegant left-hand middle-order batsman, and a very accurate medium pacer who bowled left-arm over the wicket, with an ability to swing the ball back into the pads of the right-handers. Not that he ever discussed his game with me. It was just something that he did, not a starting point for conversation. You wouldn't really have known that Dad even enjoyed playing the game. He didn't get excited before a match, he never seemed to smile on the pitch, and he was never in the best of moods afterwards. Though that could have been because I rarely got the temperature of his footbath right.

Looking back I don't know why he moved to Whetstock Cricket Club when he did. At the smaller club he was quite obviously the best player on the park by some distance. Dad cut a sort of whippet-like figure on the cricket pitch. He had a slight build and was about five feet nine tall – so there wasn't that much of him at all. But whatever he did on the field, he did it well. Whenever he moved he did so with speed, precision and economy of movement. He clearly had a good eye, because when he batted he just appeared to have so much more time than anyone else. He was never flamboyant, so he'd never hold the pose after a shot. The only real give-away that he'd nailed the ball was the sound of it coming off the bat. At that level of club cricket, the sound of leather on willow is a mixture of clonks, dull thuds and the unmistakable click of an edge. When Dad drove the ball it sounded like a cross between a pistol shot and a taut snare drum.

Dad also took a hatful of wickets for Whetstock. He could swing the new ball and he could bowl cutters with the old one. But his main weapon was relentless accuracy. Many of his wickets came when players, tiring of waiting for the bad ball, would try and smear him through mid-wicket. Again, when you looked at him marking out his short run-up, it was all too easy to underestimate him. You wouldn't have said that he was an exciting bowler to watch, but he was a very effective one.

Unfortunately for the rest of us, it turned out that Dad was a rather better cricketer than he was an encyclopaedia salesman. By the time I was seven, in 1970, Dad was still driving across Wessex in a second-hand Ford selling door-to-door. His ancient Mark 1 Consul had been replaced with an ageing Zephyr – the Consul finally died climbing the hill out of Budmouth – but otherwise his career had gone precisely nowhere. He'd still head off on the Monday morning and return to the house on Friday evening. Obviously as a seven-year-old I didn't really understand the idea of commission-based selling – but I had got the sense that Dad's job could go well or it could go badly. I don't think she meant to, but Mum created a sense of anticipation on Friday evenings when he got back, so that Dad felt under pressure to tell us all how he'd done.

Dad had a limitless number of ways to avoid answering the question. "I've told you Valerie, I'm not going to discuss business in front of the boys." "Look, just let me get into some comfortable clothes." "What's for dinner, Val?" In fact, I don't ever remember him actually giving her a straight answer to the question.

Dad didn't have the whole encyclopaedia, just the index and Volume 1, which was of course the letter A. He kept them in a neat leather case, not unlike the sort of thing a GP would have travelled with at the time. Naturally Danny and me weren't supposed to touch them, but obviously we did. Not so much the index, which was a bit of a tease without the relevant volume: a bit like Jim

Bowen on *Bullseye* when he'd instruct some failed contestant to "Look at what you could have won."

So when I was really bored on a dark or wet Friday evening, and when Dad had left the case in the living room, eaten supper and gone round to the Red Lion, I'd re-read my favourite entries. I liked aircraft carriers, atom bombs and artillery. I couldn't really raise any interest in amoebas, antelopes or Albania, wherever that was. More of a challenge – at least for a seven-year-old – was turning the pages so gingerly that the volume remained in pristine condition. Prior to Mum getting her monthly magazine subscription, and apart from the *Emminster News*, there wasn't really anything else to read lying around the house.

I didn't realise it at the time, but we were basically living off Mum's wages from her job at the local shop, which was right around the corner from our house in Whetstock's main square. It was owned and run by Mr Hendricks, a former sergeant in the Royal Marines. Over the years he sorted out the odd misunderstanding in the Red Lion, so he had a bit of a reputation as the village's unofficial policeman. Even though he was really a pretty easy-going guy, with his dark hair always cropped to a grade 3 he looked just a little bit scary.

Mum took the job with Mr Hendricks when Danny joined Whetstock Primary School. Danny was only eighteen months older than me but because of the way the school years fell, he was two years ahead. When Mum started work, Mr Hendricks seemed pretty relaxed about me coming as part of the package. I remember sitting at the back of the shop leafing through return copies of *Eagle* and *Tiger*. If he thought I'd been well behaved – and I remember that more often than not he did – he'd offer me a choice of the various sweets that were stocked in jars across the shelves behind the counter.

I didn't mind sitting around in the shop, but by the time it was my turn to go to school I was champing at the bit. I was quite a big kid for my age. Apparently when I was born, at ten pounds two ounces, I held the record for the biggest delivery in the hospital for a number of years. These days, what with richer diets and the general obesity crisis, that sort of weight isn't so unusual. But back then it was. Mum told me that the midwife had said to her that we'd have to call me *The Mayor*. Personally, I would have thought that *The Champ* or *The Chief* would have been better names for the big-baby record holder, but I'm sure she had her reasons.

Regardless, when the time came for me to go to school I was one big bundle of energy. I wanted to race other kids in the playground, I wanted to play football, I wanted to join in rounders and I even wanted to join in the girls' games of netball. In fact, I didn't really think of school so much as a place of learning, but more like a sports club with some classrooms attached.

To my shame I can't remember the names of the first couple of teachers that I had at school. And I really can't remember much about what happened inside the classrooms either. It was just endlessly tracing my own name – P E T E R –, learning the alphabet and having milk delivered every morning. In the afternoons we sat in a semi-circle on the floor, listening to the teacher read from a selection of really boring stories. But this was a small price to pay for the opportunity to get outdoors and to compete with other kids. For my age I was strong, I was fast and I picked up the skills pretty quickly. And more than the other kids in the playground I had a desire to win: be it football, rounders, running, marbles or conkers.

Or British Bulldog. I loved British Bulldog. It was the first time in my life that I remember being good at something. Not just quite good, but really good. At Whetstock we played the rule that in order to be caught the Bulldogs had to prevent the runners from moving forward for a count of three. It wasn't good enough just to tag them. I didn't mind whether I was a Bulldog or a runner – either way it was all about speed, strength, manoeuvrability and tenacity. And I just loved the physical challenge – imposing your will on others. Sure, we all got hurt a bit from time to time, but it was that sense of real danger that made the game so exciting. The risk was part of the thrill. We regularly had grazed knees and elbows. I can't remember his name now, but when some kid lost a tooth a few of us ended up in front of the headmaster. And we promised solemnly to calm it down a bit. But as you'd expect, over time the intensity levels crept back up. More problematic than the cuts and bruises were the ripped clothes. Mum had to repair the knees of my trousers countless times, and I remember her going properly mental when I'd managed to get the entire arm torn off my shirt on one occasion.

I think it was when I was playing British Bulldog that I first began to notice girls. In the classroom they just tended to be children with longer hair who were more likely to have done their homework. Not particularly interesting at all. But the ones that played British Bulldog, especially those who were a few years older than me, they were a different prospect entirely. They could be absolutely ferocious and completely merciless if they caught you. But they could also be conniving and duplicitous, often feigning injury and then coming back at you like a sledgehammer. When I was out there on the Whetstock Primary playground these girls were terrifying, unknowable and yet absolutely wonderful. The toughest of the lot was a girl called Veronica, who was perhaps three years older than me. Her family had moved down from Liverpool, and to my Wessex ears just about everything she said seemed to be some form of threat. She was strong, she'd bite and scratch, and she had this sort of banshee howl that made you think twice about tackling her. I think I had a bit of a crush on her. I wanted to do things with her. Or *to* her. But I'm pretty sure she wouldn't have let me, and anyway at that age I had no idea what those things I wanted to do actually were.

Over time British Bulldog lost its appeal. When I was seven or eight, taking on kids two, three or four years older than me was a real challenge. I could get hurt and thrown around. By the time I was ten I was the biggest kid in the school (barring some huge fat child called Joseph who was excused from just about all physical activity), so it just got too easy. Football and cricket began to fill the gap.

I think it's fair to say that Danny got me into cricket. And I think I can pretty much date it to the summer of 1970. He'd have been nine and I was seven. He'd made friends with a boy in his year who lived in one of the bigger houses on the western side of the village. His family lived in a detached period property that was set back from the road with its own gravel driveway. But more importantly, his family didn't just have a television, they had a *colour* television. And it was there that Danny watched England take on the rest of the world in a series of Test matches that later turned out, according to the ICC, not to be Test matches. And which England lost comfortably. But no matter, Danny was hooked. He got me invited around to join them on one occasion. I wish I could say that watching Boycott, Greig and Illingworth line up against a side including Sobers, Pollock and Lloyd left a lasting impression on me. But that wouldn't be true. I didn't have the patience to sit through a whole session of cricket. What I do remember being struck by though was the quality of the furniture. There was a softness and a cleanliness to the sofas in that house that was quite different from anything I'd experienced before.

While I didn't have Danny's powers of concentration to sit there all day watching the game, I definitely shared his enthusiasm for having a go at it ourselves. The most obvious course of action would have been to speak to our dad, the successful local club cricketer, and ask him to sort something out for us through Whetstock Cricket Club. But Dad wasn't around during the week. On Saturday he'd be out playing the game himself. And then he'd want us to leave him well alone on the Sunday. He was absolutely clear that his Sundays were sacred: he'd get up and buy a paper, come home to a cooked breakfast, leave for the Red Lion at midday, return at two, eat a roast dinner, fall asleep for the rest of the afternoon, and finally head out to the Red Lion again for opening time at seven. So Danny and me had to improvise a bit.

Despite the obvious lack of cash in the Legend household, somehow the two of us nonetheless still managed to lay our hands on life's necessities. Like bicycles.

The family with the colour television bought a new bike for their son. And so they gave Danny his cast-off. And very shortly after that, Mr Hendricks found a discarded Raleigh bike on a rubbish dump in Emminster. He reckoned it must have been fifteen years old, but he re-sprayed it bright red in the yard behind the shop, fixed the brakes and gave it to me. I remember him arguing with Mum about it, with her saying it was too big for me. She was right of course, because I couldn't even touch the ground from the crossbar, let alone the saddle. But Mr Hendricks persuaded her that I'd be OK, and most of the time I was.

So that summer, when Danny wasn't watching the Test series that never was, we'd get on our bikes and scour the local area for cast-off sports equipment. Physically I was no longer Danny's little brother. If you could have taken Dad and miniaturised him, with his sinewy frame, sandy hair and piercing blue eyes, you'd have got Danny. But I was already as tall as Danny, I was broader in the shoulders, and I must have got my dark hair from Mum's side of the family. It meant that I wasn't the little brother slowing Danny down, so we took those bikes all around the local area, often leaving early in the morning and getting back in the late afternoon.

Mainly we went through rubbish. We remained optimistic that somebody, somewhere would be throwing out just the sort of quality kit we were looking for. Unsurprisingly, we didn't come across a size-four cricket bat in perfect condition, but we did find a golf club. It wasn't a whole golf club; the head had somehow sheared off. But it had at least sheared off fairly neatly. So we figured that the shaft would become the handle, while the extra width provided by the grip would become the blade of our 'bat'. A handy tip-off from another of Danny's friends led us to a supply of golf balls. Some guys used a long field just to the north of Emminster as a makeshift driving range, but inevitably they didn't retrieve everything that they'd hit. So with keen eyesight and time on our side, we scoured the hedges and deeper patches of grass around the top of the field until we'd got maybe six or seven balls.

Back at Whetstock we quickly discovered that playing cricket with a golf ball on the school playing field didn't really work; the ball tended to just stick in the ground rather than bounce. It was a little bit better when we tried using the actual square at Whetstock CC, but not much. And that's when we hit upon the idea of using one of the pathways in the churchyard. We picked the path that ran up the western end of the church. We'd bowl from the southern end of the path, with the church itself to the right of the bowler. We developed a scoring system that entailed scoring fours or sixes in pretty much the usual fashion, with the churchyard perimeter and the church itself forming the boundaries. The gravestones acted as fielders. Hit them on the full and you were out caught.

The closest boundary was the church itself, but it was protected by the densest concentration of gravestones. So Danny, as a left-hander like Dad, had the toughest challenge to thread the ball along the ground to the cover boundary.

It soon became clear that I was the better bowler and that Danny was the better batsman. It's actually pretty hard to hit a golf ball using the grip of a golf club as your bat. But Danny started being able to do it pretty regularly quite quickly. His stance was pretty good right from the off, and he played with a remarkably straight bat. But as the summer wore on, the better he batted, the faster I bowled. At first I was just pleased if the ball got to the other end on the single bounce. But by watching a bit more cricket on the TV, and by bowling every day at Danny, I got to fashion a pretty good bowling action of sorts.

And that's how we whiled away the hours that summer: bowling and batting in the churchyard. I think I can also trace my aggressive batting style back to those days. As a right-hander the most effective scoring shot – because of its proximity – was a six onto the wall of the church itself. That shot remained a key part of my scoring repertoire all the way through my professional career.

In the spring of 1971 Dad intervened to make Danny and me even better. But not in a way that any of us could have anticipated. It must have been a Saturday morning and we were sitting in the living room when Dad came in from the yard.

"I've blocked the toilet. You'll need to sort it before your mother gets back."

And then he picked up his coat and left. I don't think parents today would handle the situation quite like that. Not least because there's a very real danger that in leaving a turd the size of an elongated thermos flask in the toilet and telling your kids to sort it out, they're more likely to Tweet it to the world than actually consider how to shift the thing. But the 1970s were more deferential times, so we considered it our duty to somehow get this record-breaking piece of shit around the u-bend. Given that Dad really was quite a slight man I had to concede that, biologically at least, it was an impressive achievement.

Once we'd got over the shock of the size and the pungency of the thing, we set to work. It wasn't just that the log itself was huge, but that it was also cushioned by a fair amount of toilet roll, mainly below the water line. It almost looked as though it had been carefully packed for transit somewhere. Initially we were hoping that simply with repeated flushing we'd edge the thing down the toilet. We were wrong. After half a dozen or so attempts all we'd managed to achieve was to block the water flow completely, so that we were in danger of overflowing the bowl.

We realised that we were somehow going to have to break the thing in half, to stand any chance of getting it down the toilet.

After a few minutes of silence I said, "We're going to have to use the bat."

"No way. We're not using that." Danny was already developing that batsman's thing where they get really fastidious about their kit. "Well I can't think of anything else. Unless you're prepared to break it with your hands." Danny reluctantly recognised the lesser of two evils and I went upstairs to our room to get the bat. By the time I returned, the water level in the pan had subsided to about the normal level. Danny just looked at me and said, "You do it." Then, holding the grip end of the golf club in my right hand, while standing as far from the toilet as was practical, I used the shaft to cut and break through the turd somewhere beneath the waterline.

The first couple of flushes didn't seem to do anything at all. I think we were both wondering if all we'd managed to achieve was an even bigger mess, while compressing some of our father's shit up the shaft of the golf club. But on the next flush, even though the pan was still threatening to overflow, a decent chunk of it disappeared. And after three or four more flushes we'd got everything back to normal.

Later that afternoon we tied a length of string to the grip end of the club and submersed it in a local stream for hours. But Danny never picked it up by the shaft end ever again. In fact he'd only ever hold it in one hand – his right – at the top of the grip, furthest from the end where the shit had entered the shaft. I thought he was being unnecessarily squeamish about the whole thing, but it did lead him to becoming one hell of a batsman.

When we next went back to the churchyard he just played with his top hand. Now, with only the narrow shaft of the club with which to hit the ball, he had to absolutely middle it to either get any power on the shot, or to have any control over his placement. It was as though he was using a wand: he saw the ball so well and so early, and he generated this whip-like, accurate bat-speed with his wrist. I had to admit to myself that he was freakishly talented. And I also had to admit to myself that I'd never be as good as Danny with the bat.

We'd occasionally get a better sense of how well we were progressing when a couple of the other boys from the village would join us. Invariably they couldn't lay the bat on my bowling at all. There was a bit of a scene around our house one evening when the mother of one of them came around to complain about the bruises on her son's upper body. It was really awkward when she made him take his shirt off at our door to show Mum. To be fair he did look like a piece of Swiss cheese. I was stood there behind Mum with this confusion of conflicting emotions: dread (I was clearly in for one hell of a bollocking), embarrassment (for me and the other kid) and pride (because I'd absolutely peppered him).

"Is it true Peter, did you do this?"

"Err, suppose so."

"But why, Peter?"

"It's just part of the game, Mum."

"Part of the game? I don't think so. Danny, you just stood there and let this happen?"

"Well, yes and no, Mum."

"Yes and no? What's that supposed to mean? You're as bad as he is. Right, I'm confiscating the bat and ball."

"It's not *actually* a bat Mum."

"Don't get smart with me Danny. Both of you, get back inside . . . Now Mrs Kirby, I am *so* sorry."

Mum didn't allow us out of the house after school for the rest of that week, and she said she was banning us from playing cricket in the churchyard ever again. But the following Monday night Mr Hendricks sorted it all out – I don't know whether it was his idea or whether Mum had asked him to come over. He just gave us this calm lecture about not picking on kids who weren't able to defend themselves; and that by bowling short at a kid who couldn't bat, that was exactly what I'd been doing. And then he asked me if I wanted to get a reputation as a bully, and obviously I said that I didn't. So, after we'd had to apologise again to everyone, including the kid *and* his mother, we were allowed to get back to work in the churchyard.

When we returned to school that September all seemed to be well in the world. My year had moved up to Miss Hutton's class – she was the first teacher I had whose name I can remember. She was brilliant because she'd do stuff like get us to recreate famous military engagements in the playground. And she'd make maths relevant: "If Leeds score three goals a game at home, but only two goals a game away from home, how many goals will they have at the end of the season?" That was my idea of a good teacher. I also remember thinking that she was really, really hot.

But back at home things took a turn for the worse. One Friday, when the evenings were drawing in, Danny and me were stuck in the house. Dad arrived home as usual. Nothing seemed out of the ordinary at first, but then Mum asked him how his sales had gone. And he said the usual stuff about not talking money in front of us boys. I can't exactly remember how it escalated, but I think Mum said something like, "It never goes very well, Jimmy, does it?" And then Dad started shouting something like, "Don't question me, Valerie. Don't you dare question me."

They told Danny and me to go upstairs, and then it really kicked off. I can't remember who shouted what exactly, but some of the phrases have stayed with me. "Pathetic loser." "Ruined my life." "You've brought shame on this house."

"Shame. You want to talk about shame?" And then, "Don't bring Peter into this." For a brief instant I felt guilty about the incident with the child in the village and having to make that very public apology. I clearly hadn't made the situation any better.

The row finished when I heard Dad shout, "and you can throw this shit out", followed by a loud crash and then the front door slamming shut. After we'd given it five minutes or so, when we were pretty confident that Dad was in the Red Lion and not coming back for a while, we crept downstairs. Mum was just sitting on the couch staring into space. Danny and me started slowly picking up Mum's magazines that Dad had evidently kicked across the living-room floor. Then she gave both of us a hug and said to me, "It's not your fault Peter." Though in all honesty, I really didn't think it was. Sure, I'd got a bit carried away with my bowling, but I'd had my dressing down for that and I'd apologised: couldn't we all just move on? And what it had to do with Dad being rubbish at encyclopaedia sales, I couldn't fathom.

We were dreading it when Dad came back from the Red Lion. Danny and me were both lying awake in our beds expecting it all to start over again. But it didn't. We heard Dad come in very quietly, and we heard some murmured words through the bedroom wall when he came upstairs. But we couldn't hear what was said. And the following morning it was like nothing had happened. Everything was back to normal and Danny and me went off down to the school playing fields to knock around a football with some of the other lads in the village.

I'll never know if it had anything to do with the row that night, but the weeks that followed contained some of the most excruciatingly embarrassing moments, and some of the most desperately boring evenings, of my life. It transpired that Mum had been spending her Wednesday and Saturday afternoons with the elders from the local Jehovah's Witness group in Emminster. And the magazines that had so vexed Dad were her collection of *The Watchtower* and *Awake!* titles. Previously neither Danny nor me had really paid them any attention at all. In the weeks that followed the row, Mum had first tried getting us to read some of the science articles aimed at children in *Awake!* They didn't seem particularly unusual. The illustrations didn't look so different from those in any school text-book, and the frequent references to God didn't strike us as out of the ordinary either. After all, we had prayers in assembly every day before classes began, so even though the Almighty hadn't revealed himself to me personally, I didn't doubt his existence.

But things did get a whole lot more unusual and extraordinary when Mum told us we'd be going door-to-door with her around Whetstock spreading the word of God. We tried to dream up every excuse we could think of: invitations to friends' houses, after-school clubs, football games in the car park of the village hall, but Mum was having none of it. She'd usher us up to the door of a house in the village and then, standing behind us, whisper strict instructions about being on our best behaviour. If Danny and me were praying for anything, we were praying that nobody was in.

Initially I felt humiliated, both for Mum and for us boys, when people would turn us away or simply ask us to leave. But I soon realised that a brief period of humiliation paled in comparison to the utter tedium that would follow if we were actually invited into someone's home. Every conversation started in the same way. "My name is Valerie Legend, and these are my boys Daniel and Peter." That was our cue to smile. Then she'd say, "Have you ever wondered why there's so much trouble in the world today?" And if she got any sort of agreement from the householder, her next line would be, "I've just been reading this interesting article which tells us how we can make the world a better place. I'd love to come in and discuss it with you."

And what with the Cold War, decimalisation, the nationalisation of Rolls Royce and the launch of the Morris Marina, there was no shortage of trouble in the world. Fortunately, she only really had any success with old people. Perhaps once a week she'd manage to get us into a home even more dispiriting than our own. And stinking of stale piss and cabbage. And then Danny and me had to sit there for what seemed like hours while Mum talked to frail couples, widows or widowers about politics, loneliness, and the evil that people were capable of inflicting on each other. We'd drink lukewarm cups of oily tea from filthy, stained crockery, and sit there waiting for the ordeal to end.

The most embarrassing night I experienced happened when we knocked at the door of a small cottage at the bottom of the village.

"Hello Mrs Legend. Good evening Danny. Good evening Peter."

"Good evening Miss Hutton," Danny and me replied together. Of all the doors, in all the streets of the whole village, we had to knock on this one. I just wanted to die. Mum was about to start her usual patter, but Miss Hutton got in first.

"Is that *The Watchtower* you've got there, Mrs Legend?" And before Mum could really answer, Miss Hutton went on, "Well you know we're Church of England at Whetstock Primary, so I've got to keep up appearances, but thanks for thinking of me."

And as she was saying, "Goodnight boys, and I'll see you in class tomorrow, Peter", a tall man came up to the door behind her to see what was going on, and he casually rested his arm around her waist as we turned back towards the street. The humiliation was complete. She'd not only refused – however gracefully – Mum's offer of a free magazine subscription, but it was also crystal clear that she wasn't going to become my girlfriend either.

The torture ended some time in the New Year. The whole thing stopped as abruptly as it had started. I don't know whether it was the cold, the fact that we'd run out of houses in Whetstock to knock on, or that Mum had had enough herself. By this time I was doing a small morning paper round for Mr Hendricks, and shortly after Mum had stopped taking us door-to-door he asked me if things had improved at home. He really didn't have to, but sometimes I got the impression that he was always looking out for me. Years later Danny and me found ourselves talking about it and I said that I couldn't understand why she wanted to embarrass us like that. And then Danny came out with something really weird that I remember. He said, "It wasn't us she was trying to embarrass, it was Dad." I didn't get that at all.

The end of the 1972 summer marked the end of an era for me. It was the last time we played cricket in the churchyard with our makeshift equipment, because when the new term started in September, Danny joined the secondary school over in Emminster. Over at Emminster Secondary they had a cricket pitch, teachers who played and coached the game, real bats, balls and pads, and a team at every age range from eleven upwards. So when Danny started re-writing the record books for batting at Emminster, winning proper matches and training in the evenings, I was stuck back in Whetstock.

I consoled myself by becoming captain of the Whetstock school football team, and I scored a hatful of goals from centre forward, but like British Bulldog in the years before, it had got too easy. I was ready for my next challenge.

He sounded like a real man,
and he sounded furious and
unapologetic.

2. DOUGIE COMES TO EMMINSTER

I first took the school bus from Whetstock to Emminster Secondary in September 1974. And I left seven years later in a canary yellow Mark 1 Escort Sport. Academically, I'll hold my hand up and admit it wasn't a triumph. I think that my success in the world of business has proved that I'm no fool, but three O-levels, CSEs in metalwork and woodwork, and an A-level in General Studies wasn't a great return on seven years of study. But that said, nobody in the last thirty years has asked to see even one of those certificates, so I don't know if having a few more of them in storage somewhere would have made much difference to my life.

The summer of 1974 seemed to go on forever. Danny was now spending most of his time with new friends over in Emminster. I was bored so I didn't even mind going with Mum down to Port Bredy to get my first school uniform. Mr Hendricks offered to drive us. Getting a lift with him was always pretty cool because he had an old Series 2 short wheelbase Land Rover. I remember it was a warm day in August, so I sat in the back of the vehicle with the canvas down.

It took a little while to settle into the new place. The school itself was so much bigger than Whetstock – it had two full-sized football pitches, a decent cricket pitch, a gym, science labs, a metalwork department with lathes and a forge, and apparently there was even a drama studio in there somewhere. And just as the surroundings were new, so were the kids themselves. The school playground isn't that different from the professional sports dressing room, so people are always jockeying for position and sizing themselves up against the others. Before the sports trials had been held for the different school teams everyone was a bit of an unknown quantity. Kids would think that the toughest kid, the fastest kid or the best footballer from their previous school would be the best at Emminster too. But of course it rarely worked out like that.

When I was at Emminster, the kids on free school lunches joined a different queue from the others, so it was pretty easy to see those of us who came from poorer families. I'd long since worked out that us Legends had less money than most other people, but it had never occurred to me that kids would think less of us for it. But David Channing did. He was in the year above me and he had this little posse of three other boys who followed him around. He'd obviously decided to force a confrontation to check me out. So he came up to me and said something like, "You're pretty big for a free-loader." I was confused; I'd never heard the word before.

"A what?"

"A free-loader. If your parents can't afford to feed you, they shouldn't have had you."

To be honest, like most eleven-year-olds, I hadn't given any thought to the rights and wrongs of the free-school-meals policy. So I was a bit confused, but mainly I was angry. I thought that the best thing to do was ignore them. So I just remained in the queue staring determinedly straight ahead. Which is why I didn't notice that two of his little gang had come around from behind me and grabbed my arms. I then saw Channing coming straight at me with a marker pen, saying, "You need an 'F' on your shirt, big guy, so everybody knows you're a free-loader."

I think that when you play physical sports you develop an instinctive sense of how you measure up against someone else. Sure, you can be wrong, if they're an expert in Taekwondo or something like that, but most of the time you know if you can dominate them or not. And looking at Channing I didn't see much to back up the attitude at all. More importantly, getting one of my new school shirts ruined in my second week simply wasn't an option; Mum had only bought two of them. I didn't have time to shake my arms free, so I had no option left to me other than to bring my forehead down crisply onto the bridge of his nose.

I think I probably saved myself from numerous playground fights with that one movement. My timing was perfect, and being a little taller than him, I gained decent momentum, with the contact point just beneath the level of his eyes. Initially I thought I'd failed because I didn't feel a thing, but the shock of the impact had certainly stopped Channing in his tracks, and then almost in slow motion a sort of horizontal hairline fracture of the skin opened to a red line, and then the blood started flowing down both sides of his face. I shook off the two holding me, grabbed Channing by the neck and held him against the wall; largely because I was now more concerned about getting my shirt covered in his blood.

Later, I was marched off to the first of my many meetings with Mr Harding, the headmaster, while Channing was spitting after me, "I'll fucking get you; you're fucking dead you are." Harding sent me to a detention that evening. But nobody ever picked on me again. And that included David Channing.

They say that the stuff that doesn't kill you makes you stronger, and I think there's something in that. That day I didn't back away from the confrontation; I met it head on (quite literally in this case) and I won. I was in a position where I had to impose my will on David Channing or be humiliated myself. And at the end of the day, it's that do-or-die attitude which separates the winners from the losers in professional sport: you can have all the talent you like, but ultimately it comes down to the will to win, the desire to make your opponent submit to you. And it doesn't matter whether your sport uses bats, balls, clubs, racquets or your bare hands, it's all about physically imposing your will on your opponent. So when I looked into Channing's eyes, full of shock, fear and resentment, I'm not ashamed to admit that I felt good. Very good. It was a bonus that I was in the right – he and his mates picked on me, I didn't start it – but if I'm truly honest that didn't really matter. After all, a win is a win. And ultimately this would prove to be the difference between Danny and me – Danny with his unbelievable natural skills and all his artistry, and me who was simply driven by the desire to win.

I had to wait until the summer term for cricket. I was actually nervous about turning up for training. Danny was already the school's golden boy of the sport: he was only in the third year but he was playing in the school's first team. As his younger brother I thought there might be some level of expectation about me. And then, looking at the pitch, the nets, the batting gear in kit bags and the leather stitched balls, I was aware that I'd only watched the game on television, and that I'd only bowled with a golf ball at someone trying to bat with the shaft of a broken club.

Anxiously, I queued up in the first session to bowl a real cricket ball, down a full-length wicket, in an outside net. There was no batsman, just a set of stumps to aim at, and Mr Clements standing up to them with a pair of keeper's gloves on. I think there were about ten of us bowling in that first lunch-time session. I took some confidence from the selection of utter filth that was being sent down that day. There were kids trying to bowl leg-breaks when they didn't have the strength to get the ball down the length of the cut-strip, there were others taking twenty-yard run-ups to deliver off the wrong foot, and then there were various round-arm actions and chuckers. The stumps led a charmed life. Clements had the patience of a saint that day.

I just tried to keep things as simple as possible. I took a few paces of a run-up and just looked to bowl straight down the pitch. My first delivery was a long-hop – I just hadn't factored in quite how long a real pitch is. My second was a better-length delivery outside off-stump that went straight into Mr Clements' gloves. And the third hit the top of off. At this point, Mr Clements called down the net, "Your name please, bowler?" I replied, "Legend, sir," and he simply said, "Well, let's have some more of that please, Legend."

In the subsequent weeks those of us who had some potential were given the opportunity to take part in after-school practice sessions, with a view to playing a handful of age-grade fixtures before breaking up for the summer holidays. Mr Clements encouraged me to bowl quickly, he showed me how to hold the ball properly and he emphasised the importance of getting the run-up right. By the time our fixtures came round I was established as an opening bowler and number seven batsman. I think I probably got a bit carried away with the pace I was generating – at least compared to the other bowlers in my school side – but I loved to see batsmen weaving, ducking and backing away at the other end. I took a hatful of wickets, but I also began to be aware that there was a big difference between bullying out the lads who were scared of the ball, and the more sophisticated skills required to dismiss decent batsmen. Like Danny before me, I was able to join the colts set-up at Emminster CC, so I got to spend the rest of the summer playing regularly.

In the first week back at school, at the beginning of my second year at Emminster, my world changed completely. I was sat with the rest of my class waiting for the teacher to show up. My desk was in the back row. I hadn't paid any attention to the new kid who was sat beside me. He looked small, and he had a sort of weaselly face and jet-black hair. He looked pale and almost malnourished. He wasn't going to be challenging for a place in the rugby team any time soon.

And then with no introduction he just said, "Wot sorta music yinto?"

"Errrr . . . I don't know." He'd taken me by surprise and I was struggling to work out what he was actually saying.

"Fack sake. It ain't an hard question. Must be inner sumfin."

"OK. Right. I like "Seasons in the Sun.""

"Shit."

"The Bay City Rollers? They're good."

"Fackin shit."

"And David Essex. I like him."

"Ee's shit too. But at least ee's a fackin Ammer."

No other kid in school had ever spoken to me like this. He was about half my size but somehow seemed much older. There was a confidence about him. I was intrigued.

"So what should I like?"

"The Who. Fackin awesome band. Saw em last year. They're the bollocks. And Zep."

"Zep?"

"Fack me. Led Z-E-P-E-R-L-I-N? Ain't you people got a stereo daan ere?"

And that's how I met Douglas Terrence Barrett. My best friend, my agent and life-long business associate.

It turned out that Dougie was also entitled to free meals at the school, so we used to go to lunch together and he'd ask me the occasional question about Emminster or Whetstock, but mostly he'd tell me about growing up in East London. His local football club was West Ham, and he'd been to watch a few games with his dad, so he'd actually seen Bobby Moore play. Back in the early seventies they could get as many as 40,000 people into Upton Park for the big games. That would be more than ten times the entire population of Emminster and Whetstock combined. Absolutely mind-boggling.

I really wanted Dougie to tell me about Moore, Trevor Brooking and Billy Bonds, but he was actually far more interested in music. He hadn't only gone to The Who's big outdoor show at Charlton, he'd also seen Led Zeppelin play Earl's Court that summer before his family moved down to Wessex.

"Fackin mind blowin, Zep. Now, where d'you go ferra smoke usually?"

At the time I didn't go anywhere for a smoke, because at that age I hadn't yet tried cigarettes. But I did know that the kids who smoked went to the small copse at the southern end of the school playing fields. Standing underneath the trees you were sheltered from the weather and the prying eyes of teachers and locals alike. So, while Dougie told me about the big world beyond the Wessex borders, I developed a taste for his Players Number 6.

Later that September, with the weather still holding, Dougie invited me to go around to his house on the Saturday afternoon. They were going to barbeque some meat (which suggested to me that their house must have a bit more outside space than Oxford Cottage), and I was going to hear some Who and Led Zep. "We gotta start yer musical heducation somewhere."

So that Saturday I got on my bike and headed off towards Emminster. I'm not sure what sort of place I was expecting, but following his directions I found myself cycling into a close of recently constructed bungalows. I cautiously knocked at the number Dougie had given me, and sure enough he appeared at the door. I was initially struck by the aroma of fragrant cleaning products; everything smelled new and fresh, at least in a chemical kind of a way. Dougie led me into a hallway, where he told me to take my shoes off, and then we went through into the living room.

Suddenly I understood what the words *living* and *room* actually meant. What we called the living room in Oxford Cottage was simply the ground floor space that wasn't the kitchen. It wasn't just that the Barrett's living room was twice the size, it was the fact that it was clearly designed to entice you in, make you comfortable and then entertain you. There was a leather three-piece sofa so luxurious you could sleep on it, the television was the size of the model they had at school for showing nature films, and the hi-fi looked like it had come from another planet. The record collection covered an entire wall. This truly was a room you could *live* in.

"Tell ya wot. I'm gerna stick on sumfin more than decent. And get in a quick faag before the old man gets back." And with that he rifled through a number of records and pulled out one with a picture of four men standing in front of a large concrete block. He briskly, but surprisingly delicately, removed the record from the sleeve, spun it over as it rested gently between his palms, and placed it on the record player. Then he expertly lifted the arm of the player and lowered it gingerly, but accurately, onto the beginning of the record. He then bent down and adjusted the volume dial in a separate unit, and I became aware of a whispering audible crackle coming from the sizeable speakers positioned on stands in the corners of the room.

If the equipment itself was a far cry from our little all-in-one record player back at home, what I was about to hear didn't sound much like "The Dam Busters March" either. It started with these pulsing staccato, almost clipped, synthesizer notes. And then flurries of notes began appearing above and below, like there was a hyperactive mouse dashing around the keyboard. And then, out of the left-hand speaker, came these crashing chords – simple but really powerful. I was thinking at this point it was getting a bit loud and someone would probably come around and complain, and that's when the drums came in. They weren't like the little tappy drums that I'd heard on our record player or on a transistor radio. They were like fucking cannons – huge, meaty and powerful. By the time the singer came in I could hear the glass in the windowpane creaking behind me.

He didn't sound apologetic or disappointed like Terry Jacks with his "Seasons in the Sun" either: he sounded like a real man, and he sounded furious and unapologetic. I was thrilled by the effect it had on me – with this system you weren't just listening to the song, your whole body was experiencing it. The bass pounded at you, and those parts where it broke down into quiet moments, before threatening to explode again, were exhilarating. I wanted a decent hi-fi of my own.

Dougie reappeared and said, "Right, me old man's back with Mum." He then whisked the needle off the record before the next track rocked the foundations. "Come and say hello," he instructed.

Standing behind Dougie at the front door, I could see a couple preparing to get out of a new, dark blue Rover P6. It had the tell-tale distinctive V8 badge on the grille. I don't know what I was actually expecting, but Syd and Cyn – or more formally Mr and Mrs Barrett – certainly confounded those expectations. Syd was wearing a black lightweight leather jacket, which was open, revealing a Pink Floyd tour t-shirt, which itself was straining around his generously proportioned midriff. He was no taller than me, so he couldn't have been more than about five foot four, his hair was receding at the sides of his head, and what remained of it had been greased back.

Cyn wobbled from the passenger door dressed head to toe in red, looking like a post box with sex appeal. She was wearing a leather jacket that was zipped up right to its huge pointy collar, and a pair of flares. She had an explosion of shoulder-length blonde hair, which never moved when she did. I was expecting Dougie to make some introductions, but Cyn got in first. "You dint say he waz a looka, did yer Dougie? Ooooh eees a looka, int ee Syd? Gonna ave to watch me wiv this one, Syd. Haa ha ha ha ha haaa."

I felt a bit awkward and thought I should probably explain to Mr Barrett that there was nothing going on between me and his wife, but I simply said, "I'm Peter Legend, I'm pleased to meet you both."

"Oooh you are an ansum fella. Let's take the stuff in."

So we all carried an enormous amount of food from the boot of the car to the kitchen and the utility room (that was another first for me – a utility room). There were huge quantities of crisps, fizzy drinks, beers, wines, ice creams, sausages, cuts of meat and so on. When I left several hours later in the early evening I could hardly walk – I was absolutely stuffed. When I finally got home I walked into Oxford Cottage and for the first time thought, "Bloody hell, this place is shit."

Syd was the Wessex circulation rep for a newspaper group. His job was to increase sales by ensuring that the right numbers of papers were being delivered to the right newsagents across the region, and that the newspapers were prominently displayed in the shops. Over time I learned that sales could be increased by either selling more copies or by disappearing the unsold ones so they weren't counted as returns. Syd seemed to be pretty accomplished at both tasks.

Syd also earned his *bunce*. This called for more creativity. So he might delay a price increase to a wholesaler for a year in exchange for a small personal cash payment. He might suggest to the independent newsagent outside Casterbridge station that a few cartons of cigarettes every month might guarantee timely delivery of the morning papers. He might help retailers swap their stock holding among each other – all for a small fee. He could also source quantities of duty-free cigarettes from the docks at Budmouth. The Barretts introduced me to a world where smart people with a bit of nous could get ahead. I'm not sure that everything Syd was up to was strictly above board, but nobody was getting hurt.

One thing that puzzled me though, after I'd been around to Dougie's place a few times, was how come he was in the free-meals queue with me at school? He lived in a new house, with a new car, a brilliant hi-fi and all the Golden Wonder crisps you could eat. Their version of economising was using the SodaStream rather than opening a new bottle of Coke. So one day, during one of those free school meals, I just asked him, straight out.

"As me old man says, it san illushan, Pete. It ain't real."

Over the years that followed I was able to piece it all together. Basically Syd was a contractor for the publisher, so when they'd left London to come down to Wessex he'd set himself up as an independent company. That meant the car and the property were legitimate business expenses. And of course, the *bunce* was all made in cash off the books. So, officially at least, the Barretts were scraping by on barely more than a subsistence level of income. But I liked it round at the Barrett's house.

And just as my social life was improving so was my cricket. By the following year I was noticeably stronger – although I may have been carrying the odd excess pound or two thanks to Mrs Barrett's generosity with the crisps, Coke and ice cream – but by then I was pretty close to having a full adult physique. That, combined with regular net sessions at both the school and Emminster CC, ensured that my overall game was getting better and better. Mr Clements asked me if I wanted to become a net bowler for the school's first team – an opportunity I jumped at. Testing myself against players who were a few years older could only make me a better player. I didn't yet have the pace to force decent seventeen- or eighteen-year-old batsmen back, so I had no choice but to focus on line and length. All the coaching I was getting at the colts with Emminster CC was based around developing an out-swinger to the right-handed batsman: getting the wrist and seam positions right. So I got a real buzz from getting those older players to nick-off in the nets. I knew I was making real progress.

I don't know how many wickets I took for my school-year side that season, but it was a lot. Word would get around the opposition school teams that we had a quick bowler and three or four of them would almost be ready to surrender their wickets before we'd even started. It was great fun though; watching them jump, duck, back away and wince before bowling them out. But I think I might have developed more quickly as a bowler if I hadn't played for my year side at school at all. When I went back into the first-team nets or into games for Emminster Colts (where we played a far higher calibre of opposition), I had to re-educate myself. I couldn't expect to just blast decent players out.

That summer I'd cycle over to Dougie's to watch the West Indies' fast bowlers torment the English batsmen on the big screen, in full colour, to a classic rock soundtrack. Dougie passed the time between his cigarette breaks trying to find the best music to accompany the on-field action. I think his most successful combination was timing the introduction of Black Sabbath's "Paranoid" to Michael Holding's run-up, so that he ran in to the sound of the guitar riff, and then the drums coincided with his delivery stride. Trying to drop the needle in exactly the right place at exactly the right time proved almost impossible. But it gave Dougie something to do. He wasn't that into cricket, to be honest.

I'd started smoking a bit, but nowhere near as much as Dougie, so I'd often spend time in their kitchen talking to Mrs Barrett while Dougie was pretending to get something from the shops or claiming to be looking for something in the garage. She must have known he was smoking like a beagle, but I guess she didn't really mind. Mrs Barrett would insist on me calling her *Cyn*, which I found a bit awkward at first, but I got used to it soon enough. She'd always kiss me hello and goodbye, and she was always telling me how good-looking I was. I was more than happy to get used to that too.

And she'd talk to me about anything. After a couple of years of going round to the Barretts' house I knew far more about them than I did my own family. Cyn had met Syd when she was going around Brick Lane market one day. Syd had run a pitch there since he was fifteen. Cyn first stopped by to check out a consignment of winter gloves he'd got from somewhere or other. He'd sell anything from car radios to candlesticks or even bicycles – anything where there was a margin to be had. The attentions of the police were an occupational hazard, because occasionally some of his suppliers might not be completely up front about the source of the gear. So when a friend of Syd's said that he could get him a job in newspapers, he'd jumped at the chance.

Meanwhile my own parents' lives were going nowhere. Dad still never seemed to make any money. He was now driving a late-sixties orange Vauxhall Viva: the best thing that you could say about it was that the colour made it more difficult to spot the rust in the door panels. And we still seemed to actually live on whatever Mum earned from her job with Mr Hendricks and whatever food was past its sell-by date from the shop. The truth was my parents were losers.

Danny didn't seem to mind. The way he saw it was that he stood a pretty good chance of becoming a professional cricket player for Wessex. And if that didn't come off, for whatever reason, he was determined to stay on at school and get some qualifications. He was a model teenager. He was also better academically than me – the school expected him to pass five or six O-levels – so if he wasn't playing cricket he was taking his homework pretty seriously. I could read and write, and my basic maths was more than adequate, but I really couldn't see the point of learning equations, speaking French (I hadn't left Wessex, let alone

England), quoting Shakespeare or committing the periodic table to memory. Syd had left school without any qualifications whatsoever and it hadn't held him back. But I knew if I was going to stand on my own two feet I was going to have to become a bit more entrepreneurial – I certainly wasn't going to get any handouts from Mum and Dad – so over the next couple of years Dougie helped me build up some savings.

We ran a shop on Monday and Friday lunch-times. On Saturdays we could always borrow a Cash and Carry card – on the pretext of doing a favour for any one of the newsagents that Syd needed to visit over the weekend – so we'd pick up anything that they were after and then add our own orders. It was mainly cigarettes and sweets. We could take advance orders for the Monday and hold a bit of stock for Fridays when most of the kids got their pocket money. I could easily pass for sixteen at the Cash and Carry. And at Cash and Carry prices we could easily undercut the shops in the village. Plus it was less risky for kids to buy their cigarettes from us. We also offered a short-term money-lending service with a flat rate of 30 per cent a week that was very popular. Dougie did the books and I was responsible for the collection. So even if I wasn't learning that much in the classroom, I was certainly picking up some useful skills outside of it.

Back on the cricket pitch there was a memorable day during the July of 1977 when Dad, Danny and me all turned out for Whetstock CC. It was the only time this ever happened. I'd usually be playing for the colts in Emminster, while Danny would have to ask permission from the Wessex youth set-up to be cleared for a league game. Whetstock were missing a couple of their regular players, so the club captain had dropped around during the week and asked us if we were available. The forecast was for a warm weekend, so the club had decided to make a day of it by arranging a barbeque after the game.

Whetstock Cricket Club sits just to the north of the road into the village as you approach from Emminster. The ground is overlooked by Whetstock Manor from the western side of the ground, while the clubhouse offers a view from the east. The pitch slopes a little too steeply from north to south for Whetstock to be considered a perfect village ground, but the location is nonetheless picturesque. The forecasters had got it right, and the day turned out to be beautiful, with clear blue skies. What with the weather, the promise of a barbeque and the local rivalry with that day's opponents from Cloton, we were expecting a large number of spectators to turn out from the village. I'd told Dougie that some of the Whetstock girls might show up in the afternoon, so he'd been dropped off by Syd at the ground with a rucksack containing some crisps, chocolate, twenty Players No.6 and a four-pack of McEwans.

Our skipper won the toss and chose to bat. When Dougie turned up we took the opportunity to walk around to the northern side of the ground, allowing Dougie to work his way through the contents of his rucksack without the unwelcome attentions of any busy-body adults. We sat on the bank above the outfield and I promised Dougie that some females would definitely show up later. I was also at pains to remind him that he'd arrived pretty early. After an hour or so, finally a woman did appear on the far side of the pitch.

"Fack me, oo is that? I'd facking give er one, I tell yer."

"That's my mum, Dougie. It's my mum."

She'd walked into the ground wearing a simple white summer dress. I'd never seen her wear it before. It was cut reasonably low so it showed off her cleavage and it finished above the knee. A white headband was tied with a simple bow, and she was wearing sunglasses and a pair of white plimsolls. Had it not been for Dougie I wouldn't have thought anything about her appearance at all. But he was right; she was a good-looking woman. I'd never even considered the question before: anyway I'm pretty sure you're not supposed to think about your mum like that.

Realistically, Dougie would have given just about anybody one. He was fourteen, and I don't think you could have said he was particularly choosy. He was one of those guys whose approach to getting lucky was purely statistical. He'd chat up just about every girl he met, he'd take the almost inevitable rejection remarkably well, and yet he'd still have the occasional success. That said, his assessment of my mum seemed to be shared by other players at the ground. Heads turned in the clubhouse and on the outfield to follow her as she walked.

Danny was down to bat at six, with Dad going in before him at five. After an hour or so we were three wickets down, so Dad walked out to the wicket. Right from the start he looked more comfortable and composed at the crease than the previous batsmen. When his partner got out, Cloton had some real energy in the field, and presumably thought that they were about to get into the Whetstock tail. But village sides can be deceptive. Often the batting order bears very little relation to the actual talent of the various players. The club treasurer might bat at three simply because he's the club treasurer. Someone might open, not because he's any good against a moving ball, but because he doesn't have any attacking shots. And almost invariably younger players bat far lower in the order than they should do, because unlike the older guys they haven't been paying their subs for the last fifteen years.

So when Danny went out there, even with Dad at the crease, he looked a class apart. Cloton's enthusiastic medium-pacers and honest off-spinners simply weren't good enough to trouble Danny. He played himself in, went smoothly through the gears, and scored all around the wicket, going on to complete an undefeated century. Dad got himself stumped trying to keep his scoring rate up with Danny's, when he was somewhere in the forties. He left the pitch in a right hump. He sat in the clubhouse sulking while the next man in played out the last seven or eight overs of the innings. Danny came off to warm applause from both the clubhouse and the Cloton players – it was obvious to everyone that he was a bit special. Once in a while I think you can just stand back and admire a good opposition performance. You just don't want to make a habit of it though.

Spectators were beginning to drift in from the village, including a few girls. Even Dougie had grounds to feel pretty optimistic about the rest of the day.

After tea we took to the field to defend our total. It was the first time that I'd played in a men's game of cricket. I got posted to fine leg by the skipper, which indicated that he hadn't got too much faith in me as a fielder. But at least it allowed me to get myself into the game easily, by chasing down a few balls and putting in some hard accurate throws back to the keeper. The run-rate was slow at first, but then began to rise, so that by the time of the first bowling changes the Cloton pair looked on top. Dad came on from the Manor end with his left-arm medium, so that the slope would allow him to shape the ball into the right-handers. And at the other end a slow left-armer came on, trying to turn the ball away from them, again using the slope. Dad finally removed one of their openers with a huge LBW shout, and then the new man in tamely chipped the slow left-armer to point.

By now the skipper had moved me to cover, so at least I felt I was in the game – cutting off any singles and pinging the ball back into the keeper's gloves. And then, halfway through another of Dad's tight overs, one of the batsmen went after a slightly wider ball with a drive. It was just a fraction too short for the shot, so he got the power, but he didn't get on top of it. It was coming a few feet to my right, fast and low to the ground. I instinctively dived and it went straight into my hand and just stuck there. As I picked myself up, a gaggle of players were congratulating me by slapping my back, my arse, and ruffling my hair.

Caught Legend P, Bowled Legend J.

Absolutely fucking brilliant. I'd pulled off a blinder for Dad.

Despite the wickets, the runs kept coming. They looked on course to chase down our total when the skipper told me to get myself loose. I was shitting myself. Danny had scored a century, Dad had scored runs and taken some wickets, so it fell to me not to let everybody down. I marked my run-up from the clubhouse end. The ball was in a bit of a state by now – nobody had really been looking after it – so I didn't reckon I'd be able to swing it that much. And I was looking at two set batsmen. So I thought I'd just try and bowl the first ball full and straight and as fast as I could. The Whetstock players were all making encouraging noises like I was a sympathy bowling change, just so I'd get a bit of experience. All of which worked out in my favour as I sent down the quickest ball bowled in the match so far. The batsman was setting himself to play an exaggeratedly respectful forward defensive, but the ball was through him long before he got the bat down. There was a satisfying crack as middle stump was pegged back.

We didn't quite bowl them all out, but the run chase was as good as finished for them. It turned out that they didn't have any more decent batsmen in the shed, and I took a further three wickets, all nicked off to the keeper. By the end they were nine down and still a good fifty runs short of our total. I was seriously looking forward to the barbeque. We had something to celebrate, and surely it wouldn't prove a problem getting served a few lagers at the clubhouse.

Players from both sides were asking me where I'd learned to bowl, and whether I'd be playing for Whetstock again. Danny and I both said nice things to each other about our respective contributions to the game. Meanwhile Dad just sat quietly at the back of the clubhouse drinking beer on his own. I looked around for Dougie, but I think he'd already disappeared with one of the village girls. As he'd say himself, "It's a numbers game, mate."

Mum was at the centre of a group of players and their wives, talking about the game, the weather and general village gossip. That was when Mr Hendricks showed up in his Land Rover. I hadn't realised that he was bringing the barbeque food. Before unpacking it all, he first joined the gaggle of people at the bar. I don't think anybody had really noticed just how much Dad had been drinking, until suddenly he shouted out, "Cover yourself up, Valerie. You're an embarrassment."

The whole place went quiet for a moment, and then everybody tried to pretend that nothing had happened by getting the conversation going again. It almost worked. But just when we all thought that might be the end of it, he started again.

"Go home Valerie. You're dressed like a whore."

There was absolute silence. Then our skipper said something like, "OK Jimmy, I think you've had enough."

"I haven't had anything like nearly enough. My wife is dressed like a whore. And now she's brought *this* cunt along to taunt me. Fucking bitch." He was pointing to Mr Hendricks.

Mum spoke. "You know full well that Lionel's here to bring the barbeque. You're making a scene and embarrassing yourself, Jimmy." Funnily enough, I didn't, until this precise moment, know that Mr Hendricks was called Lionel.

"Bitch," repeated Dad.

"That is enough!" said *Lionel*. "I think you should apologise to Valerie."

"Apologise for what? Coming down here dressed like a tart, looking to get fucked by any of you fuckers who'd fuck her? And you can fuck off too, Hendricks."

At this point Dad staggered forward and took a wild swing at Mr Hendricks, who just swayed easily out of the way.

"You think you're so fucking clever don't you Hendricks? Valerie, put some fucking clothes on. Right, I'm going for a proper drink."

And with that he staggered across the grass to the Viva, got in and started the engine. The car lurched forward about a foot as Dad promptly stalled the thing. This wasn't getting any less embarrassing. He then re-started the car, and began driving out of the ground towards Emminster, scraping the entire passenger side down the gatepost on his way.

Then Mum said, "We've got to go after him Lionel, before he does something stupid." I didn't really know what *stupid* could possibly be at this point. Mum, and Mr Hendricks more reluctantly, got into the Land Rover and headed off in the same direction that Dad had taken.

It dawned on the rest of us pretty soon afterwards that the food for the barbeque was still in the back of the Land Rover, and it was going to be spending the rest of the night pursuing Dad around Wessex in what would no doubt turn into a complete wild goose chase. Danny came up to me and said that he was going to spend the rest of the evening at Gillian's – Gillian was this girl he was seeing whose family lived just outside the village. And then most of the other players started drifting away. So, on what should have been a brilliant night over at the cricket club, I found myself at home on my own. Small consolation came from the latest copy of *Knave* that Dougie had got for me a few days earlier.

The Emminster paper carried a short match report the following week under the headline, "Cloton Fall to Whetstock Legends". It mentioned Danny's ton, Dad's all-round performance and my wickets. Unsurprisingly it didn't go on to cover the events after the game, or explain how I ended up having a lonely wank on what should have been a night of triumph. The following morning I was expecting to wake up in an empty house, but I pulled back the curtain to see the Viva parked in the road outside. And Danny had returned at some point during the night and was still asleep in his bed. So everything was back to normal again. I never found out if Mum and Mr Hendricks had ever caught up with Dad, and I'm not sure it really mattered one way or the other. I just felt a sense of relief. So I happily rested my cock on Danny's top lip, with it lying there like a fat flesh-coloured moustache. I'd always do that when I woke up first to see how long it would take him to notice.

I started off my fifth year at Emminster Secondary School with a renewed sense of optimism. I'd built up a substantial pot of savings, which I kept in a Post Office account. Dougie was always dreaming up new ways to make cash, and although we'd ended up in front of Mr Harding a few times over the years and received the odd detention, he'd never managed to pin anything serious on us. However, by the end of the summer term my life had completely unravelled.

The year before, we'd expanded our commercial operations significantly, when Dougie managed to persuade a newsagent in Casterbridge to sell him top-shelf magazines at the wholesale price. I think this was because Dougie was supplying him with duty-free Benson & Hedges or Rothmans – but I can't remember the specifics. Regardless, we had access to a regular supply of *Knave*, *Penthouse* and *Club International* magazines, which we could easily sell around the school. There were only three newsagents in Emminster and none of them would sell the top-shelf stuff to kids, and anyway most of our market would have been too embarrassed to try buying this stuff themselves. We were a reliable source of product, we'd take orders, and we'd keep a small amount of stock for impulse purchasers.

Everything was going just fine until the beginning of the summer term. Dougie sold a magazine to a second-year who, it transpired, showed it to his elder sister, who told her parents, who made an appointment to see Mr Harding. Dougie might have got away with it, but for the fact that unusually, on that day, he'd got three new titles in his bag waiting to be delivered and about £50 in cash. In retrospect he should never have sold the title to a kid who was just curious. He wasn't old enough to *need* a copy of *Club International*, he just wanted to see what all the fuss was about. Most of our customers understood that discretion was vital in order to protect the supply chain. Maybe Dougie got greedy, but that's easy to say with hindsight.

Regardless, Dougie got called into see Harding almost immediately. And an hour later, I was pulled out of a class to go and see him too. Harding, the wily bastard, tried to fit me up: he told me that Dougie had claimed he was just carrying the magazines and the cash for me. I could only imagine that Harding was trying to get me to incriminate myself, because there's no way Dougie would have ever done that. Harding just kept asking me question after question. Did I know anything about this? No. Did I know Dougie sold pornographic magazines around the school? No. Did I know who else bought these magazines? No. Dougie got expelled. Apparently Syd was seriously pissed off with him. Not because we'd been selling top-shelf magazines around the school – but for being careless and getting caught.

To complicate matters, the regional cricket trials were being held that Friday down at the Port Bredy ground. I knew that this was my big chance to follow in Danny's footsteps and get myself into the Wessex set-up. It was a big deal. I don't know if the Thursday evening I spent round at Dougie's drinking can after can of McEwan's affected my performance the following day. It would be all too easy to put my failure to impress down to just that one evening. But honestly I think there was more to it than that. I hadn't been training as hard as I should have been for the previous couple of years, and certainly not with the intensity that I had when I first joined the school. And I was probably half a stone overweight.

That evening I told Dougie about everything that Harding had said to me.

"Fackin wanka. You do know ees a bullshitta don'tcha?"

I trusted Dougie, I knew he'd got my back. But when I left I was somewhat worse for wear. I had to push my bike up the hill into Whetstock that night. And I had to go and throw up at some stage in the small hours. The next day down at Port Bredy there were about fifteen of us in the trial. The coaches took us out onto the pitch and had all of us bat for a few overs, bowl for a few overs and field in between times. Despite the fact that I'd already got a sweat on before my first over I was actually looking forward to having a good bowl. Obviously none of the batsmen were going to be mugs, but I reckoned I was good for a handful of scalps.

Then I speared my first delivery so wide down the legside that the keeper missed it by three feet. I'd have been pissed off with myself, had it not been for the fact that my delivery stride had somehow thrown my brain against the inside of my skull, like I was shaking pickled eggs in a jar. It was painful beyond description. For the next few deliveries I tried holding my head at different angles to see if there was any position that would minimise the trauma. It turned out there wasn't. To say that I lost my radar that day would have been something of an understatement. And to make matters worse I wasn't even fast. What I was – albeit only on those rare occasions when I actually bowled legitimate deliveries – was cannon fodder.

If my bowling wasn't embarrassing enough, then I went and dropped an absolute sitter at mid-wicket. The ball was travelling, but it was a dolly. Somehow I managed to create a perfect funnel with my hands through which it travelled freely until its flight was arrested by my soft, intimate parts. The ball rolled down my inner thigh and onto the ground at my feet. I felt like an absolute clown out there. A clown, that is, whose bollocks were stinging from both the impact of the ball, and from the particularly acidic sweat that was channelling between them and the tops of my legs.

Despite getting out a couple of times when I batted later in the day, I felt that I partially redeemed myself by smacking a few boundaries. By then I reckoned I was just badly hungover as opposed to still drunk. But I knew I was never going to get selected on the strength of my batting alone. And I knew, without having to wait to be told, that I'd failed the trials.

My best friend was expelled and my dream of playing cricket professionally for Wessex was in tatters. I wasn't going to be the boy from Whetstock who went on to make a name for himself in front of the big crowds at Canberra Park in Budmouth. I was going to be the boy from Whetstock who got stuck in Whetstock.

A few weeks later, sat in the sports hall, I wrote that the major theme of *Jude the Obscure* was the obscurity of Jude. It was a short essay. I failed the exam. And I didn't just fail that one. If it involved putting a pen to paper, I failed it. All I had to show for five years were a couple of CSE passes in woodwork and metalwork. I'd hit rock bottom.

It was easy enough to sneak
over to the caravan park in
the evenings.

3. ON JURASSIC BEACH

Later that summer my exam results were delivered to Oxford Cottage. I wanted to go and share commiserations with other people in the same boat – but I didn't know any. Dougie, after his parents managed to persuade Casterbridge Secondary to take him on for the remainder of the year, had passed five O-levels. I'd always known he was sharp like that, but even so I was impressed. He signed up for the Sixth Form at Casterbridge. He wanted to go on and get a business studies degree, so he'd need to pass some A-levels.

Danny had also done well in his exams. But the bigger news was that Wessex had offered him professional terms. I was pleased for Danny – I really was – but we had our first major row that summer. Of course we'd had our moments before, like when he really lost it with me one morning saying he'd fucking well bite the thing off if I ever put my dick on his face again. However, when he started lecturing me about Dougie, it was something else entirely. He was saying that Dougie was somehow to blame for the position that I was in – by which he meant my exam results and the fact that I'd failed at the Wessex trials. I wasn't going to take that from Mr Goody Two-Shoes. It was all a bit rich given that he'd frisked himself off to more than his fair share of *Penthouse* playmates that Dougie and me had supplied.

The thing he said which really got under my skin was this: "Think about it Pete. You're the one in the shit; Dougie's going to be fine. He's going to do his A-levels. But he's not worried about you. You're the one with the problem." That Danny would have the nerve to presume what Dougie might think about me stuck in my craw. But I think what really made the red mist come down was that he'd actually said two things that were true: Dougie *was* doing fine, and I *was* in the shit. I wish he hadn't brought the whole thing up, because I was the one who ended up looking like an arsehole. Going off the deep end in the way that I did probably made it look as though I was just jealous of his success with Wessex.

A couple of weeks later he called me and asked if I wanted to join him in the members' stand at Canberra Park to watch a day of a Championship match. I think he knew he'd been out of order with some of the stuff he'd said about Dougie, and that I, by accepting his invitation, was apologising for some of the things I might have come out with.

Sitting in the stand that afternoon, playing professional cricket seemed so near yet so far. Danny was my brother. He had grown up in the same room as me in Oxford Cottage, and now he was a professional player. Although he hadn't yet made a first-class appearance, he nonetheless earned a living playing cricket. Surely, if Danny could do it, with some application and dedication so could I. The following day I took an unused school exercise book, a pen and a four-pack of McEwan's to the churchyard in Whetstock. I needed to clear my mind, get some focus and set myself some simple goals. Because I was still feeling a bit sorry for myself, the first things that I started writing down were all a bit self-indulgent and perhaps even self-pitying. At some point during the third can of McEwan's, inspiration struck. I needed to stop whining and get something more practical and more motivational written down. So I wrote just three lines:

I _will_ play professional cricket for Wessex and England
I _will_ get some qualifications
I _will_ get laid

Sometimes I think there's a limit to the power of positive thinking and that modern sports psychologists overstate the extent to which they can help players. But there is certainly something to be said for having a simple plan with clear objectives. And happily for me I achieved all of mine in reverse order.

In the summer of 1979 my virginity was still securely intact. I hadn't even had a sniff of an opportunity to lose it. Had it not been for everything else that had gone wrong for me, I might have fixated on my still being a virgin as a major source of injustice. Girls slept with Dougie. Granted, they didn't tend to sleep with him twice, but on a number of occasions he'd had girls willingly spend time in his bedroom. And of course then he'd be telling me about *what girls like, how you should do that first*, his *favourite position* and so on. He turned into a sort of talking *Kama Sutra*. And I'd be listening to this, thinking, "I am not in need of advanced technical tips; all I want is to meet someone nice who'll let me shag her." I'd console myself with the fact that, when it came to girls, Dougie didn't have particularly high standards, or even any standards at all. But then after a few McEwan's or Hofmeisters, frankly I'd have rutted a hedge, so I didn't really have the excuse that I was just waiting for Debbie Harry to show up in Whetstock.

Danny always seemed to have a girlfriend. So he'd also enjoyed a reasonably frequent supply of sex over the previous couple of years. And that too seemed unjust, because my superior endowment had counted for nothing. Danny, I can tell you, has got a very average six inches to work with. And while I neither want to boast or get into a detailed anatomical description, I've got more to offer. But my looks and my equipment seemed to count for nothing.

The following morning I woke up early and re-read what I'd written in the notebook. It still looked good, and it still made sense. But I needed some practical advice. So I called Danny before he left for training, and asked him what he thought I should do next (about getting on in cricket rather than getting laid). Having met a number of other guys in the Wessex seconds, he said that three or four of them were local lads who hadn't come through the youth set-up at all. They'd been scouted playing in the Wessex leagues. It wasn't the quickest route to becoming a professional, but neither was it unheard of to bag a professional contract in your early twenties. This was what I wanted to hear. Danny suggested that I should initially target playing for the Emminster first team.

Later that morning I walked around to the shop to have a chat with Mum, but she was out delivering groceries to a customer in the village. Mr Hendricks asked me if I wanted a cup of tea, and given that I didn't have anything else to do, I took him up on the offer. Mum had obviously told him about my exams and the fact that I hadn't got into the Wessex development programme. I thought he might start lecturing me about it. I told him about the list I'd written (leaving out the third part), and that Danny had told me that by performing well in the Wessex leagues I could still make it as a professional cricket player. He said a couple of things that morning that stayed with me.

"Well you certainly don't need me to read you the Riot Act. You know you've let yourself down, and it sounds like you're ready to do something about it."

And then he said that Danny's idea that I should play a high standard of league cricket sounded like a good one. But of course I couldn't really do anything about that until next year, given that it was now early September. So, I was going to have to find something useful to do with myself until then.

"I know it'll feel like you're going backwards, but I think you should return to school and re-take your basic O-levels. You'll probably never ever use them, but it'll help you prove to yourself that you're not stupid. You'd be too embarrassed to fail twice, right?"

I couldn't help but like Hendricks, even though I found it a little strange that this big, tough action-guy had settled for a quiet life running the village shop in Whetstock. I could never work out what kept him there.

A few days later Mum and me went to see Mr Harding at the school. I think he was rather hoping that he'd seen the last of me, but I managed to persuade him that I was serious about turning over a new leaf and making sure that I passed the exams this time. It was his idea that I just did the classes for O-levels in

English, Maths and History. The thinking was that if I only sat three, I'd be able to really apply myself in all of them. He also said that I should join the A-level General Studies course as well. This would entail me travelling down to Port Bredy twice a week, because the course was shared between the two schools.

Travelling down to the Sixth Form College at Port Bredy to do the General Studies course was actually quite good fun. I started playing rugby and football again – I'd only been involved in cricket at the school for the previous couple of years. By the winter term I was established in the school's first team for both sports, but I was under no illusions that I'd ever be good enough to go much further at either. All the same, I enjoyed playing, and it certainly helped me get my fitness back on track.

What I found most fun though was playing five-a-side football in Port Bredy on Wednesday afternoons after the General Studies class. The standard was pretty high. We'd do training exercises in the main sports hall for half of the session and then play a game, subbing in players to ensure that everyone got some time on the pitch. I found myself invariably playing at the back, breaking things up and trying to get quick balls forward to the pair of midfielders. We had a couple of really mobile lads who proved far more effective in front of goal than I could ever have been.

During that first term, I kept hearing snatches of conversation between some of the guys that invariably went something like this: "Is BT going to play this year?" "January, I heard." "What is it *this* year?" "Right leg *and* right arm." "What happened this time?" "Hockey, that's what happened."

I was curious about this BT. Whoever he was, just about all the players seemed to agree he was something special, and that we'd be playing a better standard of football when he joined us in the winter term. But to be honest I was a little bit sceptical. All teams, whether it's football, rugby, cricket or tiddlywinks, think that they're going to be better when someone gets back from injury, holiday or whatever. Players tend to go up in most people's estimations when they're not available. However, given that this player seemed to be universally considered a cut above, I thought to myself, maybe I'm doing BT a disservice; maybe he's the dog's bollocks.

When we broke up for the Christmas holidays, I was feeling pretty good. I was fitter than I had been for a while, and I was keeping up with all my courses. And with Danny gone, I'd even got a bedroom to myself.

On 9th January 1980 Bethan Trellick joined the first five-a-side session of the new term. She didn't move like a girl, she moved like a footballer. You couldn't help but notice the ease with which she trapped the ball and the zip she put on her passes. And you couldn't help but notice the precision in her range of close control exercises – the ball just seemed to be an extension of her body. She didn't say that much. But there was an intensity about her. Your eyes always followed her, expecting her to be part of the action. In that first session we played on the same team, with her slotting into the left-hand side of our formation. Two or three times I got us into trouble by under-hitting balls out to her, allowing an opposition player to pounce on the loose ball.

"What's your name, mate?"

"Pete."

"Well come on Pete. Get some pace into your passing. Let's see some urgency." And then she was clapping her hands in front of me, "Yeah?" I nodded. "Good! Let's go!"

It must have been almost a subconscious thing: *she's a girl, go easy on her.* So I kept under-hitting my passes to her. I must have continued to think like that deep into the game, ignoring the evidence of my own eyes that she was by far the best player on the pitch. Unfortunately, however, you can't really afford to have a spectator as part of the playing line-up in a five-a-side game, and despite a couple more motivational pep talks from BT, I didn't improve much and we lost. She'd rightly identified that I'd been distracted. But I'm not sure that she had realised that she herself was the source of that distraction.

I started doing some research, which basically involved asking anyone and everyone in my General Studies class what they knew about Bethan Trellick. "There was this girl, errrr . . . Bethan I think her name was, who played in the five-a-side last week. Very good footballer. What else does she play?" And slowly I began to piece together the BT dossier. Her parents ran a caravan park a couple of miles to the east of Port Bredy, off the road to Budmouth. She was a sports fanatic. She had been captain of various school teams, and she'd led Port Bredy when they'd won the regional netball cup. She was also the best cross-country runner at the school. She was doing A-levels in Biology, Physics and Psychology. She wanted to go to Loughborough to study sports sciences.

The following week in the five-a-side session I found myself paired up with Bethan during the pre-game exercises. Seeing her close up for the first time I noticed that she was actually a little shorter than I'd remembered, maybe around five foot three. She had shoulder-length hair, a sort of dirty blonde, which she'd pulled back into a pony-tail. She had brown eyes that could be piercing, curious, enthusiastic or disapproving. One of our pre-game exercises was shielding the ball. Players would take it in turns to have possession of the ball while shielding it and looking for a passing option. Your partner just had to win it back. She started in possession, and again – just like in our first game together – I went easy on her, having the odd nibble at the ball, but not actually putting her under any real pressure. When we swapped around everything changed. I had the ball and the first thing that happened was that she clattered straight into my hip, knocking me off balance for a moment. She was surprisingly strong: it was a bit like when you go to take a stick from a dog and you underestimate how tenacious it's going to be in trying to wrestle it back. And with me off balance, she then peppered the back of my legs with kicks, searching for the ball.

We swapped round again, and this time I didn't mess about, buffeting firmly into her backside and thigh, forcing her to lean firmly back into me to regain her balance. I could hear her breathing harder. I managed to slip her body, forcing her to step backwards to steady herself, allowing me to steal across and win the ball. We changed around again and she came back at me even harder: her upper body was buffeting my back, her knees were regularly hammering into the back of my thighs and she was snapping away at my ankles. But she didn't get the ball. I wasn't going to let that stop before I had to.

A few weeks later I saw her for the first time outside the sports hall. We talked awkwardly about music. She was into noisy guitar bands like The Jam, The Clash and The Skids. There were all sorts of band names and logos drawn over her canvas school bag. For a model student, she could come across as a bit of a rebel. There was an edge to her. Although Bethan didn't look like Cyn Barrett – she certainly didn't wear make-up and use hair spray the way Cyn did – she was confident and outspoken, just like Dougie's mum. And I liked that: maybe I've just got a thing for strong women.

The school campus at Port Bredy is in the middle of nowhere so Bethan cycled to and from school. I asked her a bunch of questions that I already knew the answers to: what did her parents do for a living? What A-levels was she doing? Did she have any brothers or sisters? I, of course, already knew that she had a twelve-year-old sister called Kimberley.

"Is she like you?"

"Like me? In what way?"

"You know, into sports and stuff."

"Oh, I see. Not really. Her bedroom is a shrine to Barbie. She's got the lot: all the outfits, a house, a jeep and a Ken."

"You were never into that sort of thing?"

"I pestered my parents for an Action Man one Christmas. But they gave me a decent bike instead so I forgot all about it."

The last couple of Wednesdays that term, after five-a-side, I'd walk with her down from the school into Port Bredy while she wheeled her bike. We'd hang around the town centre for a while and then I'd get the bus back to Emminster, and make my way home from there. And then the following term we picked up where we left off, so we'd pretty much assume that when I was down at Port Bredy we'd spend the afternoon together. Her father sounded like a stern taskmaster. He was the son of a dock-worker from Port Bredy. He'd trained as a carpenter, worked hard and saved some money to buy the plot of land that he'd turned into the caravan park. He'd installed these fixed units that customers could either buy or rent. He was the first member of his family to own his own home: a thatched house in the middle of Bridestock. And he expected his daughters to be the first generation of Trellicks who went to university. Sometimes Bethan would bring a small cassette recorder with her and we'd sit on the benches behind the clock tower in the centre of Port Bredy. She'd know all the words to her favourite tracks and would be angrily singing along, "London Calling" and "Califonia Über Alles" were among her firm favourites.

In the summer term we hatched a plan. There was going to be a five-a-side schools tournament held at Port Bredy over a weekend. One of the other players in our team also lived in Bridestock, and as luck would have it his parents were going to be away that weekend. So I arranged to stay with him on the Saturday night. The tournament format involved eight teams playing in two leagues on the Saturday, with the top four coming back on the Sunday. On the Saturday we played out of our skins and won all three of our league games – there was absolutely no way I was going to allow us to be knocked out of the competition and get sent home on the first evening.

So that night Bethan and I arranged to meet at midnight in the car park of the pub in the middle of Bridestock. From there we walked for about fifteen minutes along the cliff road and then down onto Jurassic Beach below. Jurassic Beach runs all the way from Port Bredy to the Isle of Slingers. Over the years the area has been a popular destination for honeymooning couples: they stay in the villages that have guesthouses overlooking the beach itself. I've never really understood the appeal myself; the beach is largely shingle, and as I can personally testify, pretty uncomfortable. Bethan, having crept out of her house once the rest of her family had gone to bed, had brought a torch. And I had brought a handful of Durex that I'd got off Dougie for a couple of quid the previous weekend. The condoms were essential, but his advice was invaluable.

"Gonna be yer first time, Pete? Don't forget to havva shuffle first, yeah?"

"A what?"

"A shuffle. A tug. A wank for facksake."

"Really?"

"Cos unless yaw sum sorta Superman it'll be ova beforeyer even star'edd."

"OK."

"Naffing special, just a quickie off the wrist. Don't wanna be treating yerself to a total sack draining with sent'id candles and the latest Danish import stuff. Just a regulation wank."

Before slipping out of Jason's house, I followed Dougie's instructions and then headed off into the dark to meet Bethan. It was pitch black as we made our way down the cliff road and onto the beach itself. And so, to the sound of the waves running in against the shore, I set about striking off the third objective on my list. I'm not claiming to have been Casanova, but for a first go I was pretty bloody good. It must have been after about forty minutes when Bethan asked me if I was going to be much longer, because the shingle was freezing her arse off. By that point the shingle was also causing my knees some serious pain, so it was with some relief that I finished up. I think it's fair to say I was magnificent. And I owe that to Dougie. You can't buy a mate like that.

We lost our semi-final the following morning. And then we lost the play-off. But in all honesty I didn't really care. I got subbed in the first game, and I didn't play in the second. Bethan played in both, but I think more on reputation than performance.

The next twelve months flashed by. I played my way into Emminster Cricket Club's first team. I was coming on at second change and I was picking up regular wickets. I spent long hours in the nets that summer working on my batting and I scored a couple of half-centuries later on in the season. We still finished in the bottom half of the table, but I could be pretty pleased with my own contribution. But that's one of the funny things about cricket; it's a team game when you're winning and an individual sport when you're not. Bethan came over to watch me play at Emminster a couple of times, and she saw our game at Port Bredy. Most of the time she'd just take the piss, telling me that cricket wasn't actually a sport. I think I'd just about managed to persuade her that bowling demanded a certain level of personal fitness, when she saw a fifty-something off-spinner at Port Bredy bowl us out.

"He was an absolute lump of lard. A walking heart attack. He needed a breather after marking his run-up. Well I say *run-up*, it was more of *stroll* really. Have you guys sent any flowers?"

"Flowers?"

"To his widow. I doubt he made it home."

I met Frank and Moira Trellick for the first time that summer. Frank looked like he could handle himself. He was greying around the temples, but he looked seriously fit. He looked like the sort of guy that would relish bawling out a contractor or chasing up a bad debt. It felt as though he didn't ask you questions so much as accuse you of stuff. To be fair, that could have been because I was shagging his daughter.

Frank made it pretty clear that he didn't entirely approve of me as a match for his daughter. He was certainly sceptical about my plan to become a professional sportsman, and he realised pretty quickly that I wasn't exactly in Bethan's league academically.

"Bethan tells me you're doing an A-level."

"That's right, Mr Trellick. In General Studies."

"Just the *one* A-level, Peter? That's not going to get you into a university is it?"

"Well, Mr Trellick, I'm just really doing it to prove that I can. To myself, if you like."

"So, as a taxpayer, I'm funding your little academic hobby? What *do* you take seriously then, Peter?"

"Cricket. I'm going to play for Wessex."

"Well I certainly admire your ambition. So, how does it work? Are you part of their youth development programme?"

"No. My brother has a professional contract with Wessex. I'm currently playing for Emminster to get noticed."

"So you're an intellectual dilettante and amateur cricketer. Quite the renaissance man you've found here, Bethan."

He could be a patronising bastard, Frank, he really could. Despite this, he offered me cash-in-hand work at the caravan site. At first I'd just do interior painting for him, but over time, when he'd realised that I could do basic carpentry pretty well, he'd get me to complete various running repairs.

That summer I passed my driving test first time. I can probably thank Mr Hendricks for that, because on Wednesday afternoons and Sunday mornings he'd strap 'L' plates on the Land Rover and let me practise for a few hours at a time. He said that he couldn't understand why people paid for driving instructors – he'd apparently been granted a full licence by Her Majesty's Armed Forces after demonstrating that he could reverse a vehicle between a set of goal posts. And he'd never had a major accident, so by his reckoning I didn't need lessons at all. He'd occasionally tell me to change gear or check my mirrors, but most of the time he'd just ask me stuff about school, cricket and Bethan. Looking back I realise that he'd really gone out of his way to help me out, but he never made a big deal about it.

After the cricket season finished I'd often go down to Bridestock for Sunday lunch. After much wrangling Mum had helped me persuade Dad to put me on the insurance, so that I could borrow the Viva.

"You're not going to tell me you've paid money for *that* are you Peter?" asked Frank.

"No. It's Dad's."

"You didn't tell me he was a stock-car racer."

Ironically perhaps, the more work Frank sent in my direction, the more opportunities I had to shag his daughter. He kept the chalet keys locked in a safe in the house and gave them to me on a job-by-job basis. But if a job was going to stretch over a couple of weekends I'd just hang on to the keys. So it was easy enough to sneak over to the caravan park in the evenings. And through the winter months when there were very few other residents coming and going from the chalets, Bethan would bring her cassette recorder along.

By her standards at least, she'd put together compilation tapes that were positively romantic. We had "Games Without Frontiers", "Ashes to Ashes", "Going Underground", "Geno" by Dexy's (which offered some interesting syncopated hand-job possibilities) and "Atomic" by Blondie. After Christmas of that year she'd also make a point of including "There's No One Quite Like Grandma" by the St Winifred's School Choir at some point on the tape. I could only hope that she'd get it out the way early, because you really don't want to be hearing that at the business end of proceedings.

Some time in the spring of 1981 it dawned on me that soon it was all going to be over. Bethan would pass her A-levels in the summer and head off to university in the autumn. I asked her if there was anywhere in Wessex she could study instead of going off to Loughborough, but she was adamant about it.

"You've always known I was going to university, Pete. You're not going to make me feel guilty about this. I'll see you in the holidays and then we'll see where we go from there."

That put things into perspective a bit. When we were rocking one of the chalets off its foundations, it was easy for me to forget that she was the one with the solid career plans. And she certainly wasn't going to change those plans because of me. I was the one who was going to be left behind.

****

"Yer need sumfin to getcha mind ov it."

I was sat in the Black Dog in Emminster with Dougie. I was feeling a bit down on myself. Come the end of the summer, Bethan would be gone, plus I was going to have to find some way of actually supporting myself over the coming years. I reckoned that I could do painting, decorating and other odd jobs, but I knew that I couldn't rely on a regular supply of work from Mr Trellick. And I was going to need to spend most of my savings getting my own car. As ever, Dougie came up trumps. Firstly, it just so happened that he was setting up a firm called Wessex Premier: Painting & Decorating. The idea was really simple: he'd use his father's eyes and ears to find out where there might be work, Syd would pass him the contact details, and then he'd sort out the bookings. It was something he could run while he was down in Plymouth doing his business studies degree. I could be his first, and preferred, contractor. All I had to do in return was give him 15 per cent of the job fee. So we agreed that Trellick would be Wessex Premier's founding client, and that I'd send Dougie his share in cash to keep things simple.

"Now you're gonna need some wheels. Wotchcha gotta spend?"

I hadn't really thought about it, but I came up with a number I could live with. A couple of weeks later he gave me a call and asked me if I wanted to come and see a car he'd found for me in Casterbridge. He picked me up in his John Player Special Ford Capri, and when we arrived at a quiet street on the western edge of the town he pointed to a '75 Escort Sport parked in one of the driveways. It was completely impractical. But I had to have it. I took the Escort for a spin a few miles down the main road towards Port Bredy. There were a few rattles here and there, but I loved it. Dad's Viva handled like a blancmange by comparison.

When we got back to Casterbridge, Dougie said it would be better if he looked after the negotiations. In the end I think we may have paid a bit over the book price, but then an Escort Sport in decent condition didn't come up too often in Wessex.

Before we knew it we were sitting exams. Bethan's were all finished before mine. I think my maths paper was the last thing I completed. I felt reasonably good about them – it wasn't like the last time where I'd struggled to do much apart from fill in my name. I drove down to Bridestock that evening to see Bethan. She looked serious and got straight to the point.

"I was waiting until your exams were over before I told you. I'm pregnant."

In a sense it wasn't a surprise. We'd had a couple of condoms break. Maybe we could blame the inclusion of "Call Me" by Blondie on our compilation tapes. And at that age keeping all of those fluids contained was a challenge. But it still came as a bit of a shock.

"Oh shit."

In fact I went from 'Oh shit' to 'I do' in just over five weeks. I broached the idea that we might just think about an abortion. But that didn't go down very well at all; Bethan said I was a pathetic, cowardly loser running away from the consequences of my actions. I'd heard her make the case pretty strongly in favour of a woman's right to choose, but when it came to her personal situation, she couldn't just ignore the views and values of her own parents. While Bethan mocked Frank for his membership of the Conservative Party, she couldn't consider disobeying him or even lying to him about something so important.

We agreed to go and tell Frank and Moira together. Initially they either feigned surprise, or they genuinely were surprised, that we'd been sleeping together in the first place. Then there was a lecture about contraception and responsibility. We then moved on seamlessly to what other people in the village would think. But once I realised that Frank wasn't actually going to hit me, I let my mind wander a little to help the time pass. I had never before, and I haven't since, endured a three-hour bollocking. He was right. I was in the wrong. I got that. And finding ever more angles on the ways in which he was right and I was wrong just became tedious. But then I found that I couldn't get the bloody Specials' "Too Much Too Young" out of my head. It was just too damned catchy. I was hearing the chorus over and over again.

"What in Hell's name are you smirking about, Peter?"

"Nothing sir. I was just thinking that the proper thing to do would be to get married."

I don't know if I came out with that because Frank was leading me there anyway, or simply because after hearing my own rendition of "Too Much Too Young", *married* was one of the few words that I could think of under pressure. Very quickly the conversation turned to Reverend Fellows' availability, and then Moira started drawing up a catering budget.

We were married on Friday 7th August 1981. The Reverend "Call me Brian, mate" Fellows kept things in the church mercifully brief. Dougie was the best man. He managed to get us a good cash deal on suit hire from some place in Casterbridge. I just gave him some money and he took care of everything. He'd got the measurements on the trousers wrong though, so they finished about three inches above my shoes. Someone took some wedding photos, but they had the good sense not to take any full-length shots. There was one photo of Bethan and me: her in a simple white dress, flanked by Mum and Dad on one side, and Moira and Frank on the other. It was the first time that they'd ever met. Not that you'd know it from the photo; it actually looks like a pretty normal wedding shot. We're stood outside the church in Bridestock.

After the ceremony everybody walked through the village down to the Ship, where Frank and Moira had booked a buffet. Most of our friends from the school were there, Bethan's gran who lived in Budmouth had been driven over, and Mr Hendricks joined us in the early evening after closing the shop in Whetstock. The evening was warm and we sat outside with our friends speculating on exam results and listening to suggestions for the best baby names. Basically everybody just tried to pretend that this was all perfectly normal. Slowly the Ship began to fill up with regular customers over the course of the evening so there was a lovely buzz in the place. It must have been around eight o'clock when Dad came up to me and said that he'd got something he had to do. In a sense I was relieved, because with him around there was always that possibility that it might all kick off at any moment. It would be more than ten years before I saw him again.

Our honeymoon consisted of a weekend in the chalet that I'd re-decorated a few days earlier. Bethan had put a new compilation tape together for the occasion. I can't remember everything that was on it, but it included most of The Jam's more angry stuff like "Set the House Ablaze" and "Funeral Pyre". I didn't mind The Jam, but it wasn't a great weekend. What with all the references to blazes, flames and fires, I was just relieved that Bethan didn't torch the chalet with me in it. By Sunday afternoon I went into Bridestock to ask Frank if there were any jobs that needed doing. I spent the rest of the day unblocking the roof guttering of one of the rental units.

The next few weeks passed in a blur. We moved into a small two-bed house on the cheaper western edge of Emminster. Both of us passed our exams, which ordinarily would have been a reason to celebrate. But when Bethan saw that she'd achieved the grades she needed for Loughborough she broke down.

At least I had work to do. Dougie had come up trumps and found me a number of garages to demolish in Casterbridge. It was back-breaking work. I'd fill a large skip every two days, get a new one delivered and start over again. But if nothing else it got me out of the house. Other decorating jobs began to follow – people would see me working and ask me if I was available for a painting job, a wall repair, and so on. On Friday evenings I'd tot up that week's earnings and put aside Dougie's share.

My season for Emminster was unremarkable. I established myself as an opening bowler and must have averaged two or three wickets a match. But if Wessex were going to send any scouts up to Emminster I'd need to be making the local paper headlines week in and week out over the course of the season. My batting was gradually improving and I was beginning to develop a reputation as a big-hitting number seven. One of the highlights of the season was smashing one of the Abbot's Cernal openers for two consecutive sixes, clearing the houses at the western side of our ground. I was voted player of the season at the annual club review night, but in a way that made me feel even more down on myself. It was as though I'd found my level: I was a very good young club cricketer. Not one who stood out as playing several levels below his actual ability.

Then things went from bad to worse. Bethan had gone to Casterbridge for a regulation scan at the hospital, and they found that the baby's heart had stopped. She couldn't call me because I was out on a job. When I got home that night she was just sobbing uncontrollably in our living room. I couldn't even begin to untangle the mess of emotions she was going through. Of course, she hadn't wanted to get pregnant in the first place, but she really didn't want *this*. She'd lurch from telling me that she'd let us down, to saying that she just wanted them to get the fucking thing out of her. I reckon that was the worst night of my life. We'd both be hugging and crying, and then she'd tell me to get my hands off her. I realised that up until then I hadn't given much thought to what life would actually be like with a baby. I'd busied myself with work and with cricket, and it was only now, now that the baby had been lost, that I even started to imagine us as an actual family.

Bethan would have to go back to Casterbridge General the following day to have the baby induced. I got ready to go over with her but she insisted on taking Moira instead. I could understand why she did that, but I'd wanted to be there with her. She spent that evening back at home in Bridestock. She called me from Frank and Moira's house and we spoke for a while on the phone. She talked me through everything, describing the doctors, the midwife, the anaesthetic and so on. Before we hung up she described the baby. It was a girl.

I'm surprised there's any
money in drug dealing given
the length of time it seems
to take to sell the stuff.

4. ANOTHER GIRL, ANOTHER PLANET

A few weeks earlier, on the Sunday after our wedding, the police called around to Oxford Cottage. Dad's Viva had been left in a short-term parking bay outside Budmouth station. The officers were working on the assumption that it had probably been stolen and used by joyriders. Which was reasonable enough given the state of the car and the fact that nobody had filed a missing-persons report for Dad. Two or three days without him wasn't actually that unusual, nor was it particularly unwelcome. It was entirely possible that he'd caught the last train out of Budmouth that night, but we couldn't know for sure. He could have got off the train anywhere between Casterbridge and Waterloo. No bodies meeting his description were discovered in Wessex, Southampton or London during the days that followed. He just vanished. I think, after she'd got over the initial shock, Mum's biggest concern was that he might come back one day.

After Bethan's miscarriage, it wouldn't be right to say that our lives slowly returned to normal in the weeks that followed. We couldn't undo what had happened and we were certainly no longer the carefree couple of the previous summer. But we did start to do some everyday things again. We'd go to the quiz night in the Black Dog on Mondays. We'd watch television: *Bergerac* and *Blake's 7*. Bethan helped out in the PE department at Emminster Secondary, running after-school hockey and netball sessions. When she came back home after these sessions I'd see glimpses of the Bethan I'd met two years before. Some of that intense energy and enthusiasm of hers was returning.

She re-applied to Loughborough, and shortly after received an unconditional offer of a place for that year. So we knew we had another six months or so together before she went off to university. It was a bittersweet moment when the offer arrived: I knew it was exactly what she'd always wanted, but I was still going to miss her. Shortly after she received her offer, the Falklands War broke out. I don't think I was the only person to wonder how on earth the Argentinians had managed to launch an invasion off the coast of Scotland. But once I'd got the basic geography cleared up, the conflict proved a brilliant distraction. You could go down to the Black Dog and ask any of the ex-services guys in there to talk about the tactics, the logistics and all that sort of thing. Bethan could point on a map to the location of the *Belgrano* – outside the exclusion zone and sailing away from the islands – when it was sunk. It at least allowed us to take our minds off our last year. Except that is, whenever we were over in Whetstock, where I'd always try and steer the conversation towards some other topic. I got the strong sense that Mr Hendricks would have liked nothing more than to be part of the Task Force, so I didn't think that he and Bethan would exactly see eye to eye about the whole thing.

Something clicked for me at the beginning of that 1982 season for Emminster. Right from the first pre-season net session I felt good. Somehow my action had just fallen into place and I was generating real pace. Whether it was because I was simply fitter and stronger or whether it was because I was just mentally in a better place – I was finally ready to do some serious damage to club batsmen.

We started the season away at Casterbridge. I opened the bowling for Emminster from the pavilion end. The pitch at Casterbridge falls away in almost exactly the same way as it does at Lord's. The comparison between the two grounds may end there, but the slope is uncannily similar. So your out-swinger will hold its line or move away up the slope, while straight balls will tend to fall down the hill into the right-hander. I was in bowling heaven that afternoon: drop it back of a length at speed and just watch the ball follow the batsman like a Sidewinder into the ribs; push it fuller and watch it shape away. In an eight-over opening spell I'd got four wickets and gone for six runs. I'd hit all of their top order in some way or another: two of them took balls to the ribs, one actually dropped his bat when the ball jammed his bottom hand as he was trying to fend a short one off his throat, and there was a disconcerting *splatt* sort of sound when I hit a generously proportioned number five in the middle of his stomach. It was a breakthrough for me: I'd imposed myself on decent club batsmen, and used my strength and my skills to dismiss them cheaply. But I'd bowl even better before the season was out.

I took seven wickets at Creston. They may have been one of the weaker sides in the league, but we skittled them out for less than fifty. Their batsmen simply didn't have the technique to cope with the pace that I was generating. It's a funny thing being a fast bowler. Sat in the clubhouse at the end of the day, you see the game far more strategically. But in the middle of a spell it's more primeval. Maybe he's nicked off through third slip and got away with it, or you've over-pitched and he's driven you, so you want revenge. It's that simple. You're going to hurt him. Really fuck him up. And with the adrenaline flowing as you're running in, that's the plan. Fast and short and *take that you little cunt.* But if you do hit him, you come out of your bubble for a fraction of a second. *Shit that looks nasty.* "You all right, mate?" But then you're straight back into the bubble, ready to follow up that blow with another one. You can't just let the red mist come down completely, you must have some level of control over that anger, but honestly, in the moment, you are actually trying to inflict serious physical harm. Afterwards it's just part and parcel of the game. Later that day I was sat having a few drinks in the Creston clubhouse with the opposition players. They were showing me the various welts and bruises they'd got from where I'd hit them. Trophies from the contest you might say. It was a really nice evening and they were a lovely bunch of guys.

Our final game of that season was at home to Budmouth, who needed a win to retain their league title. We batted first but just couldn't get enough runs on the board. I bowled well enough, taking another four wickets, but in the end they just edged it. It was a slightly anti-climactic way to finish the season, but we had plenty to be proud of. We'd finished third in the league – Emminster's best finish in years. And I'd got the best bowling figures in the entire league, with an average of under fifteen. More importantly perhaps, people were beginning to take notice of me. Wessex hadn't sent any scouts out yet, but there seemed to be a general chat about me around the other clubs.

One Saturday that September, Bethan packed a couple of huge bags and I drove her to Loughborough. When we joined the M5 near Taunton I realised that this was the first time in my life that I'd actually left Wessex. And after getting lost a few times on the campus itself we managed to find the hall where Bethan was going to be staying. I helped carry her stuff up to her room, and sat around for a while drinking tea with her and some of the other students who were arriving. Soon I felt that I was just getting in the way, so we said our goodbyes and I headed back to Emminster. Rummaging around in the glove compartment I found a copy of Duran Duran's *Rio*, which I'd bought but never played. Well, Dougie wasn't there to tell me that it was shite, so I stuck it on good and loud. By the end of the first track with all that sax playing and the "do do, d' do do, doo doo" bit, I began to feel a bit better. And after discovering "My Own Way" – which seemed particularly relevant – I was feeling positively optimistic. Maybe things were looking up.

****

"HULLO. CAT YAR."

"Cat yar?" I queried.

"YAR. CAT. YAR."

I had opened the door to a couple. The girl had thrust her hand forward. Instinctively, I went to shake it, but I was still completely baffled.

Addressing both of them, maybe in the hope that the bloke standing behind her might translate for me, I said, "I'm sorry, what was that again?"

"Her name's Katya. And I'm Bruno."

I looked at Bruno. He looked like a total fucking freak. Starting at the bottom he was wearing a pair of red Converse ankle boots. Both had split, so large parts of his feet were visible. And from what I could see those feet didn't look as though they'd been anywhere near a bath recently. His jeans were a sort of lime-green colour, but they had various stains – probably caused by bodily fluids. His hooded top had evidently been knitted from every available colour of wool. No doubt it would have looked even more garish if he'd ever washed it. His face was the most pallid thing I'd ever seen. And on top of his head, his red hair had been formed into dreadlocks. I'd never seen dreadlocks on a white guy before. That said, I hadn't seen them on a black guy either, because to the best of my knowledge we didn't have a black guy living in Wessex back in 1982. They looked like skanky off-cuts of carpet.

And then I looked at Katya. Strictly speaking, I guess you would have had to categorise what she was wearing as a dress. However, I thought it could be better described as a wigwam with some holes cut for the arms. Actually it was more like the material from three or four non-matching wigwams that had been somehow randomly sewn together to create this confusion of clashing patterns and colours. The *dress* ended just beneath her knees. There was a brief gap where nothing dreadful happened, and then on her feet she was wearing a pair of knackered eighteen-hole Doc Martens. But unlike Bruno, who just had a sort of blob for a face, Katya was striking. She had this dark hair that hung in ringlets, high cheekbones and a pure complexion that somehow defied the couple's apparent approach to personal hygiene.

When I'd put an ad in the local paper, these weren't the sort of housemates I had in mind. But nobody else had responded, and now that they were here I thought I might as well show them around. The tour didn't take very long. I asked if they'd like a cup of tea.

"OH YAR TEA DELISH! A SAM?

"Errr no, I'm a Pete not a Sam." This wasn't getting any easier.

"AH HA HA HA. 'SCUSE ME. DO YOU HAVE ANY **ASSAM** LEAVES?"

"Assam's a tea? No, I don't. I've got Tetley. And the milk's still in-date."

"TETLEY? NO. ABSOLUTELY. GOOD. TREMENDOUS. MMMMMMMM."

"So you'd like a cup, then? Bruno?"

And as I made the tea, I was wondering what on earth we were going to talk about for the next twenty minutes and what sort of people show up to look at a house wearing fancy dress and speaking in riddles. But then it dawned on me that Katya was mentally ill, and that maybe Bruno was dressed like that to make her feel more comfortable. Everything would be a whole lot easier if I just spoke to Bruno. I brought the tea through into the living room.

"I don't think I've seen you around Emminster before," I began. This wasn't strictly true; I was absolutely bloody certain that I hadn't seen anyone who looked even remotely like this pair before. Anywhere. Ever. "Are you new to the area?"

"Yeah," Bruno (thankfully) replied. "Simple story. Met at UCL. Both read anthropology. My dissertation was gift exchange, Katya's was patriarchy. Then finals. And then two months in Goa."

"YAR. GOA. JUST WOW! REALLY. WOW!"

And then, as though this somehow meant something I should understand, Bruno asked, "So, where did you go, Pete?"

"Go? Errr . . . when?" Now I couldn't understand a bloody word he was saying either.

As time went on I found it got a little easier to work out what Katya was on about. Well, at least I began to recognise the words she was using; I was still reliant on Bruno to translate.

"SO YAR. WE'RE HERE TO, LIKE, DECOMPRESS."

"Decompress? Like a diver?"

"Yeah, Pete. You know, three years in London is a long time. It's a lot of stress. It's a lot of pressure. So we're going to spend a year getting our shit back together."

I was sensing that they were actually quite interested in taking the room. But I thought I ought to broach the subject of how they might pay for it: especially if they were going to spend their time *decompressing* rather than actually working anywhere.

"With housing benefit and our social security entitlement, down here in Wessex we shall live like kings."

"BRUNO!"

"And queens," he continued. "I apologise for the patriarchal figure of speech. While we may live in Thatcher's oppressive police state, they won't yet let the population starve. We are still worth more to them alive than dead."

"YAR. SURPLUS LABOUR. MMMMM. WHOLE THING'S BUILT ON SURPLUS LABOUR."

"Exactly Katya. And by removing ourselves from the labour market, we're actually doing them a favour."

I was going to hear a lot more of that sort of thing over the coming year, so I just clarified, "The council will pay your rent, then?"

"ABSOLUTELY. YAR. YAR."

The following day Bruno and Katya moved into the second bedroom. And after a few weeks the oppressive state, through its local representatives in Port Bredy, wrote cheques to Bruno and Katya, so that I could pay the landlord.

As soon as their cash flow was resolved, Bruno came up to me and asked me where I got my weed. I'd shared a joint here and there, but I'd never really been particularly into the stuff. That was more Dougie's field of expertise. I gave him a call down in Plymouth and he gave a name (Barry) and an Emminster address. Credentials are everything in the drugs business I discovered, so I had to go with Bruno to see Barry, tell him that I was best mates with Dougie, that Bruno was a top bloke and that he was looking for some quality product. I was hoping that Barry would get out some gear and that we could then go home. Unfortunately, weed isn't traded like that; at least not in Emminster. First Bruno had to tell Barry where he'd been getting his *shit* from in London. What he was getting. How much he was paying for it. Where it came from. The name of his dealer's cat. And so on. And then Barry, painstakingly slowly, rolled a joint. I just wanted him to light the bloody thing so everybody could try it and we could get out of there. Apparently this was *a sweet smoke maaan. Really nice. Mellow.* Barry was *glaad you appreciate it, maan.* Finally, Bruno bought an eighth and we left. I'm surprised there's any money in drug dealing given the length of time it seems to take to sell the stuff.

Over the weeks that followed, I got to know Bruno and Katya a bit better. Or rather I got to know Katya a bit better. Aside from a fortnightly trip to Port Bredy to sign on – *it's such a fucking imposition maan* – Bruno never left the house in daylight.

It turned out that Katya was the smarter of the two. Apparently she'd got the highest grades you could get on their course, while Bruno had barely scraped a pass. They had met in their first year at the university and had been together ever since. Katya still talked about Bruno as if he was some sort of genius – YAR. YAR. HE SO *SO* GETS IT. YAR – but it would seem that whatever intellect he may have once possessed had deserted him after a punishing three-year programme of weed and acid.

When I got back from work in the evenings that autumn I'd often grab something to eat and then go over to the Black Dog with Katya. Nine pm was still a bit early in the day to wake Bruno, so the pair of us would go alone. And sitting there in the pub Katya explained that what she wanted to do next was write a *thesis*. I established that this was basically a long essay. And in order to be able to sit around for another three years writing an essay she needed funding. (I'd had to write one for my General Studies A-level, but it hadn't taken me three years.)

"Someone will pay you to do this?"

"YAR. ABSOLUTELY. YAR. NEED A GOOD PROPOSAL. BUT YAR."

"So your essay. I mean *thesis*. What's it going to be about?"

"RIGHT. YAR. GRAVITY: A FEMINIST PERSPECTIVE."

"Gravity is gravity, surely? For both of us."

"YAR. WELL. NO. NOT EXACTLY. SCIENCE, MMMMMM, IS A HEGE-MONIC PROJECTION OF MALE POWER."

"H-what?"

"AH. HEGEMONY. RIGHT. WELL, MEN DOMINATE SCIENCE. SO MEN SET THE SCIENTIFIC AGENDA. IT'S LIKE EMBEDDED POWER, RIGHT? YAR? IMPLICIT IN THE SOCIAL STRUCTURES?"

I ignored the last bit. "Sure, but gravity is just a fact, right?"

"WELL. YAR. NO. NEWTON, A MAN, DEFINED GRAVITY. IT WAS *HIS* CONSTRUCT. HE WASN'T INTERESTED IN *OTHER* PROPERTIES OF THE APPLE."

"Such as?"

"MMMMMM. YAH. GOOD POINT. WELL. HMMM. FOR EXAMPLE. ITS CAPACITY TO *FEEL*."

Bethan came back to spend a couple of weeks in Emminster at Christmas. She was wearing her hair a bit shorter, and she had even more muscle definition. She was beginning to look more fit than *fit*. We went out running and I was really struggling to keep up. It was a bit of a wake-up call: unless I kept to a disciplined fitness programme I'd be struggling at the beginning of the next season. I asked Bethan if people like Bruno and Katya were typical of Loughborough students.

"None that I've met." After a pause she said, "But one thing that really puzzles me is what on earth she sees in him? She's absolutely beautiful, and he's just a whinging lump. And Pete, you'd better not shag her while I'm away."

I saw increasingly less of Bruno. But there were signs that he was still alive: he wasn't what you might call a light-touch user of the bathroom, and a large pile of spliff butts was accumulating in the garden underneath his and Katya's bedroom window. Meanwhile, Katya was becoming more active. She'd answered an ad in the paper for a second-hand typewriter and was beginning work on her university application, which itself was a pretty long essay. Seemingly neither Casterbridge nor Budmouth library possessed copies of the scientific or feminist titles she required, so occasionally I'd give her a lift to and from Casterbridge station, from where she'd go on to Southampton or even as far as London.

As it got warmer she wore the wigwam less often. In late May and into June the temperature shot up and Katya would alternate between her two summer outfits. One was a thigh-length pair of blue dungarees and the other could basically be described as a long white t-shirt, worn with a belt. Bras didn't really feature in her summer collection. With the former you'd get a full view of her tits if she ever leant forward, and with the latter, you could clearly see her nipples through the fabric. I have no idea whether she was so wrapped up in her academic world that she hadn't given her clothes any consideration at all, or whether she was consciously telling a male-dominated society that she, Katya, didn't give a fuck. Either way, the men of Emminster, and those drinking in the Black Dog in particular, were pretty comfortable with the situation.

I worked harder than ever before on my pre-season training. I was aware that everybody close to me was getting ahead, and that if I didn't make some sort of breakthrough in 1983 I'd just be left behind: forever an odd-job man. Bethan and Dougie were going to get university degrees, while Danny was on the brink of establishing himself in the Wessex first team. He'd played a Championship match and a couple of one-day games the previous season, but it looked as though he was about to become one of the club's first-choice openers.

I hadn't got to see Danny turn out for the first team before, so when he told me that the West Indians would be playing a World Cup warm-up match at Canberra Park, I asked him if he could get me a couple of tickets. Dougie was up for the weekend from Plymouth, so we arranged to meet in the ground. I had a game starting at Emminster in the early afternoon, so I was just going to hope that Wessex batted first and that I'd get to see Danny do his stuff. I arrived just after the start of play and settled into a seat beside Dougie, facing the pavilion by the side of the sight-screen. It was the beginning of the second over and Danny was on strike.

I've never actually worked out who was bowling that day. Holding and Garner sat the game out, so by process of elimination it was either Wayne Daniel or Andy Roberts from our end of the ground. I'd never seen either of them before, so couldn't immediately say which was which. I wasn't the only bloke in the ground struggling to tell them apart: I subsequently found out that the scorer that day had got Malcolm Marshall opening from both ends. Regardless, whoever bowled to Danny that day, he started with a gentle delivery wide of off-stump that went harmlessly through to the keeper.

"Fack me. Ain't you fellas supposed to be quick?"

There was no doubt that the bowler heard Dougie quite clearly. There were a few giggles in the crowd around us. The second delivery was identical to the first. Again, Danny chose to leave it alone.

"Fack sake. Ees quicker than you." Dougie was pointing to me. "Fack. *I'm* probably quicker than you."

There was another ripple of gentle laughter from the people around us. The bowler made a brief gesture in our direction, as though he was lazily flicking a fly away from the side of his face. And that's where the fun stopped. The next ball was fast. I reckon that it pitched on middle stump halfway down the wicket. It gripped on the seam and appeared to follow Danny. The ball was still rising when it hit Danny square on the jawbone. There were no grilles on the helmets back then. There was a sickening sound – not unlike when a player nails a back-cut with a really waspish bat-speed. There was silence around the ground. Danny dropped his bat and then subsided into the pitch.

For a moment or two I was just sat there, numb. Everything just stopped. The players were closing cautiously on the spot where Danny was lying. They seemed reticent to get there too quickly; maybe they were afraid of what they were going to find. Everything seemed to be happening in super-slow motion. And then I could hear Andy Farrow, the other Wessex batsman yelling, "We need a doctor, we need a fucking doctor", and the full reality of the situation hit me. I don't know what I thought I was going to do when I got there, but I got out of my seat and started running towards the middle of the pitch.

I was well beaten to the square by a youngish GP. He'd sent Farrow to the pavilion to call an ambulance by the time I got out there, and long before George the first-aider at Wessex came shambling out across the ground; no doubt carrying some plasters and a jar of Dettol. Danny looked stricken. The ball had broken the right side of his jaw and smashed a number of teeth in the process, so his whole head looked misshapen and there was a lot of blood. His legs would start twitching intermittently and he was making very disconcerting gurgling and squealing noises. The doctor kept saying reassuring things, and repeating, "It's not as bad as it looks." And I was thinking that he'd better be right, because it looked absolutely fucking awful. After what seemed like an eternity the medics arrived and Danny was put onto a stretcher and taken to the ambulance.

I went and found Dougie back in the stand and told him that I'd better get over to Whetstock to tell Mum what had happened, before driving over to Emminster to see if there was anyone else available to fill in for me in our game. I really didn't feel like playing. Mum was a bit panicked and she got Mr Hendricks to drive her down to the hospital in Budmouth. When I got to the ground back in Emminster I went to find Dennis, our skipper. But before I could get a word out, he said, "See that bloke sitting on the northern bank." I looked where Dennis was pointing and saw a chunky-looking guy, probably in his mid-fifties. "Do you know who that is?"

"No, idea, Skip."

"That's Jeff Carter. And I'm pretty sure he's here to see you."

Jeff Carter was the bowling coach at Wessex. And it was a pretty safe assumption that if he was touring around league sides, he was there to do a bit of scouting.

"He said he's going to watch the first ten overs or so before going back to Canberra Park to see how his bowlers do against the West Indians."

Carter's timing was absolutely terrible. I was in no mood to bowl whatsoever, but the chance to impress the Wessex bowling coach might not come along again any time soon, so I resolved to just get on with it. I couldn't exactly ask Jeff if he'd like to come back next week.

It was really hot and muggy that afternoon. You could sense that the ball would hoop around nicely, but bowling was going to be hard work. Dennis lost the toss and the opposition skipper decided to bat. So I got into my kit and did a half-hearted warm-up routine. I was worried because I really wasn't up for it at all. I always bowled best when I was feeling a bit spiteful and nasty, when I used intimidation to get on top of a batsman. But right now, I felt that I'd seen enough intimidation for one day.

I opened from the northern end of the ground, so I could see Jeff clearly as I walked back to my mark before each delivery. With the humid conditions the ball was swinging prodigiously, but it was actually going too far and too early. So the batsmen weren't unduly troubled and I couldn't really control it. In fact, I ended up bowling cross-seam just to get the thing going down a useful line. But in so doing it was now gun-barrel straight, and even targeting the top of off, I wasn't much of a handful for the batsmen. I must have bowled six or seven fairly innocuous overs – nothing to suggest that I was ready to step up to the next level.

I was pretty down on myself at the end of that spell. It really had been a bad day. First Danny, and now I'd only gone and stuffed up my chance to impress Wessex. But as I jogged around the outfield between various fielding positions, I noticed that Jeff hadn't headed off back to Canberra Park. And I could also figure out why. Katya had pitched up – without Bruno obviously – to watch the game. And miraculously, from my point of view, she'd also decided to sit on the north bank. It was the sawn-off dungarees that day. I could even see that Jeff was asking her to point out the various sites around Emminster, which no doubt created all manner of more locally interesting viewing opportunities. But Jeff didn't just hang around for my second spell; he hung around for several more entire games at Emminster that summer. Despite Katya's assertion that cricket was a tool of the oppressors in the class war that she assured me was raging across the country, she seemed to genuinely like watching the game. And Jeff Carter, more understandably, loved watching Katya watching cricket.

My second spell that day was more menacing that my first. But in the subsequent games – when I knew that Danny was going to be OK – I put in some of my best, most spiteful and most effective bowling performances to date. And Jeff, while also enjoying other distractions, saw all of them.

I drove down to the hospital in Budmouth that evening to see Danny. He looked dreadful and he couldn't speak, but he wasn't in any danger. His cricket season was certainly over, almost before it had begun. He would need a plate in his jaw, he would have to spend weeks with his face wired, and finally he would require some serious dental surgery to replace the smashed molars. I drove back to Emminster feeling somewhat relieved. I parked the car outside the house and asked Katya if she wanted a quick pint in the Black Dog before closing time. Walking back home from the pub we could both sense that the weather was about to break. The air was still and heavy; you could feel the tension in the atmosphere.

I don't know whether it was the thunder, the lightning or the blow that slammed into the pillow beside my head that woke me that night. Silhouetted by the lightning flashes coming from outside, a heavily bearded, naked figure was attacking my bed with a weapon. Without hesitating to consider my likely state of arousal, I spun out of bed, leapt up and grabbed the implement. It was my own bat. And, although I didn't recognise him at first, it was Bruno. I just started yelling.

"What the fuck are you doing, you could have killed her."

"So you *have* been sleeping with her."

"No Bruno. I said that because *you* thought that she was there. And if she had been – which she wasn't – you'd have fucking killed her."

"So you haven't been sleeping with her?"

"I'm married, Bruno. Of course I haven't been sleeping with her."

"So where is she then?"

I stared out of the window into the garden where Katya had become one with the storm. She was wearing merely a white t-shirt that was by now completely soaked and completely see-through. She was standing in the torrential rain looking up to the sky. She was oblivious to the ruckus inside the house. And as we both stood there, with me now firmly in control of the bat, we watched her. I really don't think Katya had any idea of the effect she had on men.

Later that summer Bethan called to see if I'd mind if she spent a few weeks travelling around Europe with one of the girls I'd briefly met at her residence. I was a bit pissed off when she first called, but then I reckoned it might be for the best anyway. I really needed to focus on whatever remaining opportunities I'd got to impress Jeff, so I didn't want anything to stop Katya from watching the games.

I bowled brilliantly over the rest of the 1983 season for Emminster and we beat the big teams when they came to our patch, and we beat pretty much everyone else at their place. And on the first weekend in September we won the league for the first time in the club's history. Finally I looked like the real deal – a player ready to step up a level.

Katya got a letter in July of that year telling her that she'd got the funding to write her essay. I don't reckon she ever did discover a feminist version of gravity that works any differently from the regular women-oppressing kind, but she was thrilled when the news came through. I realised that I was going to miss her, even though she was without a doubt the weirdest girl I've ever met. It had become clear over the course of the summer that she and Bruno were no longer an item. He got an offer to study teacher training and left Emminster in early September to head down to Plymouth. It must have been the last Sunday in September when I drove Katya over to Casterbridge station. I waited on the platform with her until her train arrived, and as it pulled into the station we shared a brief hug before she got into her carriage. It was like she'd come from a completely different world, and she was returning to it. She leant out of the window and waved as the train pulled away. And that was the last time I ever saw her.

October came and went. One Saturday, when I was thinking that I really ought to get round to putting a new ad in the paper to let the second bedroom again, I saw a letter on the front door mat. It was from Wessex Cricket Club.

Dear Peter,

Following reports of your exceptional season for Emminster this year, I am delighted to offer you a one-season development contract at Wessex Cricket Club – commencing on April 1st 1984 and terminating on September 30th of the same year. Payment will be £70 per week plus any match-related expenses. I very much hope you will accept this offer and I look forward to you joining our playing staff next year.

Yours sincerely,

Sebastian Welland-Flanders

Fucking yes. Get in there. I was going to be a professional cricket player. But I had to have a wry smile thinking about Jeff Carter – waiting for Katya to show up week in, week out. Maybe I owe her my entire career.

There was the tell-tale aroma
of stale cigarette smoke.

5. INSIDE CANBERRA PARK DRESSING ROOM

Wessex Cricket Club was officially founded in 1891. It can trace its history further back to the eighteenth century when The Gentlemen and Players of Wessex would tour the South West taking on all comers. By the 1870s a team calling itself Wessex was playing at a permanent ground in Casterbridge. Then in 1895 Captain Richard Thornton, a Wessex ship owner, bequeathed the club a significant plot of land called Canberra Fields in Budmouth, and the club moved there from Casterbridge the following year.

It is rumoured that, as a young man in the 1860s, Thornton was heavily involved in smuggling French brandy into Britain. Using his sailing skills to avoid the attentions of the Royal Navy, Thornton reputedly landed shipments up and down the length of Jurassic Beach. It is said that he was a cricketing fanatic and that he wanted Wessex CC moved to his hometown of Budmouth. His story lives on today with the club playing as the *Wessex Smugglers* in the modern Twenty20 competition. The garish purple strip worn by the players has divided opinion among the members: as has been pointed out on more than one occasion, the chances of them smuggling anything unnoticed these days would be remarkably slim. Bethan says that from a distance they look more like a collection of Ribena bottles than a cricket team.

As generous as Captain Thornton may have been, and as much as he might have wanted to atone for his criminal behaviour, he couldn't have bequeathed *that* much money to Wessex Cricket Club: Canberra Park is on the very out-skirts of Budmouth, just off the main road to Casterbridge. If Canberra Park hadn't been built there, you could very easily imagine the site being used for an out-of-town garden store; the sort of place with a separate pet shop and good parking facilities.

The members' stand and pavilion at Canberra Park is at the southern end of the ground, and it faces the Dinsdale Stand to the north. Mervyn Dinsdale was possibly the greatest Wessex player that never was. A fast bowler, he almost certainly would have been the first Wessex player to win an England cap, but for the interruption to his career caused by the Second World War. But by the time the County Championship resumed in 1946, a combination of age and a shrapnel wound to his right leg (inflicted by the Luftwaffe in Malta), resulted in him losing his pre-war zip. Nonetheless, until the emergence of Herb Brunton, Dinsdale's bowling records set the standard at Wessex. Behind the Dinsdale Stand is the Wessex Indoor Sports Hall (known to players as the WISH) where there are full winter and bad-weather training facilities. Uncovered stands flank the rest of the ground.

It was Monday 2nd April 2nd 1984. Colin Beresford and me were standing in the members' room at Canberra Park, getting the official tour of the place from Len. Every club has a Len. He was about a hundred and four when I joined Wessex and he was still there when I left: he didn't age appreciably over that time. Len's primary job seemed to be the opening and closing of the players' gate out to the pitch during games. He was also supposed to help out around the dressing rooms, but he wasn't exactly the fastest mover, so you were generally better sorting things out for yourself. Unfortunately he didn't smell great. Nonetheless, Len possessed an encyclopaedic knowledge of Wessex Cricket Club.

I'd met Colin the day before. When I say met, I rather mean that I'd been in the same place with him before. Col had the appearance of a rather tall wardrobe with a storm-damaged haystack balanced on the top. Occasionally you'd get a glimpse of his nose, or maybe his mouth, if he made a particular point of brushing a portion of his mane aside to say something important. But, up until now, that hadn't happened so I couldn't really say that I'd *met* him. Col was a foreigner. Actually he was from Devon, but as far as Len was concerned, that amounted to much the same thing.

"You're not a Wessex boy then, son? Don't know about that. Last one of your lot we had was Franny Dawkins. 'Course, he's dead now."

Col didn't seem to be bothered by Len's apparent hostility. In fact, Col didn't seem to be particularly bothered by anything. It turned out that Col's journey to Wessex Cricket Club wasn't that dissimilar from my own. He hadn't excelled at school cricket and consequently hadn't been picked up by the Devon set-up. He had suffered from a seriously wonky radar – something that would continue to go on the blink throughout his professional career – so he'd ended up playing league cricket for a club on the northern edge of Dartmoor. Having variously dismissed or hospitalised scores of decent league players over the previous couple of seasons, Col, it seems, had occasionally torn Jeff Carter's attentions away from Katya's tits to watch him bowl in a few games.

I can't say that I've ever liked the members' room at Canberra Park. It had dark-green carpet, and a similarly dark shade of thick contoured paper covering the walls. There was also a lot of dark wood panelling around the room. Most of the surfaces – the tables, the bar, and the shelves surrounding the edge of the room – were coated in a thin film of grease, the residue of countless greasy buffet meals served in there down the years. The walls were covered in framed paintings and photographs – starting with pictures of tubby men in top hats posing with hockey-shaped bats, right up to the present day. Overall the décor had more in common with a run-down seafront bed-and-breakfast establishment than an elite sports club. All that wood, leather and lack of light served as some sort of monument to former glories. Not that Wessex really had that many former glories. Aside from the odd piece of silverware to commemorate the defeat of a pre-war university side or the Bristol Lodge of Freemasons, Wessex had never won anything. The club's greatest achievement was that it hadn't, in its entire history, ever picked up the wooden spoon in the Championship. But they don't hand out silverware for not coming last.

As Len continued to bang on about the club's history I just found myself staring out the window, down towards the pitch below. Now *that* looked magnificent. The playing surface was much larger than anything I'd ever set foot on in anger before, and the outfield looked superb. Gus Jackman, the head groundsman, was working on the square with one of his assistants. There were sprinklers in action across several areas of the field. The sun was out and the drops of water shone and sparkled through the air. To me it just looked like a beautiful stage – waiting for the players to come down the pavilion steps and take up their positions. That's where I wanted to be, not up here in a stuffy, dark old museum.

The club had arranged some accommodation for us, so me, Col and another player, Phil Grey, were sharing a three-bedroom bungalow in a very quiet residential street at the back of Creston. The club could no doubt argue that Creston was ideally located for us, what with it being a couple of miles around the bay from Budmouth itself, and an even shorter distance around the wetland reserve to Canberra Park. But in truth I think they'd put us there, rather than some other equally affordable area closer to the city centre, because in Creston there was absolutely nothing to do. There were no nocturnal temptations of any kind whatsoever. Just by moving in we must have halved the average age of the local population.

Maybe we'd have shared the house with Danny if he hadn't already quit the game. Physically he was back in one piece by the end of the 1983 season – albeit with a little extra metalwork to hold his jaw together. But by the time he was cleared to play again, the season had finished. So the club suggested that he go down to Australia during our winter to play a high standard of league cricket. He joined the Camberwell Magpies in Melbourne.

He loved the weather. He quite liked Australians. But his batting had simply fallen apart. He says that, even today, he can *feel* his jaw. It doesn't actually hurt or ache, it's just that he's always physically aware of it. He claims he senses changes in the weather through his jaw, long before he sees any changes in the sky. So when he was batting for the Magpies, he was thinking about his jaw, not his footwork or his shot selection. Stroke-making, which had been a sub-conscious, carefree, natural thing for him to do, had become conscious, stressful and a chore. At first he thought he'd be able to bat himself back into form. But the more he worked at his game, and the more he analysed it, the worse he got. He'd been reduced from a batting god to a mere mortal like the rest of us. One by one he lost all of his attacking shots, until he was just left with a tentative forward defensive prod.

By the time he got on the return flight home, he'd decided that his cricket career was over. Maybe if he'd always been a grafter at the crease, he'd have stuck at it for a couple more seasons to see if he could fight his way back. But that wasn't the sort of player Danny had ever wanted to be. It would be like Viv Richards waking up one day to find that his natural ability had been swapped for Chris Tavaré's. Still. I tried to talk Danny out of it. I even got Dougie to drop by and see if he could change his mind. Dougie suggested that he could take on Danny as a client and find him a new start at a different club. But it was all to no avail. Danny landed a job with Davison's, an estate agency in Port Bredy. He got on well with old Bill Davison who owned the business, and he threw all of his energy into his new career.

Not many people have ever said this of the city, but Plymouth had a civilising effect on Dougie. His clothes were completely different. Gone were the jeans, trainers, leather jackets and classic-tour tops with venues and dates down the back, to be replaced by chinos, deck shoes, cotton blazers and button-down shirts. Sometimes he'd even do that eighties thing where he'd roll up the sleeves of his jacket like John Taylor in the *Rio* video or Don Johnson in *Miami Vice*. Clearly, he wasn't going to quite match either in the looks department, but he'd certainly had a wardrobe re-think – no doubt it all helped with the seduction of the numerous ex-public schoolgirls he'd been meeting. He spoke differently too. Meeting him in 1984 you'd have never suspected that his parents were Syd and Cyn from East London. Whereas once he might have said something like, "Fack me, ain't you erd a single fackin word I said, you cloff eared cant," he'd now say, "Fuck me, haven't you heard a single fucking word I said, you cloth-eared cunt?" He'd got a new look but it was the same old Dougie underneath.

Since graduating the previous summer he'd rented a flat in Casterbridge. With the new sales and marketing skills he'd picked up he wanted to move into sports and music management. I was going to be the first professional sportsman on his books. He was also looking to represent other players, as well as managing some of the better bands working in the region. His first music act was Captain Reckless and the Wreckage. It turns out the captain wasn't particularly reckless at all; by day he was a supervisor called Simon Coleman in the Budmouth council housing department. By night he was a good vocalist and he fronted a crack band of local musicians. They'd play covers really well, working the latest chart material into their act. And more importantly they'd learn pretty much anything you wanted if you booked them for a function.

Col and me settled into life in Creston. And when he wasn't away with the first team we were joined by Phil. Phil Grey was a batsman who'd been in the Wessex youth set-up since he was about fourteen. He was a little bit younger than us two, and because he'd been on various development contracts since he left school at sixteen, he'd never had to go out and find work or anything like that. Col, on the other hand, had done just about every menial, soul-destroying job that Devonshire farming had to offer. So he'd repaired miles of fencing in the middle of January, he'd worked in an abattoir, he'd got up at four-thirty in the mornings to move milk herds; you name it, he'd done it. Like me, Col came pre-knocked in.

Phil had led a charmed life up until 1984. His father was something in the main branch of NatWest in Budmouth. Phil had been coached from the age of eight in the colts set-up at Budmouth CC. He was expected to become a mainstay of the Wessex top order for some years to come. Col and me didn't get to see that much of him during the early part of the season because he'd been fast-tracked into the first-team squad.

In pre-season Brian Gunnell, the club coach, worked with the first team in the WISH. But those of us destined for the second eleven had to drive up to the club ground in Casterbridge, where Jeff Carter led the sessions. For me it was a little bit anti-climactic: I'd played league cricket for the previous four seasons on this ground, so I was a bit disappointed to find myself in early April jogging laps of the outfield and doing various conditioning exercises with a medicine ball on what, to all intents and purposes, was a public recreation ground.

In the early part of that summer, Col and me found ourselves touring around the first-class counties' second-tier venues, playing a surprisingly high standard of cricket in front of an unsurprisingly low number of spectators. Second-eleven cricket isn't really a team game. Nobody remembers or cares about the results, it's all about the individual players' performances. You've got young players on development contracts mixed in with older guys who are either out of form, coming back from injury or reaching the end of their careers. But none of them want to be there. Given the choice between winning games versus getting out of the second string, all eleven players would choose the latter.

When you're walking out in front of three men and a dog it's easy to forget just how close you could be to playing first-class cricket. You're just one guy's injury, or another's loss of form, away from your first-class debut. There were some decent players turning out for their county's second teams in 1984: young players waiting for a first-team opportunity included Alec Stewart, Gus Fraser, Devon Malcolm and Phil Tufnell, while seasoned old pros like Chris Old and David Graveney were still on the circuit. You certainly couldn't just expect to show up and run through one of these sides.

For Col, bowling was always a battle: first with himself and then with the batsman: always in that order. Cricket is one of those sports that can accommodate players who aren't what you'd call *natural sportsmen*. And Col certainly wasn't a *natural sportsman* – he was useless at football – he had no feel for the ball whatsoever. He was also a proper traditional number-eleven bat: he was as fearless as he was useless. He could find any number of ways of playing around a dead straight delivery. But given licence and a lot of luck, he could deposit just about any bowler back over their head for six. That said, I don't think his success rate would have been hugely hampered had he played blindfolded. There was a whole lot of Col to coordinate.

Typically he'd start a bowling spell by berating himself with the back end of some expletive.

"'k sake Col. 'k sake."

And then if he didn't improve he'd start chanting his way back to his mark.

"Get it right you stupid cunt. 'king get it right."

And if that didn't have the desired effect, he'd take things up to the next level.

"That's fucking shit Col. Total shit. Fucking come on. COME ON!"

He never played with a smile on his face.

However, when the gods chose to smile on Col, and when the stars were aligned, he was lethal. He could be both physically intimidating and close to unplayable. He could get the ball to rear up from just back of a length, and he could get significant movement off the seam. But even a wicket-taking over from Col could easily include a four ball, a no-ball for over-stepping and a massive wide. Somewhere in that giant frame, and underneath all that hair, was potentially the most fearsome strike bowler that Wessex had ever produced. And every time he played, Col put himself through hell trying to find him. But away from the cut-strip Col was perhaps the most chilled-out, relaxed person I've ever known.

"Do you want pizza or the lasagne tonight, Col?"

"Don't mind."

"Lager or the last of those John Smiths?"

"Whatever. It's all good."

Back in Creston we'd settled into a very comfortable evening routine. We'd plough through about six cans of beer each, and I would follow the instructions on whatever ready meals we had in the freezer. Col, meanwhile, would prepare his evening spliff. After a few weeks we'd given up ever opening the living-room curtains, so we'd just sit there in the dark, chilling out and listening to music. Col was a big Pink Floyd fan. But not so much the more popular stuff like *Dark Side of the Moon* or *Wish You Were Here*; Col preferred those meandering records they made after Syd Barrett left, without any actual songs on them. I would then liven things up by playing any number of cracking pop singles. Even Col could sing along to "Pale Shelter" by Tears For Fears, or "Don't You Want Me Baby" by the Human League.

And then occasionally Phil Grey would come back and intrude on our domestic harmony. He always had the look of someone who had just got off a force-seven Channel ferry crossing, having puked himself down couple of trouser sizes. He'd usually ask us two questions, and usually in the same order:

"Has Belinda rung?"

Belinda was his girlfriend.

"No."

In truth, she might have rung, but the phone was in the hallway, which made answering the thing, if not impossible, certainly very difficult. Col couldn't get up either mid-spliff or mid-Floyd, and I reckoned that, since I'd already prepared the food, it wasn't right that I should have to go. So Phil would move on to the second question.

"Can I play some music?"

"Sure."

He'd grab a beer from the fridge, put on "Perfect Circle" and then just sit there staring into space.

Then Col would invariably ask, "Phil, who is this again?"

"R.E.M."

"Right, right. Oh yeah. You said."

I didn't know what they'd been doing to Phil in the first team, but they had clearly knocked the stuffing out of him. He was actually scoring a few runs and his stats didn't look too bad at all. But whenever he returned from a match, especially when he'd been away on the road, he came back looking absolutely shell-shocked. Never having been inside the first-team dressing room, Col and me didn't really have any advice to give him, so instead we just offered weed, beer and ready meals; and we let him play as much self-pitying, dreary music on the hi-fi as he wanted.

I found myself wondering how different the first-team dressing room could be to anything that I'd experienced before. It might even have been at that very moment, when I was sitting there watching Phil endure his psychological agony, that a few miles away in Budmouth Regis, first-change seamer Craig Holland experienced agony of a more physical nature. Craig was walking barefoot to his garden shed, to find a spare light bulb. And in the dark he had absolutely no chance of seeing the circular saw he'd left, and forgotten, in the middle of the floor. The surgeon at Budmouth General actually managed to save the big toe on his left foot; but not the rest of his season, and not much of the rest of his career.

Sometimes one man's excruciating, indescribable pain is another man's opportunity. I would experience that first-team dressing room soon enough.

Before I got the call from Brian Gunnell (strictly speaking he sent a message via Phil – if he'd relied on phoning me I'd probably still be in the second eleven today), Bethan showed up in Creston. She wasn't very impressed. Arriving, as she did, unannounced one Saturday morning in late June, both the house and its inhabitants were in something of a state. The previous night Col and me had hosted 'album face-off'. Basically this just involved each of us playing an album of our choice really loud and then trying to persuade the other that it was better than his album. Given that neither of us was ever going to change our mind, Phil always held the casting vote. And I can only put it down to his fragile state of mind that he declared Pink Floyd's tedious, dull and self-indulgent *The Final Cut* a better album than Michael Jackson's *Thriller*.

I'd only just gone to bed when Bethan started hammering on the front door the following morning, so I was feeling pretty shabby as I made my way down the hallway, holding on to the walls for support. We hadn't really got a system for dealing with the rubbish, so there was a six-foot pile of old pizza boxes leaning against the garden door. Every kitchen surface was covered in either used crockery, scraps of food or ready-meal packaging. The living room was full of crushed beer cans. That had started innocently enough. Col and me finished a couple of beers one evening and were trying to decide whose turn it was to get the next pair out of the fridge.

"Tell you what Pete. Whoever lands their empty tightest in the far corner stays put."

"And I can crush it a bit to stop it rolling back?"

"Sure. Whatever you like."

"Fuck. That's harder than it looks. Have you played this before?"

We never picked up any of the cans we threw, and pretty soon it didn't even work as a game because you couldn't identify the can you'd just thrown from the rest of the pile. But it meant none of our finished cans ever left the house. Col had also stopped emptying the ashtray he used in the living room because the bin in the kitchen was already overflowing. He'd come up with a short-term solution, which involved using a massive fruit bowl as a giant mega-ashtray.

"You look awful. Are you ill?"

"It's good to see you too, Bethan."

"No really, you look a fucking state, Pete. And what *is* that smell?"

"Ah that. Yeah, well, you get used to it after a while. Anyway, how are you?"

"Shocked. Appalled. Disgusted. I think that covers it."

Bethan had edged past me into the hallway and glanced into the living room and the kitchen. I was trying to come up with a convincing explanation for the overall state of affairs, when Bethan noticed the mouse droppings across the kitchen floor. I hadn't seen them before. Whatever position I was going to take, it was going to be indefensible. So I agreed to her plan of events for the day. We went down to the local shop and cleared them out of cleaning products and bin liners, and then I woke up Col and Phil to get them to help out. It was the first time that Bethan had met either of them.

"So you're both professional sportsmen, eh? Well, I'd shake your hands, but I haven't got my rubber gloves on yet."

After about five hours of concentrated physical exertion, we'd managed to return the bungalow to some sort of presentable state. Once Bethan was assured that we were going to stick to our allotted tasks, she drove off to the market and retuned with some sea bass. To celebrate our deliverance from domestic hell (and ignoring the fact that this hell was entirely self-inflicted), we thought we'd make an evening of it and invite Dougie and Belinda around to join us. I always think of Belinda as Dougie's first wife. Back in the summer of 1984 she was actually Phil's first girlfriend. Belinda was a mousy little thing, but quite cute with delicate little features and a small up-turned nose. She had this exaggerated movement, where she'd hold her head at a strange angle, to demonstrate that she was listening to someone. This had the effect of making her look, almost permanently, either fascinated or surprised. She worked as a paralegal in Budmouth for Riley and Sharpe: something that maybe Dougie hadn't considered when she took him to the cleaners in the divorce courts a few years later.

Bethan grilled the fish, prepared a salad and roasted some vegetables. We shared some white wine and some rosé. Col even had a night off from the weed. It was all so grown up. Bethan made good use of the moral high ground she was on, by suggesting to Col and me that if we washed up right there and then, it wouldn't take too long and it would be easy to keep on top of things. So we quietly got on with it while the others drank coffee. We never quite lived up to Bethan's exacting culinary and hygienic standards while we lived in Creston, but never again did we plumb our previous depths of depravity.

Dougie was on top form that night. Full of stories about how he'd discovered these great vineyards in France the previous summer, and how he was going to import their wines. How he'd ended up with a seat in the director's box at Plymouth Argyle when he was down there. I'd had no idea of all the things he'd been getting up to while he was away. He was also remarkably well informed about Wessex CC – he was congratulating Phil on several of his innings that season. Again I had no idea that he followed the club so closely.

"Yeah Phil, the sixty-eight at Taunton could have just been a flash in the pan, but when you followed that up with the eighty at Chelmsford, that's when you really got *my* attention."

Christ, I didn't even know that we'd already played Essex this season: and here was Dougie talking in some detail about an individual player's performances. Incredible. He went on to say that in his opinion what Wessex really needed was to shake things up by giving the captaincy to a quality young player. Like Phil. I think he was going a bit far there, but I suppose Phil really needed to hear that someone believed in him. Dougie then had Belinda in hysterics by demonstrating how Captain Reckless had got an entire wedding party to perform the dance routine from Adam Ant's "Prince Charming" the previous week.

The evening eventually ended after he got us all to perform an a cappella version of "Stand and Deliver". He got me and Bethan doing the *da diddley qa qa, da diddley qa qa* bits, Col just had to master the baritone *orrrooooh* notes, while Dougie himself, Phil and Belinda sang the main chorus bit in a round. Then we'd all have a turn at ad-libbing stuff, attempts at the whistled bits and general yelping.

On the following Tuesday, Phil came home with the message from Brian Gunnell. I was in the first-team squad for the next day's home Championship match against Derbyshire. I'd like to be able to say that I coolly took this news in my stride, prepared a healthy chicken salad for dinner, worked though a few positive visualisation exercises and then got a good night's sleep. But my mouth and my bowels had other ideas. I spent most of the evening running from the telephone in the hall, which I was using to tell everyone I'd ever met about my news, to the bathroom where I was repeatedly performing industrial-scale evacuations. I think I maybe slept for an hour that night. I spent most of the time lying awake yo-yoing between bouts of euphoria and humiliation. *I've made it! I'm a professional! I'm going to take ten wickets!* But then some other voice in my head would take over. *What if you can't even hit the cut-strip? What if you're just going to carry the drinks? Then what are you going to say to everyone?* By the time I finally got up I was absolutely knackered.

In the morning I hauled my coffin up the stairs and then followed the signs down the corridor. I didn't want to get caught out without the right kit, so I'd put just about every piece of cricketing paraphernalia I owned into the container. It weighed a bloody ton. I dumped it in the far corner of the dressing room and sat down on the wooden bench. The room was smaller than I'd imagined: a lot smaller. I could tell that by the time an entire team was in here it would be pretty cramped. It was also pretty knackered. There were a number of bat-sized dents in the plasterboard wall that separated the main locker room from the even smaller shower room. The cream paint had yellowed with age, and was peeling off the ceiling in places. There was the tell-tale aroma of stale cigarette smoke. I got up and opened the door that led to the players' balcony. It too was small; I guessed that you could maybe fit four players out there at a time. Then I heard a clattering behind me; another player was dragging his coffin into the changing room.

"You can't put that there Sonny. That's the skip's spot."

I recognised Laurie Kelly immediately. He looked like an earnest welterweight who was on the wrong side of his win:loss ratio. But he looked fit. There was a hyperactivity about everything he did – from the quick jerky movements of his limbs to the staccato bark of his voice. I held my hand out and was about to introduce myself, but he just sat down and started rummaging through his kit bag for something.

"That one," he said without looking up, pointing to a locker in the opposite corner of the dressing room. Whatever it was that he was looking for seemed to have the lion's share of his attention.

I dragged my coffin across the room to the spot Kelly had just pointed to and sat back down. I considered trying to introduce myself again, but thought better of it. So I sat there silently while Kelly carried on feverishly scratching around at the contents of his bag. The noise he was making sounded like a rodent foraging feverishly for scraps of food in a rubbish bin.

"Sorry old bean, but unless I been given the chop mid-season, that's still my locker. David Collister." The newcomer offered his hand, as I started moving my coffin for the second time. "I think you'll be fine there," he added pointing to another spot a few feet away.

I was about to introduce myself to Collister when Kelly, without taking his head out of his bag, shouted a muffled, "No. No. No. Down one more." With one free hand he was pointing to a space a few feet further down the wall.

I used my feet to kick my coffin into its new location, while offering my hand to Collister. In the flesh, he looked even older and even more donnish than he did from the stands. Collister had been Wessex' first-choice spinner ever since I could remember. So I guess he must have been in his mid-thirties and that his gallows humour about getting dropped was based on the reality that, at some point over the next season or two, the management would call time on his professional career.

Andy Farrow appeared at the dressing-room door. He momentarily looked like a normal human being, before noticing exactly where I was sitting. He then looked at me like I'd shagged his wife or something, and then he just let out this howl: "WHY?"

I jumped up from the bench and moved another couple of spaces down the wall. Farrow had grabbed a handkerchief from his jacket pocket and was manically polishing the spot that I'd just vacated. At this point I had no intention of attempting to introduce myself to him because he was simply mumbling, "What have you gone and done? What have you done?" over and over again. I'd heard some stories about Farrow before, but I'd assumed they were all exaggerated for effect. It would have been funny to watch if it weren't so disconcerting: Wessex's leading batsman on his hands and knees furiously scrubbing the bench, while the rest of the players ignored him.

Kelly looked up from his coffin with an air of frustration. "I didn't say there, did I?" I was about to tell him that I'd been sitting *exactly* where he'd pointed to, but I thought better of it. He then stuck his head back in his kit bag, so I was left standing like a spare part in the centre of the room holding my coffin. Without waiting for further instructions, I just picked a new location on the facing wall and sat back down.

Herb Brunton came in and sat down opposite me. I breathed a sigh of relief. Herb was my hero and my inspiration, so I was enormously pleased that I hadn't gone and sat in his space.

He leaned across the gap between the benches and offered his hand. "Herb. You going to be bowling for us today?"

"Well, errrr… sure. If I'm asked, sir. Yeah, errr… I'm Peter. Peter Legend." I don't normally get star struck, but I was a young player sat in a dressing room opposite Herb the Curve. Herb the Swerve. Whatever you called him, he was the best swing bowler Wessex had ever produced. Every decent league batsman in Wessex who ever played in the 1970s claimed to have scored runs against the young Herb Brunton from Port Bredy. My dad had scored a fifty against him – allegedly. But if all these stories were true, he'd have leaked so many runs and taken so few wickets that he'd have never gone on to play for

Wessex. I'm sure a lot of league players remember facing Herb, but I reckon they might be misremembering quite how well they played against him.

In 1984, Herb must have been in his mid- to late thirties. He was smaller than I expected, and not so much older as timeless. He looked like he could only be photographed in black and white. Herb wasn't so much a sportsman as a craftsman – put a ball in his hand and he could make it talk.

I thought I'd made a bit of a fool of myself, but just meeting Herb had made my day. I think I had, for the first time that morning, a smile on my face. Carl Musgrove wiped it off quickly enough.

"Day one and you think you're ready to take the number seven spot, eh big guy?" He held out a hand and, catching me slightly by surprise, gave me one of those test-of-strength handshakes. "Carl Musgrove," he said, before adding, "Now do us a favour and fuck off out of my locker space."

Carl and his brother Alan were non-identical twins. They had already developed a bit of a reputation as the closest thing Budmouth had to playboys. Their father ran Musgroves, the biggest car and van rental business in the area. Carl was a middle-order batsman and seam bowler. The fans liked him: even if the game wasn't going Wessex's way he'd still be there, getting in the faces of the opposition, making his presence felt. I couldn't help notice his clothes: the chunky watch, and the highlights in his hair. Carl looked expensive. His brother Alan grunted a brief hello, and settled into the space beside him. Alan seemed to have spent a little less time on his hair, and he wasn't quite as physically imposing as his brother, but it was clear that he too spent a fair bit of money on his appearance. They both looked as though they belonged on a breakfast TV couch.

I dragged my coffin back across the room to where there were a couple of free spaces left. I sat down. Again.

"Sorry mate, that one's mine." I looked up to see Justin Bridges. "I imagine you've been on a bit of a journey this morning." He introduced himself and offered his hand. I didn't know that much about Bridges. He'd been at the club for a couple of seasons and had carved out a reputation as a fairly reliable player near the top of the order. Without drawing any attention to it, he briefly pointed to one of the last empty spaces with the thumb of his left hand.

I thought he'd stitched me up when club captain Tony Sinclair came in through the door and made straight for where I was sitting. I was about to groan with disappointment, but he just came up to me as said, "Sit down, no need to stand. Tony Sinclair. Good to have you on board."

"It's a record everybody. It's a new record," Kelly was shouting across the dressing room. "That was fully six moves, and you Alan, owe me five pounds."

As various players were congratulating Kelly on a new record, David Collister asked me, "Just to be clear, you weren't in on this were you?" I shook my head. I was feeling a bit embarrassed that I'd been played so easily, but when I noticed that I was back in the very first spot I'd sat in, I had to see the funny side.

Brian Gunnell stuck his head around the dressing-room door and harried everyone down onto the outfield to do some warm-up routines. There wasn't a massive amount of enthusiasm among the rest of the players, but they obediently started filing out into the corridor and down the stairs. We started with some stretches, then some jogging and finally a number of fielding exercises. Tony Sinclair ambled across the outfield towards me.

"Peter, you're playing today. Enjoy it." And with that he just wandered off.

Tony won the toss and we batted first. Coming in at number ten, I scored a handful of runs in the late afternoon before running out of partners at the other end. The following day I made my bowling debut. I'll admit it, I was terrified. By the time I came on all I wanted to do was keep it tight and not embarrass myself. I bowled half a dozen overs in my first spell and I didn't try to do anything other than bowl my stock out-swinger. It wasn't the best ever spell in world cricket, but neither was it the worst. Tony chucked me the ball again after lunch, and I got a little bit more confident. I started trying a few variations, my in-swinger and the occasional bouncer.

And then, on the last ball of my fourth over, it happened: my first ever first-class wicket. I'm not bitter, but I think Carl Musgrove basically stole the moment from me. He was fielding – or he should have been – at long on, in front of the pavilion, when I tried my split-finger-grip slower ball. It was a peach of a delivery, even if I say so myself. Such was my disguise on it that the batsman was about an hour and a half early on the shot. The ball just ballooned down to long on like it was catching practice. Only Musgrove was either signing programmes or flirting with some girl in the stand, so he didn't even start looking for the ball in the air until he heard the cries of 'catch' coming from the middle. To be fair, he rescued the situation quite well and, in sprinting back to where he was supposed to have been in the first place, took the ball one-handed at full stretch. The catch should have been regulation, but it ended up being spectacular. In the following celebrations it was David Collister who had to remind everyone that it was also an important moment for *me*.

At least Bethan was there to see it. And there too when I wrapped up the innings by trapping their last man plumb in front. She'd come down with her parents for a few hours to swell the numbers in the crowd. I slept well that night and I was looking forward to the third day, but it was washed out and the match was drawn. Nonetheless, I had reached a milestone: I was now a professional first-class cricketer and I wasn't looking back. My name, Peter Legend, was now a permanent fixture on the Wessex CC team sheet.

I spent much of the rest of that summer on the back seat of David Collister's enormous Citroen CX, which was sponsored by a local car dealer. I was in the back because David always drove Herb to matches. I soon realised that David wasn't just Herb's driver; he also seemed to work as his personal assistant. He'd do all the paperwork for Herb at every hotel we visited, he'd keep a tally of Herb's expenses, and every morning when we'd set off, he'd talk us through the various scores from the other games taking place across the country. Whenever we were on our way to a fixture, David would preview the batsmen we were going to confront by regaling just how far they'd whacked him out of the ground previously. So if we were off to play Northants David would say to Herb something like, "Do you remember when Larkins just popped me over the Dinsdale?"

"That's right. All in the footwork that. Lovely player."

"But I think Lamb's taken me for more runs of late."

"Good eye. Powerful shot on him, that one."

It was interesting to hear the pair of them talk about great players who had smeared David all over the ground, but it wasn't exactly inspiring. That said, the suspension system in the Citroen was so smooth that invariably I fell asleep after a while.

The figure of £6,500 had
been increased to £6,501.

6. THE NOTE IN WELLAND-FLANDERS' OFFICE

Bethan finished her degree that summer. She also decided to go straight back to Loughborough for another year to do a teacher training course. In August she and a couple of friends from the university had taken a car and a tent on the St Malo ferry, with the aim of driving down through France and on into Spain. She'd be returning in time to head back off to Loughborough for the start of her course in September. So I didn't quite know when she'd be arriving back in Budmouth. Which partly explains why she got home to find me in bed with Kirsty on the Saturday morning. At least I think it was Kirsty. It could have been Tracey. The whole incident was, of course, perfectly innocent. I'll explain exactly how it happened.

The Wessex team would always meet on the final Friday of the season, in the Black Horse in Litton Bredy. It was supposed to be a low-key affair, just for the players. I imagine that the location was originally chosen because it lies between Budmouth, Casterbridge and Port Bredy. Litton Bredy also has the advantage that it's well off the main roads. So, with a little care, most people could safely drive home reasonably pissed without having to risk running into the police. Of course, attitudes to drink driving have changed since then.

Col, Phil and me got into my now somewhat battered Escort and I drove over from Creston to the Black Horse. We were among the first to arrive at the pub. The Black Horse is actually about a mile from Litton Bredy. A stream runs alongside the road. There is parking for around fifteen cars. There's a small terrace of three period houses on the other side of the junction. It may not be quite in the middle of nowhere, but it's very close.

Kirsty and Tracey were the closest thing that Wessex CC had to group-ies. I don't think that they were actually club members, but they were usually in the pavilion come close of play at Canberra Park. They looked like two-thirds of Bananarama, but not the two best-looking thirds. Or to be fair to Bananarama, not even the worst-looking two-thirds. But what they had in common with the band was a significant volume of (often) blonde hair, a wide range of headgear, plenty of over-sized striped shirts and stonewashed denim jeans.

It was a pleasant evening, so us players gathered around the tables in the front garden of the pub. We had all seen the girls inside, sat at the bar. Col was so curious about the duo that he was actually moved to speak.

"So, who's been there, then?"

"Beresford my dear boy. The ladies' virtue should not be the subject of discussion among us. To even raise the issue does you a disservice." David Collister was looking gravely at Col. After a pause Collister went on in that donnish way of his, "But seeing as we can't put this particular conversational genie back in the bottle, which of you fine athletes have generously given of yourselves to the girls?"

"Rumours have it that they've been kept busy enough," suggested the wicket-keeper.

"Eurgh ha ha eurgh. Busy enough! Eurgh ha ha." Andy Farrow, I had realised by now, found just about anything Laurie Kelly said side-splittingly hilarious.

"And you, Andy," Collister continued, "have you kept either of the girls busy?"

I'd swear that a panicked look of guilt shot across Andy's face. But before he had a chance to deny that he might have ever shagged either of them, Laurie saved him.

"Unlikely I reckon, 'cos if he had, he'd still be sat at home wiping down his dick."

"Eurgh ha ha eurgh." I think Andy only found this funny because Laurie had said it.

"I'm just a little disappointed that they're here tonight." Tony wanted to change the topic. "This is supposed to be just a team night, a chance for us to all get together and reflect on the season. Someone's obviously told them we'd be here."

"But you know what they're like Tony. They know everything. If I can't find Brian, I just ask them which hotel I'm supposed to be staying in when we're travelling." Collister was simply trying to pacify the skipper.

"Yes David, I know," snapped Sinclair. "But they're not fucking telepathic are they?"

The sudden sound of aggressively driven performance cars killed the conversation. A blue Audi Quattro screamed into the car park and then squealed to a halt, throwing up a fine cloud of dust. The Quattro was followed by a bright red Mazda RX7. The Mazda driver gunned the engine unnecessarily a couple of times before switching it off. Alan Musgrove got out of the Quattro wearing a baggy pair of chinos and an over-sized white t-shirt with the words CHOOSE LIFE on the front. Alan was always the more sensible one. Carl got out of the Mazda in a lime-green linen suit. Whatever shirt he was wearing was unbuttoned down to pretty much his navel, revealing a large gold medallion.

He'd evidently had his mullet re-permed since we'd last played.

I was sat beside Justin Bridges. "Oh shit," he said to nobody in particular, "this isn't going to end well."

"I'm telling you Al, I was all over your fucking arse in the RX. I'd got you in my pocket."

"I don't think so Carl. That thing's just a show pony. The Quattro is pure class."

"Pure class? Oh *do* fuck off." By now Carl had reached the tables where the rest of us were gathered. "Now," he continued, addressing the whole group, "I heard that the girls might somehow be finding their way out here this evening."

I nodded in the direction of the bar. Tony scowled as he watched the pair of them disappear inside.

After a couple of minutes the twins and the girls emerged from the pub and Alan called across the car park to the rest of us. "The girls want to know what a decent ride's actually like." He gave us his best pantomime wink, just in case the innuendo was lost on anyone. "So we're going to take them for a quick spin. Mine's a Holsten when someone's next going to the bar."

A Musgrove and a heavily accessorised girl got into each of the cars, and in an orgy of revving, more dust and flying gravel, they shot out of the car park.

"Are they coming back?" I asked.

"Unfortunately," replied Bridges.

In the brothers' absence we talked a bit about the season. We had finished sixteenth in the Championship, in the bottom half of the table in the John Player League and we had failed to get out of our group in the Benson and Hedges competition.

Phil spoke up. "Well, we're one of the only teams who haven't got a big overseas star at the club. I mean, no offence to the bowlers, I think you're all great, but we don't have a Khan, a Holding, a Marshall or a Garner, someone like that. I thought Sylvester Clarke was trying to kill me at the Oval this year."

"I'm a Wessex man and I play for Wessex. Not some fucking multi-cultural, or whatever it's called, collective. We're Wessex." Kelly was suddenly very animated.

"But he's from Devon," said Bridges, pointing to Col.

"Yeah but he's basically one of us. Aren't you Berry?" *Berry* nodded nervously in agreement.

"And I'm from Buckinghamshire via Durham," continued Bridges.

"You know full well that's not what I mean. Shall I spell it out for you?" Bridges nodded, so Kelly continued. "Frankly, I would rather we lost every game we ever played than share a dressing room with any of that lot."

"How come?" Bridges' question didn't seem loaded in any way; he just sounded genuinely curious to know the answer.

"Well I'm sure they've all got their own teams and we've got ours. But it says *Wessex Cricket Club* at Canberra Park, not *The Dirty Fucking All Comers Eleven.*"

"But the world's moved on Laurie. It's 1984." Bridges wasn't going to drop the subject. "Every other team welcomes overseas players. And it makes them stronger sides."

"*Welcomes*? What sort of word is that? You should be working for the council or something. *Welcomes*." He'd repeated the word with heavy sarcasm. "They don't fucking *welcome* them. They're just fucking mercenaries. And they don't belong here. It's that fucking simple."

Bridges looked as though he was about to say something, but we could hear the Musgroves returning, so he just dropped the subject. This time the Mazda arrived first, closely followed by the Audi. Again, both drivers threw gravel and crap everywhere as they slammed on their brakes. And once again, a film of dust then gently drifted over the pub garden.

I heard Carl saying to one of the girls, "If you find yourself in something like that at the end of the night, then you know it's gone badly wrong." He was pointing to my Escort. The girls disappeared back inside the pub, while the twins finally came to join us in the garden.

"Which one's my Holsten, then?" enquired Alan. Sometimes the pair of them made picking a favourite twin really quite tricky.

"Well, thank you Carl, and thank you Alan. Now we're all here, I'd just like to say a few words about the 1984 season." Tony Sinclair was a well-meaning skipper, but you couldn't exactly accuse him of being charismatic. He then droned on, describing the various achievements of our best bowler and our best batsman without actually naming either of them. As though somehow we'd be kept guessing who he was talking about. To be clear, Andy Farrow topped the Wessex batting averages by a country mile. He may have been borderline special needs with OCD, but in 1984 he was by far our best batsman. Similarly, Herb had taken maybe twenty more wickets than anybody else, at the best average, and at the best strike rate. It simply wasn't possible to talk about them without their identities being glaringly obvious.

I can't have been the only player thinking, "Just say the words *Andy* and *Herb*. Just say the fucking words. And then for the love of God please just stop talking."

Finally he wrapped it up. "And so with great pleasure I can reveal that this year, the captain's man of the season award is to be shared between Andy for his fantastic batting and Herb for his superb bowling performances."

There was a sort of stifled hurrugh from the rest of us and a half-hearted clinking of glasses.

Kelly had a question for Carl. "Now then you flash poser, which of the girls is going home in that car of yours?"

"Which girl? Which? Laurie, my friend, your problem is that you lack ambition. Tonight I shall be entertaining the beautiful Kirsty." He paused for effect. "And I shall also be entertaining the gorgeous Tracey."

"Bollocks you are." Alan was obviously pissed off.

"Look, I'll be doing you a favour Al. You're the one with the fiancée. I'm just going to have to take them both home to keep your conscience clear. There's no need to thank me."

"You're right there isn't. But I wouldn't be too confident if I were you."

"What's your fiancée called, Alan?" Col sounded as though he was genuinely interested in her name.

"Rachel."

"Uh, Rachel. What does she do?"

"She's Welland-Flanders' personal assistant."

"Uh, the blonde girl who sits in that office on the top floor of the pavilion?" Alan nodded in agreement. "Right, she's pretty."

There was an awkward pause. Nobody – including me – could work out if Col was making some big moral point, or simply getting the facts straight in his own head. Either way, someone needed to change the topic.

So Alan did it himself. "You're married aren't you, Herb?"

"Yes."

"What's her name?" Alan continued.

"Mrs Brunton."

That got a small laugh around the group.

"No, Herb, *her* name."

"To you, Alan? It's Mrs Brunton."

"OK, OK." Carl was bored. "Guys, what's better than Jenga?"

"What's better than *what*?" someone asked.

"What's better than Jenga . . . is Giant Jenga!"

Before the 1984 season began, the twins had been to Florida on holiday with their parents. They'd discovered Jenga, which they'd played with some neighbours in their condo, and they'd tracked down a giant set when they got back. None of the rest of us had played Jenga before: either giant or regular sized. So when Alan came back from the Quattro with this large bag over his shoulder, he had to explain the principle of removing wooden blocks, one at a time, from the bottom half of a tower and replacing them higher up, without toppling the whole thing over.

"Right," he continued, "it's top half of the batting order versus the lower half. Laurie, you come and join me."

"Well if you've got the extra man," Carl replied, "I think the girls should join my team. Kirsty! Tracey! Come over. You're going to help me thrash Alan at Jenga!"

"Where am I supposed to be?" Tony asked without any great enthusiasm.

"Top order with me, Skip," called Alan.

Someone grumbled something about shoving one of the blocks up his fucking arse. But I didn't catch who said it, nor which brother's arse he had in mind.

It sounds boring – pulling wooden blocks out of a tower and putting them back somewhere else – but once we were playing I think pretty much everyone got into it. One of the twins had decided that the losing team should buy the winning team's next round, so in a sense there was more riding on the result than on a typical Championship game. Very quickly we'd got to the point where the tower was standing about seven feet tall and looking about ready to fall.

It was our team's turn and Herb carefully studied it from all angles. Then suddenly he knelt down, and in a swift movement plucked out a block without so much as a quiver from the rest of the tower. Gingerly he placed it on the top of the tower and stepped back.

Us bowlers celebrated with a few rounds of "There's only one Herbie Brunton." He just gave us his wry wicket-taking smile.

But it had to go wrong for someone, and it went wrong for Phil. Like Herb he carefully studied the tower from all angles, he selected his move, but just about on touching the block the whole thing collapsed around him. Alan had a right old go at Phil.

"Fuck sake Phil. You've run me out Christ knows how many times this season, you never tell me which way it's moving, you've played all the best bowlers from the non-striker's end and you even screw this up."

Most of us thought he was joking. But he just carried on. "Jesus Phil, do you ever get anything right? I'd be averaging close to Andy if I didn't have to go out there with you. You're a fucking liability. Fuck it, *you* get the drinks in. *You* fucked up."

"This is just a game, right Alan?" Collister enquired. "Maybe you want to apologise to Phil."

"Yeah sure. Sorry Phil. Right, best of three!"

Having figured out the game, the early moves on the second tower were made rapidly by both sides. By the time the whole thing looked really dicey it was David Collister's turn for our team. By now we'd all become self-appointed experts and were giving him all sorts of conflicting advice. He calmly ignored us, elegantly slipped out a redundant block from near the very bottom of the tower, and balanced it vertically, well above head height on the very top. The chances of Alan's team managing a successful move after that looked pretty slim. Unbelievably, it turned out to be Phil's turn to go again for Alan's team.

"Jesus fucking Christ Phil. It's like watching you bat. No bottle. I'll do it." Alan held Phil by the shoulders and briskly manoeuvred him back into the middle of the group of batsmen. He then slid out a block from about halfway up the tower. The whole thing shifted noticeably, but nothing fell. Somehow Collister's vertical block at the very top stayed in place. Then, after a theatrical set of stretching exercises, he gingerly placed the block across David's, creating a T-shape at the top of the tower. It seemed to vibrate there for some time, but it didn't fall. Surely they'd got us beat. Col was up next for us, and frankly with his physical dexterity, I didn't give us a prayer. Carl walked up to the tower. It stood about a foot above him now. Even his footsteps set the top blocks vibrating.

"I think the slightest gust of wind might do for you, Al." Carl was now fanning the air around the top of the tower with his free hand; holding his pint in the other.

"Don't you fucking dare," Alan threatened. "Col, it's your turn. You've got to step up and take a block."

Carl, however, continued to fan the air. He was ignoring Alan, and just smiling at the rest of us in his team.

That was when the man with the slightly shorter mullet, in the CHOOSE LIFE t-shirt, rugby-tackled the man with the longer, blonder mullet in the lime-green suit. To be fair to Alan it was a good hit, and the pair of them went flying down the bank at the front of the garden, sliding down into the stream below. Remarkably, the tower was still standing in the garden above them. Carl's pint glass had smashed on the stones at the top of the stream's bank. Down in the stream the pair of them were struggling to get up and find their footing. After a few moments of slipping and staggering, they were facing off a few feet apart, both standing thigh-deep in the water.

"Not funny Alan. Not fucking funny. This ends now."

"I am so up for this Carl. I'm going to fucking kill you."

They inched their way through the stream towards each other, screaming more threats as they went. The rest of us watched from the top of the bank. Carl's suit was hanging soaked off his body, while Alan's t-shirt was smeared with grass stains from his trip down the bank.

Just at the point when the pair of them had got close enough to start actually throwing punches, the landlord came running out of the pub shouting, "I'm not having this, I'm calling the police." And then he disappeared back inside to get dialling.

I don't know whether or not the twins heard him, but it made no difference. Neither was backing down; they'd both adopted a guard and were looking for an opening. Then, seemingly in one graceful move, Col slid down the bank, and launched himself at the pair of them, grabbing whatever clothing he could grasp around each of their necks and pinning them both to the far bank.

"Alan," he said, looking at the twin who was closer to the car park, "I'm going to let you go first. You're going to get in your car and go home." And he said it with such quiet authority that Alan just pulled himself out of the stream and did exactly as he was told.

When Alan's car was out of earshot Col simply said to Carl, "OK. You can go now." And without saying anything to the rest of us, Carl did.

Given that the police had been called, we figured that we'd better get on our way before they arrived. Otherwise we'd all have to get taxis home and pick up our cars the following morning. I said to the girls that they could come back with us. Carl was certainly right about one thing though: the girls had ended up in my Escort because the evening had gone wrong. It turned out that they both lived somewhere near the centre of Budmouth, but I didn't want to risk driving into the middle of the city on several pints of Holsten. So I suggested that they stay at Creston overnight. And that's how I ended up sharing my bed with one of them.

So, it was all perfectly harmless. Though I admit that it didn't look great when Bethan arrived the following morning. Things were still a bit frosty when I drove her back to Loughborough the following weekend. But I think our relationship has always been strong enough to get over the occasional misunderstanding.

****

Some time later that month I got a letter from Wessex CC offering me a three-year deal at the club. All I had to do was sign my name at the bottom of the page and £6,500 a year would be mine. It was good news. But it wasn't really much of a surprise either. My place in the side didn't seem to be under any genuine pressure, so it seemed reasonable that I'd be offered a full contract.

"Don't sign a fucking thing Pete. I'm coming round."

Within the hour Dougie was sat in our living room reading the offer.

"It's good Pete. It's good. But it's also derisory. They're treating you like a total cunt. You're a fucking star! You're the future! I'm going to earn my 15 per cent, and make you some proper fucking money."

Dougie decided that the best thing to do would be to fix a meeting with Sebastian Welland-Flanders. Dougie picked up our phone. Alan's fiancée answered.

"Dougie Barrett here, representing my client, Peter Legend. I need to meet Sebastian asap."

A look of irritation flashed across Dougie's face as he listened to the voice on the other end of the line.

"Sorry, I didn't catch your name, love."

There was a brief pause.

"OK Rachel. Let's start again shall we? We seem to have got off on the wrong foot. It's pretty simple. Your boss has made an offer to my client. And I'm not exactly going to be doing my job if I just advise my client to accept the first offer that your boss makes."

Rachel spoke at some length. Dougie kept flexing the fingers of his free hand, evidently in frustration.

"Well, here's the thing Rachel. If you want to explain to your boss why Peter Legend's turning out for Somerset next season because *you* took the decision not to bother even opening contract negotiations with Wessex, so be it. It'll make good headlines that. Something like, "Local Legend Teams Up with Botham's Somerset". Do you think Sebastian wants to read that?"

There was a brief pause. Dougie was smiling. He loved this sort of thing.

"That's perfect Rachel. Eleven tomorrow. You are a sweetheart. Bye. Bye."

The following morning I was stood with Dougie outside Welland-Flanders' office at the top of the pavilion in Canberra Park. Between flurries of furious typing, Rachel occasionally stared across at Dougie with undisguised hostility. I was actually quite nervous. I'd seen Sebastian Welland-Flanders around the ground often enough, but I'd never spoken to him before. The phone rang on Rachel's desk. She answered it, said, "OK", and went back to her typing. Dougie looked at her with a face that said, "Well?" She just ignored him. After what seemed like another quarter of an hour, she stopped typing and looked up at us as though she'd only just noticed us standing there.

"Excuse me," she said, beaming cheerfully at Dougie. "Sebastian's ready for you now." Dougie shot her a filthy stare as we entered.

"Peter. Mr Bartlett. This is most irregular, but do take a seat. This won't take long will it?"

Sebastian Welland-Flanders was in his late fifties. He wore tweed. In fact he always looked as though he was just on his way to a grouse shoot. If he'd had a twelve-bore shotgun mounted on the wall behind his desk it wouldn't have looked out of place. He permanently projected the air of somebody who really ought, at that very moment, to be doing something much more important, but who was just too well mannered to actually say so.

"It's Barrett. Dougie Barrett."

"Mr Barrett, please accept my apologies. Now, what can I do for you?"

"Well, Mr Welland-Flanders," Dougie started. "May I call you Sebastian?"

"I'd rather you didn't."

"Well, anyway, you've made an offer to my client."

"Your client?" Welland-Flanders sounded momentarily confused. "Oh I see, you mean Peter."

"Now we're obviously thrilled that you've opened negotiations on behalf of Wessex. But I'm here to explore the potential for flexibility on the part of the club."

"Negotiations? Mr Barrett, when . . ."

"Please, call me Dougie."

"Mr Barrett, I think you misunderstand. We put our best and final terms in our offers to all players. Consider it a sign of respect if you will. Players are not some commodity to be haggled over."

"I absolutely understand. However I don't believe that the figure in the contract represents the *very* best offer Wessex could make. And I don't think it is a fair assessment of my client's value to the club."

"Do you understand what is meant by a superlative, Mr Barrett?"

"I do."

I was glad that Dougie did, because at the time I didn't.

"So you'll understand that, by definition, we cannot improve on the notion of *best*, can we? We have outlined not only our best offer, but also our *very very* best offer."

Up until this point in my life I thought that Frank Trellick was the most patronising man I'd ever met, but I was realising that Welland-Flanders had got him beaten all ends up.

"I have no doubt, Mr Welland-Flanders," Dougie countered, "that you are looking at Wessex's first ever England player. He is going to put Wessex on the map."

"Last time I looked Mr Barrett, we were already there. But I digress. You are asking me to value Peter *today* in terms of what he may achieve *tomorrow*."

"What he *will* achieve."

"Your confidence in Peter's prospects . . ." Welland-Flanders stopped himself for effect. "Sorry. Your confidence in *your client's* prospects is admirable. However at Wessex we're in the business of making the best offer possible, based on the value of the player to our club *today*."

"Peter is the best young seam bowler at Wessex."

"I'm sure there are others who might contest that accolade. However, even you, Mr Barrett, qualify your claims about Peter's ability." Then Welland-Flanders turned directly to me. "Peter, how many Championship wickets did you take for us this season?"

"Thirty-one," I replied.

"And how many did Herbie take for us this year?"

"I'm not sure, but I'd imagine it was around sixty."

"And that, Mr Barrett, is the difference between a promising player and the finished article." He turned back to me. "Peter, I do so hope you sign the contract."

But Dougie wasn't to be beaten. "I don't believe the figure in that contract does represent your best offer. And I can't leave until you've made it."

"Do you know what my other line of business is, Mr Barrett?" Welland-Flanders asked Dougie.

"No."

"My family builds yachts Mr Barrett. We build luxury ocean-going yachts to the highest specifications for the most demanding clients in the world. But none has proved as tenacious or demanding as you have been today."

I wasn't sure if this was a compliment or not.

"Never in the history of this club have I had an offer rejected by a player. But never before have I heard a player represented so passionately. So, for the first and last time, I am going to amend an offer. You have bested me today, Mr Barrett. However, I implore you to accept my new terms. These are final. Wessex Cricket Club will make no further offer. Peter, can you please pass me your copy of the contract?"

I handed Welland-Flanders the letter and he briskly made an alteration to the salary amount and initialled the change. He then reached inside his tweed jacket and pulled out his wallet. And from inside there he produced a pound note. He handed the contract letter back to me, and the pound to Dougie. I immediately noticed that the figure of £6,500 had been increased to £6,501.

"Peter. Mr Barrett. This is my very very best offer. And I'd like you to enjoy your first year's increase today. Consider it an advance. Now, can we shake on this?"

I said to Dougie, "Well, you certainly earned your money today."

I made a point of smiling to Rachel on the way out. Dougie handed me the pound note. I was never much one for collecting memorabilia – balls, stumps, that sort of thing – but I kept that pound. It was just about my hardest won trophy in the game.

I always used a two-pound-ten
Double-L Beef-Cake.

7. THE CASTERBRIDGE DEVELOPMENT

Canberra Parkas' Pitch-Perfect Delivery

Exciting new Wessex musical outfit The Canberra Parkas debuted at the Firestation in Casterbridge last Friday in front of an enthusiastic full house. The band played a short set of mod classics. What sets the band apart is that three of the energetic five-piece are cricketers from Wessex CC. Peter 'The Ledge' Legend on vocals and Colin Beresford on bass both broke into the first team last season. Steve Braithwaite on drums is a promising batsman who has been in the club's youth development programme since he was fourteen. The group also features guitarist Dave Wilde, now a veteran of several Budmouth-based outfits, and blonde bombshell Ellie Radcliffe on keyboards. Legend's high-energy performance got the crowd going, while the statuesque Beresford and the sharp-dressed Braithwaite provided a tight rhythm section to drive the songs forward. Wilde and Radcliffe added the musical flourishes and backing vocals. The Canberra Parkas are a great addition to our thriving local music scene. This reviewer was bowled over. Catch them when you can.

Casterbridge Gazette, 21ˢᵗ March 1985

1984 had been a massive year for both Col and me at Wessex. But come October, we found ourselves standing on the steps of one of Frank Trellick's chalets, sharing a roll-up. In August we'd been bowling to Viv Richards, Imran Khan, Mike Gatting and Geoffrey Boycott, testing ourselves against some of the world's best batsmen. And now we were re-painting the interiors of over forty chalets. I'd gone from running out in front of crowds at big grounds like Trent Bridge, to checking that I'd packed the turps in my work bag.

Of course there were some things there to remind me that it hadn't all just been a dream, or simply a figment of my imagination. Dougie had been looking after all the sponsorship stuff for me, and I'd just taken delivery of a red Ford XR2. It was somewhat smaller than most of the sponsored cars the other players were driving, but as Dougie pointed out, it was a fun drive and it was pretty economical. I'd had to work on my signature a bit for the stencil on the door panels, because my handwriting has always been a bit of a mess. The rest of the wording simply said, "Creston Motors is proud to support Peter Legend, Wessex CC". Phil Grey had got a black one because Dougie was looking after him too by the end of the '84 season. Dougie had taken one of the XR2s for a spin and liked it so much that he sold the yellow TR7 soft-top he'd been driving, and ordered a white XR2 for himself: all of them supplied by Creston Motors.

Dougie also sorted my bat deal for me. Layton Landy has been making cricket bats in Budmouth since before the war. Whenever you go to Canberra Park, you'll usually see at least half of the players using kit with the distinctive yellow Double-L logo. All Double-Ls are handcrafted in the Layton Landy workshop, which is now situated on a small industrial estate about a mile from the ground. Back in the eighties most manufacturers would just have one or two basic blade profiles, and then offer them in a range of weights. I always used a two-pound-ten Double-L Beef-Cake. It was a bit like the Stuart Surridge Jumbo, in that it was skinny at the top and really meaty for an extended portion of the blade in the middle. Phil Grey, like Danny before him, preferred the Double-L Standard, with the old-school weight distribution. That tended to be the choice of the more delicate touch players. But my batting game was based around power. Plus I had the guns to work with a decent-sized piece of wood.

But even with new bats in my kit bag and new wheels in the driveway, it still felt like it was going to be a long winter. For the first couple weeks after our final game Col and me didn't really do anything at all. During the season you simply don't have to think for yourself. You're told where to go, where to stay, when to train and when to go home. But then, when the season's over, nobody tells you to do anything at all. So we didn't. Phil went back home to stay with his parents in Abbotsea, while Col and me sat in Creston. When Frank Trellick rang to ask if I wanted to take on a big job that winter, it actually came as something of a relief. The work itself was dull beyond belief, but it got us out the house, and we earned some money. And as we painted the chalets we hatched the idea for The Canberra Parkas. I always knew I was a pretty good singer, but I didn't know that Col could play bass. Turned out he was probably a better musician than he was a cricketer.

Back on the field the following season I went from strength to strength. I was named the 1985 Wessex player of the season. I took over fifty wickets in the

Championship and scored over six hundred runs. I tried to learn as much as I could from Herb that year.

"There's more to seam bowling than meets the eye. It's a craft like any other and you just have to put in the hours to master it." Herb certainly wasn't going to teach me everything he knew, but I picked up useful nuggets just from being around him and watching the way he prepared and played.

We never had speed guns down at Canberra Park back then, but I'd guess that Herb used to bowl somewhere around seventy-five or seventy-six miles an hour. So he certainly wasn't in the business of blasting anyone out. Rather he was looking for every little possible advantage that could help him move the ball through the air or off the seam. Obviously he did the basics really well. He'd come in off a rhythmic twelve-pace run-up, and he had the most economical action. It hardly seemed to take anything out of him at all. It must have been his perfection of the basics that had allowed him to extend his career so long – he continued taking first-class wickets well into his forties. He had a lovely whippy wrist action to impart backspin on the ball, so it would always have a perfectly vertical seam position in flight. That meant he only needed to make the subtlest of changes to his technique, to alternate between in-swing and out-swing.

However, not all of his methods were strictly above board. For example, the nail on his left thumb was basically a seam-lifting tool. Hardened and thickened by years of picking at cricket balls, it was as good as having a decent knife blade out on the pitch. But he was so careful in the way that he went about it. Over the course of a Herb spell with an old ball, the seam would just become that little bit more pronounced, and one side of the ball would begin wearing that bit quicker than the other: but an umpire would be hard-pressed to identify when or how it had happened. Then there was his knowledge of Canberra Park. Herb always bowled from the pavilion end. This gave him two advantages. The first he told me about. I hadn't noticed it before, but there is a very slight ridge, just full of a good length when you're bowling from that end. A fuller-length delivery can get the smallest fraction of extra lift that can result in batsmen either nicking off or playing the ball through the air. The second advantage I had to figure out for myself. The pavilion sightscreen was never in quite such good condition as the one at the Dinsdale end. It could have been purely coincidental: the south-facing screen would have obviously needed re-painting more often as it faced the sun. Or perhaps Herb had shared a quiet word with Gus Jackman. It wasn't obvious, but if you ever made a point of comparing the screens close up, the one in the pavilion was always just that little bit greyer. It would make the ball that fraction more difficult for the batsman to pick up when facing a bowler from that end.

Of course, some people might see these techniques as cheating rather than being part and parcel of the seam bowlers' legitimate armoury of tricks. But then spectators didn't have to work out how to stop players like Graham Gooch from scoring freely. As Herb was always fond of saying, "What do they know of cricket? Those that don't play the bloody game?"

To this day I don't know what Herb used to do in the close season. I knew that he lived in Port Bredy. And I knew that he lived with Mrs Brunton – although I was still no closer to knowing her actual name. But beyond that, it was almost as if he didn't exist when he wasn't playing. He may as well have been hibernating for all I knew.

Herb never actually said that much to me, but he helped me become a far smarter bowler. I got a bit better at setting batsmen up, so that my in-swinger or my slower ball was more likely to take a wicket. I made more conservative use of my effort ball, particularly the short one. I knew I was never going to be a master-craftsman like Herb – I was always going to be bowling quicker with more adrenaline flowing – but he helped me get some guile into my game.

Meanwhile the club's advice to Col was somewhat simpler: just bowl it as fast as you can. I thought it was funny. Col was a really good bass player; he had a real feel for the instrument and complete control over the tone he got out of it. But put a cricket ball in his hand and it may as well have been a bar of soap. There was no point trying to work with him on subtle variations – the best thing that could happen was that he let go of it at the right time and released it in the right direction. His battles with both himself and opposition batsmen continued. But over the course of the season he had more good spells than bad (though he had some absolute shockers along the way).

Carl Musgrove was our fourth seamer. Ordinarily you might have thought of him as quite a handy bowler: he got it down there at around seventy miles an hour and could wobble the ball off the seam. He was pretty good with an old ball, and if under strict instructions from Tony to do so, he could bowl a really tight line that would force batsmen to take risks if they wanted to score freely. But in his own mind, and in his mind alone, Carl was England's natural successor to Bob Willis. Somehow, in Carl's world, the ball left his hand about twenty-five miles an hour faster than any batsman ever thought it was travelling. But we lost count of the number of times his looping bouncer was smashed into the square-leg boundary by bemused batsmen who'd had to wait for the thing to arrive. He also seemed to be very pleased with himself as a bowler – he had this sort of prancing run-up to the crease that made him look as though he was trotting in on a horse. His mullet bounced along behind him like a curly mane.

Unlike Col, Carl wasn't plagued by self-doubt, so all of his verbals were directed at the batsman. Just about every ball was followed by an "Argh!" as though it was some kind of a miracle that the batsman had survived the delivery. And this would happen regardless of whether the ball had gone anywhere near the outside edge of the bat or was currently being retrieved from the car park by a member of the ground staff. And all of his wickets were accompanied by a blast of, "Now, fuck off!" Again, it didn't matter whether the batsman had gone for a duck or had just fallen after an otherwise chanceless double century. Carl was a popular player with our home crowd, because he gave them something to cheer. Whatever the match situation we found ourselves in, Carl would go to war with the opposition and put on a bit of a show.

Meanwhile Alan Musgrove had begun the 1985 season pretty much where he'd left off the previous one; at least in terms of the way he was treating Phil Grey. In 1984 and 1985 Phil and Alan were opening, with Andy Farrow coming in first drop. If Alan got out before Phil, then invariably he'd find some way to blame Phil for the loss of his wicket. For example, if Phil had turned down a suicidal call for a single, leaving Alan on strike, and then Alan went and lost his wicket, it would be Phil's fault. By way of contrast, if Alan ever got out when Andy Farrow was at the other end, it would never be Andy's fault. But, for even more complicated reasons, it might still be Phil's. "Fuck sake Phil, you just let him find his length, didn't you? No footwork, no positive intent, you just sat there like a fucking lemon while he figured out the pitch. You Muppet."

In this situation you can ask another player to cool it a bit, but you can't act as someone's bodyguard: it merely draws even more attention to the fact that they're not looking after themselves. Phil's main problem was that he just wouldn't get stuck back into Alan. It could have been because he was a few years younger or it could have simply been because he was the smaller guy. But week-in, week-out, Alan would bawl out Phil in front of the rest of the team. Phil was by far the more promising batsman of the two, but his form was beginning to suffer.

Things came to a head on 13th July 1985. A round of Championship matches started that day, and we were playing Sussex at Canberra Park. Just our luck really: the day of the biggest concert event of all time, and we'd have to miss the first half of it. The line-up at Live Aid was unlike anything that we'd ever seen on television before. Maybe if you've grown up with the BBC's wall-to-wall coverage of Glastonbury – with pretty much every band accessible via the red button – Live Aid doesn't sound so extraordinary. But back in 1985 the whole thing was immense.

Carl Musgrove had successfully persuaded Sebastian Welland-Flanders to get a big television set installed in the members' room for the day, so that we could watch the show. It was quite a big set – even by modern standards – and it was mounted on this stand that could be wheeled around the floor. Then, the rest of us prayed that Tony won the toss, sent in our batsmen, and allowed us bowlers to put our feet up and watch the whole thing. It looked like a good day for batting, so for once all eyes were on the skipper as he walked out to the middle. Where he promptly lost the toss. So we were bowling. Because global music events don't involve generating lateral movement with a cricket ball, Herb wasn't too bothered either way. I think David Collister was more of a classical man, so he didn't really see what the fuss was about either. But for Col, Carl and me this was a bitterly disappointing outcome. And to add insult to injury, the Sussex bowlers would no doubt enjoy the entertainment that we'd inadvertently laid on for them in the members' room. So our plan was simple: bowl out of our skins and dismiss Sussex as soon as possible, in order to get ourselves in front of the television and watch the concert.

If we had bowled all season as well as we did that day, we'd have been up there challenging for the Championship. The batting conditions were superb, but we still managed to dismiss the Sussex batting line-up shortly after tea. Herb did what Herb does and took a couple of wickets with the new ball. I took three more, generating an extra yard or so of pace in all of the spells I bowled. Col was especially fiery and bounced out a couple of middle-order players. And when it really mattered Carl kept it tight – he didn't bowl any of his comedy bouncers – and he got a couple of batsmen to nick-off to Laurie Kelly. Finally David chipped in with a neat caught and bowled and we'd run through a good side on an excellent wicket for just under two hundred. After a quick trip to the showers we were in front of the screen in time for the Bryan Adams set from Philadelphia, followed by U2, the first act we saw on the Wembley stage.

Of course, this wasn't good news for everybody. Our batsmen had to go out and play for an hour or so; exactly the sort of prospect openers hate. Phil and Alan almost completed a perfect job for the team that afternoon. I don't know exactly *how* they batted, because I was watching Live Aid, but the scorecard suggests that they made solid progress, right up until the penultimate over of the day. On the first ball of that over it's recorded that Phil Grey took a single. And on the second, that Alan was bowled. Andy Farrow was never one for hiding behind a night-watchman, so he went out to bat with ten balls remaining in the day's play. Unfortunately he only survived four of them. In turn, this meant that Justin Bridges had to go out for the final over of the day. Again, the scorecard shows that Phil Grey played out the first three balls of the over, before taking three runs off the next one. This left Justin with two balls to survive not out overnight; a task that he only half finished. So, a very respectable 37-0 had become 41-3 in the space of two overs.

Needless to say Alan thought that the entire mini-collapse was Phil's fault, and he didn't exactly beat around the bush telling him so.

"Two overs to go and you take a single. What was going through your tiny little fucking mind? You were supposed to be facing Khan. Fuck's sake, are you ever going to fucking learn?"

"Alan, we never discussed not running. We never discussed each taking a bowler."

"Because we shouldn't fucking well have to, should we? This stuff is fucking obvious. Once again we're in the shit and, as fucking usual, it's your fucking fault."

Alan was ranting all the way through the Dire Straits set featuring Sting, but I got Carl to have a word to calm him down a bit. I think we all wanted to watch Queen without Alan yelling his head off all the way through their act. It was a shame there was such a tense atmosphere because I remember thinking that Freddie Mercury and the rest of the band were absolutely brilliant.

Most of the team had gathered around the television by this point, even if they weren't particularly into music. We watched the David Bowie set, and Laurie Kelly made some typical remark of his, about helping our own before we gave money to other countries. In a sense, you had to hand it to the guy; here he was watching a film showing starving Ethiopian children, and he could still stick to his principles.

In truth though, I think most of us were watching the show for the bands, and not the starving millions. And the one act most of us were really excited about was The Who. I'd been listening to The Who ever since Dougie had introduced me to them more than a decade earlier. They hadn't played together for a few years so it was being billed as the big event of the night. It turned out that Alan was really into them, and even some of the older guys like David and Tony wanted to see what they were like.

If I remember rightly, their set was actually a bit of a mess. I found myself thinking that The Canberra Parkas were the tighter band. Phil even looked a little bored, and he got up to go to the bar shortly after they started. When he returned to his seat he took a route around the back of the screen, so as not to obscure anyone's view. Just as he stepped behind the television, Daltry and the rest of the band didn't so much fade away as just disappear.

Alan was incensed. "What the fuck have you done now, Phil? Jesus fucking Christ!"

Phil stared out at the rest of us from behind the television with an under-standably startled look on his face.

"You've gone and pulled the fucking aerial out, you fuckwit. Don't just fucking stand there looking gormless. Plug it back in. Jesus! During the fuck-ing Who as well."

Phil disappeared back behind the television. After a couple of moments he reappeared. "The aerial's still in the TV. I didn't touch it."

"Bollocks. We lost the picture when you walked behind it. Are you telling me I've got to get up and sort it out myself? Fuck's sake, mate." Alan was sat in the front row of the group of us around the set. What happened next was unexpected.

A very cold look came over Phil's face. He lost the resigned and apologetic expression he usually wore for Alan's bollockings. "You want the telly, Alan? Well you can have the fucking thing." He was still talking as he used his left foot to prevent the stand from wheeling forwards, while he used both hands to topple the whole thing over in Alan's direction. As the screen landed – just short of where Alan was sitting – there was an almighty crash and a few wisps of electrical smoke drifted across the room.

For a brief moment there was silence. Phil was staring at the rest of us. I think he was actually more shocked by what he'd done than anyone else. Even Alan was lost for words. Then a voice came bellowing from the far end of the mem-bers' room.

"What in heaven's name is going on? Who is responsible for this?" It was Welland-Flanders. Given that Phil was the only person standing, Welland-Flanders addressed him directly. "Did you do this? Frankly, I'm speechless." I'd never seen him look so furious before. It looked as though he was ready to explode. I was thinking that we could be thankful he didn't *actually* keep a twelve-bore on his office wall.

"It was just an accident, sir." Herb spoke up from the back of the row of the chairs. ""Phil was getting me a pint and he got his leg caught in the cable. Just an accident, sir."

Herb seemed to have some sort of special power over Welland-Flanders. I doubt that if any of the rest of us had said anything he'd have listened or calmed down.

"You can swear to this, Herb? That this was just an accident, not an act of vandalism against Wessex Cricket Club property?"

"I swear, sir."

"Very well, let that be an end to the matter. But you'll all have to pay for it." At this Alan started, as if about to say something, but Carl just squeezed his shoulder.

The thing between Alan and Phil cast a cloud over what would otherwise have been a perfect season for me. I'd been bowling really well, I was taking wickets, and I'd scored more runs that Carl Musgrove, who was batting above me in the order. Terry Le Saux, one of the local sports reporters who covered Wessex CC, did a big profile piece on me in the *Budmouth Echo*. It was the first time that I'd done an in-depth interview.

> *There is something pleasingly uncomplicated about Legend's game.*
> *Give him the ball and you know what you're going to get: he'll run in*
> *all day and put as much into his third spell as he did his first. Blessed*
> *with a good eye and a small repertoire of aggressive shots, Legend*
> *also has the ability to compile runs quickly in the lower middle order.*
> *He has proved an effective performer for Wessex this season, and*
> *who knows, perhaps could one day go on to represent his country.*

But someone needed to resolve the issue between the openers. Tony Sinclair didn't do anything because he hated conflict. Brian Gunnell didn't do anything; as he saw it, the coach just carried the training gear. And Sebastian Welland-Flanders didn't do anything because he was too busy entertaining clients and selling yachts.

So it was left to Dougie to stand up and resolve the situation. For him, it was remarkably simple. Phil and Alan couldn't continue playing at the same club. In an ideal world, he pointed out to both Phil and me, it should be Alan who moved on. But the world wasn't perfect, and Dougie represented Phil, not Alan. So the best thing that could happen would be for Dougie to find Phil a new club. After making a number of enquiries, Dougie struck a good deal with Leicestershire. The problem was that Phil didn't really want to go. He felt that he was in the right and that Alan was in the wrong. He'd also been in the Wessex system for over seven years and, as uncomfortable as Alan made his life there, he still felt at home in Canberra Park.

Dougie asked me if I'd speak to Phil with him, so the three of us got together at Dougie's new flat in Budmouth. It was something of a classic bachelor pad. Everything was black: the kitchen, the bathroom and even his duvet. He had that Athena poster *L'enfant* framed on the wall of his living room: that was the one where a topless guy with overly developed pectoral muscles cradled a baby. He'd also recently bought himself a new CD player. He put on *Brothers in Arms*.

"I'm not going to claim to love Dire Straits," he said, as Phil and me tried to make ourselves as comfortable as we could on the pair of futons in the room, "but you've got to admit that the production's awesome."

He'd got a new hi-fi; with the right CD the whole system sounded fantastic. But there only seemed to be one right CD: *Brothers in Arms*. I've never even owned a copy, but getting on for thirty years later I still find myself singing bits of it when I'm in the shower, with its mist, mountains, mean old towns and colour TVs. There was simply no avoiding that album in 1985.

"Right Phil," Dougie began, "I'm not going to lie to you. I'll get a fee from Leicestershire if you join them. I'm telling you this, just so we're absolutely clear."

I liked the way that Dougie conducted his business: open, honest and putting his cards right there on the table.

"Sure, I'd like the money. But I'm in the business of long-term relationships, not one-off deals. But let's look at the facts. You averaged thirty-nine in your first season. And this year it was only thirty-four. This whole thing is clearly affecting your game."

"Agreed," said Phil.

"And if this decline in your form continues, you'll be struggling to hold down a place in the team. And once you're not playing first-team cricket for Wessex, I'm not sure how I'm going to be able to help you."

"I understand all that. But why don't I give it another season at Canberra Park? I think Alan's backed off a bit since the thing with the television. And I don't want to leave Belinda. She's got a career here in Budmouth."

"Pete," Dougie interjected, "do you think that the atmosphere in the dressing room has improved since Phil lost the plot back in July?"

I couldn't, in all honesty, say that it had. Perhaps Alan had become a little less obviously aggressive, but both he and Carl were always chipping away with little comments. "See the little red thing with the stitching on it. You want to be hitting that with your bat, Phil." "You need to be getting down the shops to buy some better shots." "The only thing going down better than this pint is Phil's average." "And Rachel I hope, Alan." Phil was constantly being undermined. I liked him, and I would have rather that he had stayed and Alan left, but I thought that Dougie's plan was the best thing that could be done in the circumstances.

"In truth," I said, "I think that the atmosphere in the dressing room is possibly even worse now. Alan may shout and swear a bit less, but the chirping is now almost constant."

"Listen Phil. I've got you £7,500 on a three-year deal from Leicestershire. It's a fucking good deal. It's more money than you are on now. Another season at Budmouth like this one though, and I won't be able to help. You'll be fucked. I'm sorry, but that's how it is. So you can sit around waiting for Alan to retire, or you can take control. I know what I'd do."

"I know you're right Dougie. But it feels as though I'm giving up."

"Fuck off! You're not giving up. You're starting over. It'll be the fucking making of you. I wouldn't be saying this if I didn't believe it."

"OK. Let's do it. I guess I've been thinking about Belinda as much as anything. It'll take her a while to find something in Leicester so we could be apart for a bit. At least we've got the close season to figure something out."

"Ah. That's something else I meant to bring up," Dougie continued. "Leicestershire think it would be great if you spent the winter playing some league cricket in Australia. So, we've already sorted out a club in Perth for you."

And right there, sat underneath *L'enfant*, Phil made the decision to leave Wessex. I don't think that any of us in that room could have foreseen what would happen next; but I think that even to this day Phil thinks that I'm somehow to blame for it. So I want to set the record straight.

Phil left for Australia towards the end of October. Dougie had promised that he'd look up Belinda from time to time, just to see how she was doing. As I understand it, they soon had this regular arrangement where he took her out for lunch on Fridays. Riley and Sharpe, the law firm where she worked, is only a short walk from the various restaurants dotted around the harbour, so Dougie would go and meet her there and then they'd choose a place to eat. One week around Christmas, she had to cancel their regular appointment. So that week they met for dinner instead. And that became their new arrangement. Dougie already had enough to worry about in the evenings given the amount of music promotion he was doing at the time, but he understood that representing a client was about more than just money.

And after a while they didn't just have dinner; Belinda would go on with Dougie somewhere afterwards to watch one of his bands. The pair of them might show up to see us at the Warehouse or Captain Reckless in the Underground. And I can only guess that one night, one thing led to another, and they both ended up spending the night at Dougie's. By the time Phil got back from Perth, Belinda had moved in with Dougie, and the following September they were married.

Phil didn't know that anything was going on between the pair of them until he got back from Australia. I don't blame Belinda and Dougie for not telling him. It's not as though they could have really resolved anything over the phone.

Phil came round to Creston to talk to me before he had to leave for pre-season training with Leicestershire the following spring. Actually, he didn't so much talk, as shout at me for an hour, somehow implicating me in a devious, long-planned scheme to split him up from his girlfriend.

"You were part of this Ledge, weren't you? Just doing a favour for your great pal, so he could make a move on my girlfriend. What does it say about the greasy little fucker that he had to send me halfway around the world for five months to stand a chance of getting her into bed?"

"I really don't think it was like that Phil." I was just trying to calm him down a bit. "Honestly, he was simply trying to do you a favour, and unfortunately one thing just led to another. But at the end of the day he's only human."

"No. No. No. At the end of the day he's a total fucking cunt. A total fucking cunt who has gone out of his way to get me out of Wessex just so that he could get it on with Belinda. And do you know what really gets my fucking goat?"

"No Phil, I don't."

"What really gets my fucking goat is that I've basically paid him to fuck her. I was already giving the little shit 15 per cent of my income, and now he's trousering even more cash from Leicestershire so that I can fuck off to the Midlands and leave them alone together. You told me he was OK."

"Listen Phil, if it makes it any easier, this was all about your career. There was no conspiracy. Dougie's not like that. Sure he's not an angel, but then none of us are. It's tough, but it's just one of those things."

"If you actually believe that then you're a thick cunt Ledge, you really are. But I don't think you *are* that fucking stupid, and I reckon you knew all along that Dougie was planning to make a move on Belinda."

I'd done my bit. I'd tried to set the record straight, but clearly there was no talking to him. So I decided to wrap things up. "Two things, Phil. Firstly, if you ever call me a cunt again you'll be looking for a dentist, not a new cricket club. And secondly, fuck off out the house."

Whenever we met on the cricket pitch after that he'd just behave as though he'd never seen me in his life before. He actually went on to do pretty well. After a few fairly successful seasons at Leicestershire he moved on to play for Gloucestershire, and then Worcestershire. He ended up as a well-respected county pro. All in all it wasn't a bad return on his talent.

Looking back, the whole episode feels like ancient history now. Sadly, Dougie and Belinda's marriage only lasted a few years. Dougie blew it when he got involved with a lounge singer he was representing, going by the name of Camara. Of course, it was unfortunate that Phil and Belinda's relationship broke down, but it's not exactly that unusual among cricket players. These things happen.

It could have all turned out very differently. It transpired that there hadn't been anything wrong with the television in the members' room at Canberra Park: well at least not until Phil tried to throw it at Alan. Some fuse had blown at Wembley, and the BBC had lost the whole transmission. I'm sure that's not much consolation for Phil though.

****

"My name is Bethan Legend and I'm pleased to meet you." She offered me her hand.

"Errr, hello." I hesitantly accepted the handshake.

Bethan and me had just sat down in a fish restaurant on the south side of the harbour in Budmouth. It was November 1985 and she'd been back with me in the Creston bungalow for a few weeks. I think I knew what she was getting at. To all intents and purposes we'd been living apart for almost four years. In a way, we'd really just got to begin our relationship all over again. I realised that some of the basic house-sharing stuff would prove a bit of a problem. Bethan quite simply had more demanding standards of cleanliness and hygiene than Col and me, so we'd had a few heated debates about that sort of thing.

But it was about more than just how clean the bathroom needed to be before Bethan could agree that it was indeed clean. The previous evening we'd been in our local video shop: I wanted to watch *Indiana Jones* and she wanted to see *The Killing Fields*. I thought that movies should be about entertainment, pure and simple. She thought that films should deal with big political and social topics. I said that I didn't need to spend two hours getting depressed to know that sometimes bad things happened in the world. Then she said that I'd never really understand anything about the world at all if I just watched movies made for children. I thought that was a bit harsh. And when it came to books, Bethan read them and I didn't.

I was aware that her time away at university had put some distance between us. She'd always be talking about long-term plans, what we should be doing next, and what we should be looking to achieve in our careers. I, on the other hand, was happier to take things as they came. I'd achieved my initial goal of becoming a professional cricket player for Wessex, so I found the idea of constantly setting myself new targets simply exhausting. She never said it in as many words, but I sensed Bethan thought that The Canberra Parkas were an unnecessary distraction.

"You've made a great start at Wessex, Pete." Whenever she said something like that I knew that a motivational talk was coming. "But you're going to have to ask yourself if the rest of your lifestyle is giving you the best opportunity to become the player you want to be."

Yes, she was definitely talking about the Parkas. Brian Gunnell at Wessex had suggested to me that I could really benefit from a winter's cricket to capitalise on the good season I'd had. He'd made some preliminary calls to a couple of grade clubs in Sydney. As a club pro I'd just about cover the cost of the airfare and my food bills. Chances were that I'd actually end up out of pocket at the end of the trip. I liked the idea of going to Sydney, but by then we'd already got a number of gigs lined up and I didn't want to walk away from the band.

I'd spoken to Dougie about it. "Listen mate, if I was worried about your game, honestly I'd tell you to pack your bags and get down there. But let's look at the facts. You had a solid first year at the club. And now you're player of the season. Fuck's sake Pete, how much more improvement do you need? You're on a roll, Buddy."

Funnily enough, Bethan hadn't seen it that way. "Listen Pete, it's all about momentum," she said as we waited for our mains to arrive. "If you lose it, you'll seriously struggle to get it back. Top athletes have one thing in common: they prepare for success."

"Sorry Bethan," I interrupted, "I don't want to sound like a wanker, but what do you know about professional sport?"

"Well. Let me see. I spent three years studying it at a university that specialises in the subject. I had lectures every week from people who have worked with the UK's top athletes, footballers, rugby players, and even the occasional cricketer." She continued, "The more you learn now, the more experience you have to draw on, the more it will help you in the future."

Of course she was right. But then Bethan was always right. However, at the time I was still only twenty-two. I just wanted to play cricket in the summer and get on-stage with the band in the winter. And if I went to Australia I'd only be playing for a league club, not for one of the big state sides. So I'd be flying all that way to turn out in front of three men and a dog again: I didn't think that turning out in front of three Australian men and an Australian dog was any more appealing than playing in front of a similarly-sized English crowd.

"Look, let's talk about something else," she said. "You're not going and that's the end of the matter. I'm just saying that you can't afford to be complacent about your preparation, that's all."

I'd won the argument. Well, I'd won in the sense that I didn't get on a plane bound for Sydney. Looking back, I have to say that Bethan probably made the better points: it's just that she couldn't exactly handcuff me, take me to Heathrow, and get the crew to lock the plane door once I was on board.

By this time, Bethan was already working as a PE teacher in Casterbridge Secondary School. I knew right from the beginning that she was going to be brilliant at it. She was determined that more Casterbridge pupils should go on to represent Wessex in their chosen sports. It was obvious that she was putting everything into the job. She also had an idea to share with me. Putting aside our disagreement about the Australia trip, she wanted to sound me out on a new plan.

"OK Pete, it was your decision not to play cricket this winter, and I respect that. But I don't think you'll be in a band forever." Of course she turned out to be right about that too. "And I don't think you'll want to be a full-time painter and decorator when the cricket is over."

I hadn't given my post-cricket career any thought at all; after all I was yet to play my third season for Wessex. But I did at least recognise that professional sport doesn't come with any guarantees.

"So I was thinking, why don't you take on a renovation project and try to make some real money from your painting and decorating experience? I think I can persuade Dad to help out with the financing."

Bethan was suggesting that we buy a dilapidated residential property, restore it to its former glories, and put it back on the market. I was a little wary of owing Frank anything more than I had to, but it sounded like quite a good plan. So the following week I drove down to Port Bredy to talk to Danny about the idea. Davison's was one of a number of estate agents at the top of North Street in Port Bredy – only a stone's throw away from where Bethan and me used to sit on the bench listening to songs on Wednesday afternoons.

Danny had clearly learned a lot in the time that he'd been there. After I'd talked him through the rough plan, he grabbed a bunch of various property details from the steel filing cabinets that surrounded the office. Very quickly he worked out the sort of money you might expect to make from a renovation project, by comparing the asking prices of similar properties in different states of repair.

"OK Pete. This isn't definitive, but I think if you take a terraced property which is structurally sound but a mess inside, you could maybe add somewhere between 15 and 20 per cent to the value."

"That sounds good."

"But." Danny's voice sounded a note of caution. "You've got to factor in not just the cost of the materials and the specialist trades you'll need, but also interest rates, maybe capital gains tax, legal fees and the planning consents. And of course," he added with a little smile, "an agent's fee when you come to sell."

Danny really knew what he was talking about. I was both disappointed that this was sounding more complicated that I'd hoped, but impressed with Danny's grasp of the property business. He did have some good news though. "On the other hand, if you were to buy a sizeable terraced house and turn it into flats, then you might be looking at a much larger return on your investment."

While we were talking the phone rang on his desk. "Excuse me," he said. "Davison's, Daniel Legend speaking. Uh-huh. OK. Well I'll take that down." Danny pencilled a figure on the large sheet of paper that covered most of his working area. "Well, as his agent I'm duty-bound to pass that on, but I'm not going to recommend accepting that figure Mr Kirby. We haven't sold anything on Lime Grove at that price in probably a year or more. And as you know, twenty-nine is in exceptional condition. Uh-huh. Sure. I understand that. I will of course pass it on, but you should know that's some distance short of what my client is looking for."

Up until then I'd always thought that estate agencies would be boring places to visit and even more boring places to work. I'd never really thought about the role of the agent: as a dealmaker, getting the best possible price for his client. Danny was doing *business*. It was exciting and it didn't involve getting covered in paint every day.

Over the next couple of weeks Bethan and me re-thought the renovation plan, taking on board Danny's suggestions. We found a large Victorian terraced property in Casterbridge on Duchy Road, opposite the County Gardens with the bandstand and the tennis courts. The house had four floors including the basement. Our plan was simple: we'd turn each floor into a separate one-bedroom flat, then we'd sell three of them to cover the cost of the project and move into the fourth.

A couple of days later Bethan, Dougie and I met Frank over at Bridestock. With our combined salaries Bethan and I could raise about half of the required money on a mortgage, but we'd need a loan from Frank to make the project possible. We sat in the living room while Bethan outlined the overall plan, shared pictures of the property and so on. I chipped in with the odd comment about the materials we'd want to use and that sort of thing. I'd also got a bunch of particulars from Danny to show Frank what the asking prices for one-bedroom flats were in Casterbridge. Frank seemed impressed: there was a first time for everything.

Then Dougie chipped in. "Yeah, at Wessex Premier we're really excited about the potential of this development and would be happy to come on board to run the project management."

"Sorry?" replied Frank, "I don't think I understand."

"OK right. I'll tell you a bit about Wessex Premier."

"I can't wait."

"Well, I founded Wessex Premier about five years ago. And since then we've worked on numerous period properties all over Wessex, completing various renovation tasks over that time."

"It sounds brilliant. But I'm still struggling to understand why you're telling me this."

"Well, for our usual 15 per cent project fee, we've got the experience to bring this conversion in on budget, and within the planned time-frames."

"I'm still a little confused. Correct me if I'm wrong, but I think that you're suggesting that Pete here is going to do the work, and that you're going to bill him and Bethan, or me – I'm a little unclear on this – 15 per cent of the overall cost of the project."

"No, of course not Mr Trellick. Just 15 per cent of the cost of the materials and labour."

Frank was beginning to get riled, but I sensed that he was warming to his theme. "So, if I'm understanding this right, you'd like to be paid for the labour that he," Frank continued while pointing to me, "is going to otherwise be doing for absolutely nothing."

"Well, that labour has a book value. But the real benefit will be the project management skills I can offer. Budgeting, cash flow, management of the trades and all that sort of thing."

"Peter," Frank began. "If I remember rightly, you actually passed that Maths O-level at the second time of asking, didn't you?" I nodded. "Which gives me a certain level of faith in your academic ability. Academic ability which means that you have the required acumen to add numbers together, multiply others, and possibly, right out there at the very frontiers of your computational capabilities, calculate a percentage."

Dougie was about to speak, but Frank continued. "And such is my faith in Peter, and by extension our entire educational system, that I have no doubt in my mind whatsoever that if he were to drive a van down to Stan Bamber's Building Supplies and fill it with the necessary goods for the task in hand, he'd be able to work out – in advance no less – what he'd likely be paying for those aforementioned goods."

"Frank, Frank," Dougie butted in. "I really think you're down-playing what I can bring to this. But more importantly perhaps, Pete already works for me at Wessex Premier."

"Don't be daft, son." Frank now sounded irritated. "This project has got nothing to do with your firm – if indeed it is an entity familiar to the people at Companies House. Let me be perfectly clear. If I lend my daughter and her husband the money to do this project, I will do so only on the condition that not a penny of it ends up anywhere near your pocket."

"I really don't think you understand what me and my team can bring to this project . . ."

"Team? Team? I'll bet that *he* is your team. And *he* will be working on this for nothing. And *he'll* plan and budget it for nothing. And the last time I checked, 15 per cent of nothing was nothing. Am I making myself clear?"

"But Pete has been a member of my . . ."

"Bethan! Listen to the little man! He's still talking!" Bethan was trying not to laugh, and I was really hoping that Dougie didn't see her because this was just getting embarrassing. "I don't think he understands that this conversation is over. So you two," he said, addressing Bethan and me directly, "I like the scheme, I think it's sound. I'll lend you half the money. But I'm not a charity, so I'll match the rate you're getting from the building society. I'm assuming that's somewhere around 12 per cent. Happy?"

"Very happy. Thank you Dad," replied Bethan.

Dougie and me left Bethan with Frank and went down to the Ship to talk. He got straight to the point. "Pete, I've been backing you for something like ten years now. I helped you build up those savings for your first car, I set you up in the painting and decorating trade, I got you the highest ever starting package at Wessex and I've turned the band into a nice little earner."

"I know Dougie, you don't have to remind me. But this is Frank's cash. He's going to watch it like a hawk."

"You know I could help you on this project don't you?" I nodded in agreement.

"See, that's the problem with someone like Frank; he just can't see where I can add value."

I felt guilty. And I easily could see it from Dougie's perspective. As soon as someone else had offered me backing, I'd just cut Dougie out of the deal.

"And now that you're going to spend the next four or five months doing this project, we're not going to have any money coming in from your side of the business at Wessex Premier."

Maybe I'd been selfish, but what could I do? I had an opportunity to show Bethan that, beyond professional sports, there was more to me than just a painter and decorator. Get it right, and we could have a mortgage-free flat in the centre of Casterbridge. And I'd always had the sense that Frank didn't think I was good enough for Bethan, so this was a big opportunity to prove him wrong.

"I know this doesn't look great Dougie, but we need Frank's money so that's the end of it." Nonetheless I really wanted to get Dougie back onside. "So how about I help you sign up a few of the younger players in the Wessex system? I know they won't pay back immediately, but once they break into the first team you'll be in business."

"Who are you thinking of?"

"Well Steve Braithwaite for starters."

"The drummer in the Parkas?"

"That's the one. He trusts me and I can easily get him to sign on with you. Now that Phil's left he's going to be a regular starter from next year, and if he doesn't screw it up he'll be on a full contract by '87."

"Who else have you got?"

"Alex Durrant. He's an eighteen-year-old leggie in the seconds. Wessex has never produced one before, but he's really promising."

"Pete mate, I've told you before about the jargon. What's a *leggie?*"

"A slow bowler. Spins the ball away from the right-hander. Anyway, shouldn't you know this sort of stuff by now?"

"That's not my job Pete. I care about what they can achieve, not how they do it. Is he taking wickets for the seconds?"

"Truckloads by the end of last season, apparently."

"Very good. Give me one more"

"Marcus Tomkins. Keeper for the seconds. Natural successor to Laurie Kelly once the old bastard's knees finally explode."

"Is he good?"

"He'll play professionally. No doubt about that."

"Pete, you're a good mate. I appreciate it. What say you make some calls and set up a meeting with each of them next week? Sorted."

****

The renovation was hard, hard work. And despite Frank's declared faith in my maths skills, Bethan looked after the budgeting. She also dealt with all the planning applications and that sort of thing. By the beginning of the 1986 season I was knackered and we'd pretty much exhausted our budget. So, in order to save the cash to finish the project, we moved out of Creston and into the top-floor flat, which by April was more or less liveable. Drummer-batsman Steve Braithwaite took my old room in the house with Col.

The 1986 season wasn't particularly memorable. I was pretty pleased with my performances, but I took a few less wickets and made a few less runs than the previous year. Justin Bridges had come back from a winter in New Zealand a better batsman, and I could see that his confidence was increasing over the course of the season. Alan Musgrove didn't magically increase his average now that Phil had gone, but neither did he get any worse. Herb took loads of wickets, but David Collister was really beginning to struggle. He couldn't put his whole body into his action any more, so what turn and drift he might once have been able to produce, had more or less deserted him. I think it was a relief for everyone when he announced halfway through the season that he'd taken a job teaching history and sports at Sherton Abbas. In many ways he looked as though he'd been born to walk the grounds of a historic boarding school dispensing words of wisdom to the boys.

David had always been the butt of his own jokes, but you could tell that being regularly launched out of the ground by solid county pros was a bridge too far even for him. He put a brave face on it, "Guys," he called out in the dressing room one lunch-time, "Tony's going to have me on at the Dinsdale end this afternoon, so you might want to move your cars." Being smashed around the park by Clive Lloyd makes for a good anecdote, but being deposited into the top tier of the pavilion by Phil Grey first ball doesn't. Though perhaps Phil had a point to prove on his return to Canberra Park.

In early December 1986 Bethan and me were able to throw our first dinner party in our new place, shortly after we'd completed the sales of the three other flats in the building. We'd re-paid Frank and come incredibly close to owning our place outright, but we had needed a very small mortgage to cover the shortfall. It had been tough and it had been stressful, but we were pleased with the way the whole thing had turned out.

There were eight of us there that night. It was the first time I'd seen Dougie and Belinda since their wedding. Belinda was now doing a little less of her head-tilted, enthusiastic listening thing, preferring to spend rather more time talking herself. This wasn't necessarily a good thing.

Danny came over with his new girlfriend, Angela. She was a mortgage advisor at Barclays in Port Bredy. She was blonde, attractive and very earnest. She had mastered that slightly disapproving look that bankers used to use back then, especially in front of young couples looking for their first major loan. The pair of them looked like they belonged with each other; and that's how it turned out. Nearly thirty years later their marriage is solid and both of their kids are going through university.

I'd invited Col over, so Bethan suggested that she ask Leslie Rogers, an English teacher at her school, if she'd like to join us too. Leslie was the last to arrive and I buzzed her in and told her to make her way up to the top flat. I'd had some faint hope that Leslie and Col might hit it off, but I rapidly revised that view when she arrived at the top of the stairs. I always try to focus on someone's most attractive features. But Leslie seemed determined to make that as difficult as possible. She had dark brown hair. At the sides and at the back it was cut to a uniform length, somewhere around the level of her jawline. At the front she had a severe fringe. It looked as though she was staring out of an open-face motorbike helmet. She was wearing NHS glasses. But not just regulation NHS specs; it was as though she'd gone and asked for the chunkiest, ugliest frames available. She passed me her donkey jacket to hang up as she came in, revealing some sort of green item of knitwear that I can only describe as a button-up sack.

Leslie was the least able to hide her boredom when Belinda was taking us through the honeymoon photos. She almost let out an audible groan when it dawned on her there was still a fourth album to get through. I could see that the next shot was Dougie posing in a pair of shorts and sunglasses beside a sports fishing boat holding up his catch.

"Well, it's very good that you can afford all this." Leslie seemed to shoot the words out of her mouth rather than just say them. "This holiday must have cost a few quid."

"And then some," Dougie replied. I think he deliberately ignored the hostility in Leslie's voice. "Bells, find the shot where I'm in the fighting chair. That one's brilliant."

"Well it *was* our honeymoon," Belinda chipped in as she searched through the photos. "I think we deserved something special."

"So Leslie," said Dougie. "What's your story?"

"My story? Right. OK. Born in Rusholme Manchester. Brought up by my mum. Dad left when I was two. Mum's on benefits. My elder brother's on a methadone programme. And my little sister's on the tills in Asda." She fired this at us as if we were somehow responsible.

"And yet, here you are. A teacher in Casterbridge." Danny sounded impressed. I don't know if he actually was that impressed or whether he was just trying to lighten the mood a little. It wasn't as though we'd exactly been brought up in luxury ourselves.

"Books. That was my thing. My escape," Leslie continued. "You open the cover and you're somewhere else. Away from all the shit. Away from all the pain. That's why I love books. I always knew I wanted to work with books." She now sounded a little bit less like a Gatling gun and a little bit more like a human being.

"I know exactly what you mean," said Dougie. "When we were away I took *Red Storm Rising* by Tom Clancy. It was fucking brilliant. It's about NATO and the Russians getting it on big time over access to oil. The Soviets are going to take the whole fucking thing nuclear. It starts . . ."

"I was more thinking Jane Austen. Or Dickens, Thackeray or Eliot. But anyway," Leslie said, changing the subject, "what do you do for a living, Dougie?"

"A little bit of everything: sports, music, import, export, marketing, consultancy. I'm a businessman."

"But what do you actually *do*?" pressed Leslie. "Give me an example in sports."

"Well, I represent a number of Wessex cricket players, including Pete here," he said, pointing to me. "My role is to ensure that Peter maximises his revenue opportunities throughout his playing career and beyond."

"And he touts players from the Wessex youth system around the other clubs to see if he can net himself a transfer fee." Danny sounded unusually hostile for a moment.

"Well," replied Dougie slowly, as if he was explaining something really complicated to a child, "if that player and I agree that he could benefit from a move – either to increase his earning potential or to advance his opportunities within the game – then that's something we'd consider. But Danny, you talk as though I'm moving players all the time."

"You're trying to," Danny said tersely.

"And how would you know that, Danny?"

"I still have some friends in the game. I know you were at the Oval last week trying to pitch them Steve Braithwaite. He's only just broken into the first team here at Wessex. He's doing well. He's among people he's known for years. Why's it in his interest to move to London?"

"I'm not going to talk about individual clients with you."

"Well the funny thing is Dougie" – my brother now had a mischievous smile on his face – "the story about Steve is doing the rounds because it came out in the meeting that you didn't even know he batted left-handed."

"That's a lie. And I don't need to be lectured on my business by someone who couldn't hack it as a professional."

The evening ended well, and everyone agreed that Bethan's Thai curry had been a triumph. It was just a shame that there was so much needle between Danny and Dougie. I wished that they could both simply drop it. But that night turned out to be merely the beginning – things were going to get a whole lot worse between them yet.

The beer lasted a good while.

8. THE INFAMOUS INCIDENT AT MIKE'S PLACE IN THE NIGHT-TIME

I hauled my coffin into our dressing room for the first game of the 1987 season. I was the third player to arrive. Laurie Kelly was, once again, feverishly looking for something in his kit bag and Michael Andrews was sat in my locker place. I didn't know much about Andrews: all I'd been told was that he was joining us from Surrey. He was a late addition to the squad that year. Consequently, he'd missed our pre-season training and was going straight into a game on his first day at the club. The previous year Kelly had managed to get Steve Braithwaite to shift his coffin eight times, before St-t-t-teve (he was afflicted with a terrible stutter) finally located the spot vacated by Phil Grey. Over time a couple of unspoken rules had evolved in relation to Kelly's little game: the rest of the team wouldn't give any useful hints to the newcomer, but neither would we help Kelly by further misdirecting him. This seemed fair enough, given that money would be riding on the result. The Musgroves and Andy Farrow would usually bet him a tenner each that he couldn't get the new player to move at least five times.

"Hi, I'm Peter Legend." I offered my hand. "But, unfortunately, there's been some confusion and you're in my locker space."

"Michael Andrews," he replied. "But please, call me Mike."

He sounded like Jeremy Irons in *Brideshead Revisited*: I'd reluctantly become familiar with the series because Leslie had been coming over to our place to watch it on video with Bethan. He then stood up very slowly, as though it had taken every last bit of energy from his body, and began to move his kit one locker space down the room.

"Not that one." Laurie's voice sounded muffled, coming from the depths of his kit bag. With his free hand he was jabbing at another space further down the row.

"*That* one."

"It's Laurie Kelly, right?" enquired Andrews of the kit bag.

"Mmmmm," came the reply.

"Well, here's the thing Laurie. I got up at four-thirty this morning to get here on time. And if I'm honest, I'm flagging a little right now." Andrews continued, "I realise that it'll be pretty damned side-splitting if you get me to shift my kit around the dressing room countless times, but it would be really tremendous if you could just point me to a free spot."

"Yes, that one," came the reply. Kelly was still pointing at the same spot.

Andrews glanced suspiciously at what he could see of Kelly, but nevertheless he began shifting his kit to the new locker. Justin Bridges' locker.

And Bridges was the next player to arrive. "Justin Bridges. Sorry mate, but you're in my locker."

Andrews slowly got back to his feet, rising gingerly like an exhausted pensioner. He shook Bridges' hand and then moved both himself and his kit into the middle of the room. Kelly started gesticulating to another spot, but Andrews just ignored him. Which only made Kelly's pointing become all the more frantic.

"As I said, I'm feeling rather jaded," Andrews announced to nobody in particular in his cut-glass voice, "so I'm just going to stand here like a cunt, and wait for the rest of the team to show up."

"I'm telling you, *there*!" Kelly was pointing to yet another vacant spot. Which was, after only a short wait, soon occupied by Herb. Andrews allowed himself a wry smile.

Over the next ten minutes or so the rest of the team arrived. In turn Andrews introduced himself to each of them, but stayed standing in the middle of the room. The Musgroves and Andy Farrow were the last to arrive. Carl, on seeing Andrews just stood in the middle of the dressing room, scented victory.

"You owe us money, don't you Kelly?" Carl sounded unusually cheerful. "How many was it? Not five, that's for sure."

"Two," Kelly reluctantly admitted.

"Two? That's fucking useless Kelly. You've lost it." This was Alan. "Well let's have the cash then. Hand it over."

"I haven't got thirty quid on me right now. I'll have to owe you all." Kelly sounded really irritable. He hadn't lost this bet for a while and he clearly wasn't very happy about it. "Fucking outsiders, that's what's cost me. Posh boy from Surrey there" – he was pointing at Andrews – "shouldn't even be here in the first place."

"I shouldn't be here?" asked Andrews with mock surprise. "Well perhaps you could direct me to where I should be." He then started searching in his pocket for a scrap of paper, which he then pulled out. "No, this is definitely right: Canberra Park, opposite Canberra Crescent, Budmouth, Wessex."

"That's not what I mean Smart-arse and you know it." Kelly was getting seriously riled. "This club is Wessex. We're all Wessex down here. You weren't good enough for Surrey I heard, so why that makes you good enough for us, I don't know. You've got a lot to prove, son."

"Hey Laurie, calm down." Tony Sinclair had finally decided to step in. "I don't want you and Andrews getting off on the wrong foot."

"No, we wouldn't want that," said Andrews.

"I'm just saying, Posh Boy, we'll be watching you. Best thing you can do is keep you mouth shut and play some bloody good cricket."

"Yeah," added Andy Farrow.

It would have been late April or early May and we were playing one of the university sides that day. Generally the quality of those college sides wasn't great, but occasionally they'd include a promising player or two. Mike Atherton turned out for Cambridge around that time, and obviously he went on to do alright. Most of the players in those teams weren't exactly up to county standard, so we'd expect to win, and win by a healthy margin. Nonetheless it was always useful preparation for the season.

I can't recall too much about the morning session of that game, but I certainly do remember the lunch interval. The opposition won the toss and chose to bat. I think they must have been three or four wickets down by the break, because we left the field considering it a morning's work well done. Us bowlers tended to get off the field first, making the time for a quick shower before lunch. So I arrived back at the dressing room first, opened the door and was almost knocked back by the smell of shit that engulfed me. A dressing room is a stuffy place at the best of times, but this was something else entirely. The stench of crap was so intense it felt as though I was eating the stuff.

Carl Musgrove was coming down the corridor behind me. "Ledge, what the fuck is that smell?" he asked.

Holding my nose, I peered around the dressing-room door to look inside. I instantly saw the source of the problem.

"Well," I was now speaking to most of the team who had, by this time, arrived in the corridor. "Something, or someone, has taken a dump on Laurie's bench." It wasn't a monster like Dad's effort that had blocked the toilet back in Whetstock, but it was still a pretty good-sized log. Conceivably it could have been a dog-turd, but I didn't think so.

"Where is that posh cunt? I'm going to rip his fucking throat out." The veins in Kelly's neck were standing out, he'd thrown his gloves on the floor, and his eyes were bulging with fury.

Tony Sinclair was reluctantly forced into the role of peacekeeper. "Laurie, we don't know that it's got anything to do with Michael, do we? Look, most likely some dog's gone and got in there."

"Oh yeah, I'm sure that's right Skip. It's opened the door, jumped up onto the bench, taken a shit and then left, shutting the door on its way out." Kelly had a point; it was unlikely to have been a dog. "I'm going to fucking batter him."

"I'm sorry Kelly, were you looking for me?" Andrews had nonchalantly arrived in the corridor and was pretending not to have noticed that the wicket-keeper was about ready to kill him. Kelly didn't say anything, he just started sprinting towards Andrews, baring his teeth and making some sort of gurgling war cry.

Carl Musgrove and Col easily held Kelly back: like most keepers he wasn't a big guy. But even though they restrained him, he was still struggling furiously and ranting away. Meanwhile Andrews was looking incredibly calm, as though he didn't have a care in the world: that just seemed to wind up the keeper even further. Kelly's chin was covered in spittle from the various insults he'd spat in Andrews' direction.

"Listen, old chap," began Andrews very gently. "What's the problem?"

"Fuck you, you cunt. You *know* what the fucking problem is you fucker."

"Kelly, really I don't. What's got you so wound up, fella?"

"You fucking know full fucking well. You shat in my place, you cunt."

"Why on earth would I have done that?" Andrews sounded genuinely perplexed.

"Because you're a fucking arsehole."

"Well that doesn't sound like a very good reason to me," Andrews replied. "But let's just imagine for a moment that I really did want to take a shit on your locker space, *how* exactly would I have been able to do that?"

"Don't play fucking games with me, son."

"Really. How am I supposed to have done that? We've been out in the field for the last two hours, and as you can see, I'm the last person to have arrived here."

"You obviously came off the field earlier, you fuck."

"How could I possibly have just left the field without anyone, including your good self, seeing that I'd gone?"

It may well have only been a university side we were playing, but this didn't exactly reflect very well on any of us – if Andrews had simply been able to leave the field for a couple of overs without anyone noticing.

"Well if I were to have done it . . . let me see." Andrews paused for effect. All the players were gathered around Andrews in the corridor, as he explained the only way in which the crime could have possibly been committed. "I imagine I'd have waited until the skipper came on to bowl from the pavilion end," Andrews continued. "Skip obviously wouldn't have been able to watch the whole field, so I'd have had a chance to jog off the park, get to the dressing room, do my business and then creep back into my position unnoticed."

"You're admitting it now, are you?" Kelly was still seriously rattled, but he had regained a measure of self-control.

"Admitting it? Absolutely not." Andrews sounded almost offended. "Surely when Skip's bowling there's an even greater weight of responsibility on the keeper to run the team in the field. So this just doesn't stack up does it? Think about it: from deep mid-wicket I'd have had to jog quarter of the way around the ground to get to the pavilion. Any keeper worth his salt would have noticed that." It was beginning to dawn on Kelly that he was being stitched up beautifully by Andrews.

"So," announced Andrews, indicating that he was about to draw his little speech to a conclusion, "the only way it could have been me is if you'd spent all of the skipper's spell yakking to first slip, and ignoring everything that was going on around you. I realise that we're only playing a bunch of students, but I find it impossible to believe that a player of your standing could possibly have done such a thing."

Kelly didn't know what to say. Most likely he *would* have been yakking away to Andy Farrow at first slip. We were lucky that Farrow was our best close catcher, because he was also the only person in the team who found Kelly's *jokes* funny. So the chances were that Kelly had been in a world of his own, telling Andy that the various batsmen looked like *fucking Guardian-reading, shirt-lifting, vegetarian nonces*, and had simply failed to notice that Andrews had buggered off to shit in the dressing room.

"Which leads me to conclude," said Andrews with a flourish, "that any faecal matter deposited in the locker room must have been left there by some other culprit. I think we can rule out the opposition. Even though I attended the other place, I just don't think it's the sort of thing that these chaps would do. So, in all probability we're looking for a canine perpetrator."

"What the fuck?" Kelly just couldn't believe that Andrews was going to get away with this.

"Well, as I suggested earlier," interjected Tony Sinclair with some relief, "it most likely was a dog. I don't know how it got in the dressing room, but there you go, it's just one of those things." The idea that it was a dog suited Tony just fine.

"A dog. It was a fucking dog." Kelly by now had enough self-control to be able to lace his words with sarcasm.

"It's karmic though, isn't it?" said Andrews brightly.

"It's fucking what?" asked Kelly.

"Karmic, my friend," Andrews explained. "Well, earlier today, when I'd told you that I was tired from a long drive, you treated me like crap. But then, within a matter of hours a dog takes a crap in your locker space. I'm not really a spiritual person myself, but then something like this happens and it really makes you wonder, doesn't it?"

"Fuck you," replied Kelly before shrugging off Carl and Col and making his way back down the corridor in the direction of the dining hall.

Sinclair summoned up the most authoritative look he could manage. "Don't screw this up before you've even bowled a ball for the club, eh?"

Given that it had been officially concluded that we were dealing with dog shit, it fell to poor old Len to clean it up. We all knew he loved the club, but that day he must have surely been wondering if there were limits to his devotion. Later that season Len told me that Andrews had cleared his bar tab for him, but Andrews himself denied it.

****

Mike threw a house-warming party some time in May of that year. He had rented a three-storey period property in Divinity Street, which is on the southern side of the harbour in Budmouth. The area contains some beautiful family homes, but it's also just around the corner from all the pubs, bars and restaurants.

"Do you think Budmouth's ready for some Mikey time?" asked Andrews.

"Uh, what?" replied Col.

I was driving the pair of them back from Edgbaston early on a Friday afternoon. Our Championship game had finished early and we weren't due to play again until the Sunday in the Refuge Assurance League. By the beginning of the 1987 season I was driving a five-door Sierra – again supplied by Creston Motors. Bethan had pushed me to get something more practical than the XR2: when I'd been working on the redevelopment I found that I spent half my time trying to borrow vehicles that were actually big enough to carry building supplies. So I'd made numerous journeys in the XR2 over to Bridestock, just to get the keys to Frank's Toyota pick-up truck.

Mike had arrived in Canberra Park in a mid-seventies red Lotus Elan +2. Apparently the '+2' signified that the car had an additional two seats in the rear, but those *seats* weren't much use for anything other than a place to put your map and a packed lunch. Some days the Lotus worked, and some days it didn't. It was a luxury car in the sense that owning it was a luxury: if you wanted a reliable set of wheels, big enough to get you and your kit to game after game around the country, you were going to need another car. And that other car was my car.

So, for much of 1987 and the seasons that followed, the three of us travelled together in my Sierra estate. Col and me would take turns in the driving seat; Mike would always sit in the back.

"Mikey time! Party time!" explained Andrews with evident enthusiasm. "If I throw open my doors to the good people of Budmouth, will they come?"

"Uh, if you've got beer, then sure," replied Col.

"Well, that's settled then. I'll buy beer and then we shall have a very good time."

"OK," Col and me agreed.

We got back to Casterbridge late in the afternoon. Col and Mike picked up their cars, which they'd both parked in the streets behind our flat. Bethan was still at work, so I left her a note saying I'd be spending the evening over at Mike's, and then I travelled down to Budmouth with Col. Mike pulled up in front of an off-licence on the outskirts of the city. Ten minutes later we were again following the Lotus into Budmouth, but now Col's sponsored Renault 5 was weighed down by twenty Holsten slabs and several bags of ice that Mike had just paid for.

I didn't understand why Mike had bothered to rent a whole house; it must have cost most of his Wessex salary. He basically just lived in the bedroom at the top of the property, and left the rest of the place largely unfurnished. We carried the beer and the ice up to the first-floor bathroom, ran a few inches of cold water into the freestanding tub, and then unpacked all of the cans and covered them in the ice.

"Who are you going to invite?' I asked Mike.

"Everyone of course! It's very simple. We go out for an evening in Budmouth and sample everything that this charming, yet slightly run-down provincial backwater has to offer, and along the way we invite everyone we like to a party at 21 Divinity Street. The fun starts at eleven."

"This could get really messy," I said.

"Messy? Brilliant! That's the spirit. Now, where can I find a band who'd like to entertain my guests?"

I suggested that we start at the Warehouse where I knew that we'd find an act or two sound-checking for their performances later on in the evening. When we got there a young guitar band was on-stage running through a couple of songs in front of the sound engineer, a small gaggle of girlfriends and a handful of hangers-on.

"I like them enormously!" Mike screamed in my ear over the band's rather messy cover version of "Holiday in Cambodia" by the Dead Kennedys. Thanks to Bethan's pre-university taste in music I was familiar with what the track was supposed to sound like. But Mike looked happy enough. "Great energy! I think they're exactly what we're looking for."

After they'd finished the sound-check and were milling around aimlessly on the stage, Mike jumped up to join them. After a few minutes he came back to join Col and me at the back of the venue. "They're really keen to be part of it," he announced. "They're called The Boys From Brazil."

With The Boys From Brazil booked, we then spent the next few hours going from venue to venue around the Budmouth harbourside, inviting pretty much everyone we met to Mike's party. I can't honestly say that I remember the whole night in great detail. I know for sure that we started out on a pub-crawl around the harbourside, and that we definitely stopped off in one place for some time to join in a game of skittles. That would certainly explain the bruising on my shoulders and hips that I noticed when I was warming up for Sunday's game.

Mike hadn't seen the Wessex Flop skittle bowling technique before, so he was keen to play until he perfected it. I don't know exactly how the Wessex Flop evolved. When you're preparing to take your turn you hold the ball with both hands, and stand with your legs some distance apart. You then swing the ball forward from between your knees, and as your hands come up to around waist height, you throw your whole body forward. If all goes well, the ball runs true and fast down the track towards the skittles, and you land face down at the top of the lane. There could be some sporting rationale for the technique: after all, the ball is right underneath the bowler's eye-line at all times, which should make aiming easier. But I think the real attraction is that it's simply an excuse to perform a series of drunken belly flops in a pub, all in the name of competitive sport.

I've no idea how long we were bowling for, but suddenly Mike declared that we hadn't invited enough women to the party, so we set off again to spread the word. I think I tried to tell Mike that we didn't really want to go as far as the ferry port, but he was insistent. That bit of the evening remains a little hazy, but the fact that we definitely went down there goes some way to explaining the more salacious elements of the subsequent reporting in the *Budmouth Echo*.

When we got back to Mike's place, the street was quiet. I went upstairs and grabbed three beers from the bath and we sat on the sofa downstairs. It was just about the only piece of furniture in the living room. But it didn't look as though anyone was going to show up. There wasn't even any sign of The Boys From Brazil.

But we couldn't have been sat on the couch for all that long, because people started to arrive before we'd finished our first round of Holstens. And then the band turned up shortly afterwards. Col and me helped them bring their kit into the house. Mike, meanwhile, was playing the part of host to perfection: greeting his guests at the door and directing them to the bath of beer upstairs. I think it must have taken The Boys From Brazil about an hour or so to set up their kit. I remember thinking that they seemed to be quite particular about their equipment for a band that could barely play.

Soon the ground and first floor of the house were absolutely rammed, and people were spilling out into the street outside. The beer lasted a good while through the night, simply because the journey to the first floor was proving a major undertaking; such were the numbers of people in there. This turned out to be great news for the various drug-dealers who'd made their way to Divinity Street: they were doing a roaring trade among people who couldn't be bothered to fight their way upstairs to the beer. People were openly rolling up in the street outside the house.

I can only guess that it was around one-thirty when The Boys From Brazil finally began their set. Within the confines of a Victorian terraced house, the band was unbelievably loud. Unsurprisingly, they hadn't somehow improved since I'd first seen them a few hours earlier, but I had to admit that there was something quite exciting about the way they tore into their songs. Nonetheless, they had a divisive effect on Mike's guests. Those that hated them joined the ever-growing crowd of joint-smokers in the street, while those that loved them went absolutely crazy, turning the entire ground floor of the house into a mosh pit.

It was somewhere around this stage of the night when the police turned up. Initially it was just a couple of beat constables, so Mike gamely tried to persuade them that he'd tell the band to turn the music down a bit, and that the rest of the crowd were all close personal friends. He could vouch for the good character of each and every one of them.

However, it was no more than a stalling tactic: the distinctive musky but sweet aroma from countless joints was drifting all the way down the street. (Col would have been able to describe it better than me because he's got more words for the smell of a spliff than the Eskimos do for snow.) And a crowd of furious neighbours was by this point threatening to out-number the revellers, so it was only a matter of time before the constabulary arrived in greater numbers.

Unfortunately for us, a photographer from the *Echo* arrived before the police, so he was able to get some good shots of Budmouth's partygoers, drug-dealers and hookers legging it from the scene. They also got shots of Col and me standing by the front door looking rather worse for wear. Mike was arrested and taken down to the police station. After a few hours in a cell, he managed to talk his way out of being charged with a breach of the peace. We made the headline story in the *Echo* the following week.

Hell in Divinity Street

The residents of Divinity Street were last Friday subjected to a living hell as a large crowd of young troublemakers, drug-dealers and sex workers descended on this usually quiet residential area. Eyewitnesses confirmed that drugs were openly sold and consumed on the street, while prostitutes were thought to be working inside the property at the centre of the disturbance.

Residents were further disturbed by the sound of punk rock band The Boys From Brazil who began playing a live set at 2am. Families were woken by the music all across the southern harbourside area, placing numerous calls to the police. Some of the band members are understood to have Nazi sympathies.

Three prominent Wessex cricket players were caught up in the events of last Friday night. New signing Michael Andrews is understood to be renting the property at the centre of the mayhem, while teammates Colin Beresford and Peter Legend were photographed at the scene. None of the players were available for comment.

The article went on to quote those residents whose lives had been made a living hell. The main photo accompanying the article was a shot of about fifty people running away from an approaching police car down Divinity Street. There was a dreadful inset picture of Col and me standing by the front door of the house: they'd had to blow it up so it was very grainy. I looked like the suspect in a murder trial.

Sebastian Welland-Flanders summoned the three of us to a meeting. It transpired that the local papers and radio stations had been calling him all week, asking him to make a statement. After a few days he felt compelled to issue a short press release. It basically said that the club didn't condone any anti-social behaviour on the part of its players, but equally that the club believed that its players were adults, responsible for their own conduct. Behind closed doors in the pavilion he was somewhat less measured.

"Do you know what?" he began. "In truth, I don't give a damn what you do with your lives when you're not on duty for Wessex. You can rob banks, shag ladyboys in Thailand or sell heroin to school kids. Really, it's all absolutely fine by me. But when you drag the club . . ." and here he paused for a moment, "and when you drag *me*, into your seedy nocturnal proclivities, you have crossed a line. Your little escapade has ruined my working week, and that's something that I won't stand for. If anything like this ever happens again, the consequences will be severe. Am I making myself clear?"

"Yes, sir," we all replied in unison.

Even Mike didn't seem to think that this was a particularly good moment for some smart-arse comment. We'd prepared a toned-down version of events for Welland-Flanders: that we'd invited a few close friends around to Mike's for a house-warming party, but because of our celebrity status in Budmouth, word had got around, and an unexpected number of people had showed up on the night. Obviously we were in the process of trying to defuse the situation when the police arrived. This didn't quite explain why The Boys From Brazil started their set in the early hours of the morning, but it at least sounded vaguely plausible. Welland-Flanders however, seemed to be genuinely sincere when he said that he really didn't care what we got up to when we weren't on duty for Wessex.

"Now get out and go and play some cricket. And you can apologise to Rachel on the way. Poor thing's been fielding calls all week because of you lot."

It was a useful lesson for me in the way that the media works; they way they twist the details to make a story sound more interesting or shocking. For example, there may well have been some prostitutes at the party, but it was inconceivable that they were working: every room of the house was absolutely jammed full of people, so it simply wasn't a physical possibility. The Boys From Brazil were actually an *anti*-Nazi band; so that's just an example of the newspaper getting its facts completely wrong. Overall the piece was trying to make out that us cricket players were drug-taking, prostitute-using, members of the far right. We weren't the first sportsmen to be victims of the media twisting things to create a sensational story, and unfortunately we won't be the last.

Welland-Flanders must have subsequently said something to Tony Sinclair and Brian Gunnell, because the following day they issued some new club rules about appropriate behaviour when we were on match duty. To be honest, they weren't asking for very much: basically that when we were playing away from home we should be back in our hotel by 11 o'clock, and that after this time the hotel bar was off limits. I was relieved that the new rules wouldn't impact on most of the other players. That wouldn't have been fair. The older guys like Herb, Laurie Kelly and Andy Farrow never tended to stray very far from the hotel when we travelled anyway, while the younger batsmen such as Justin Bridges and Steve Braithwaite tended to take their fitness pretty seriously, so you'd be more likely to find them coming back from the hotel gym at 11 o'clock rather than trying to get into a club. The Musgroves weren't too happy about the new rules, but I wasn't going to feel too guilty about making their lives a little bit more difficult.

Unlike Col and Mike, I got my biggest shellacking back at home. Bethan was, understandably I suppose, pretty mad that I'd been out all night in the first place.

"It shows a lack of respect, Pete. That you think you can just stay out all night without letting me know where you are. You didn't call. You just don't think, do you? I just get a note, which might as well have said, 'Tough shit, you're on your own tonight, love.'"

"I'm sorry," I replied. "Did you spend the evening on your own?"

"Well as it happens, Leslie called round and we got a video out."

"What did you watch?" I reckoned that if it was any good I could at least see it myself before it was due to go back to the shop.

"*A Room with a View.*"

"Oh." I'd noticed that Bethan was watching a lot more period drama since she'd met Leslie.

Bethan's focus changed a bit a few days later when the *Budmouth Echo* came out. It didn't help that she'd first picked up the paper in the teachers' staff-room, so she was all too aware that most of her colleagues would have seen it. And they'd likely be thinking that she was married to a racist, prostitute-visiting junky. When I got in that day she gave me both barrels.

After some considerable length of time I think I managed to explain just how much of the story was exaggerated or factually incorrect, but she still accused me of throwing my career down the toilet.

"Pete, you've gone from player of the season to someone who is only one step away from disciplinary procedure at the club. Even if we forget the party, you're not giving yourself the chance to reach your full potential as a player. I'd thrash you in a five-mile run right now."

Bethan was right about that. She was certainly fitter than me at the time. But then, as I explained to her, cricket is a skills-based game; it's not a form of athletics. She'd have also thrashed Herb in a five-mile run, and Ian Botham too for that matter, but it didn't make her the better seam bowler.

"Pete, with the best will in the world, you're not in Botham's league when it comes to the skills though, are you? You can't judge yourself next to him. He's freakishly talented at what he does. So much so that he's *never* had to look after his fitness."

I thought that was a bit harsh, coming from my own wife. Over the previous few seasons I'd taken far more Championship wickets than Botham. Obviously he was away playing for England for some of the season, but for her to suggest that he was somehow in a different league as a player was a bit insulting. And on the subject of fitness itself, Botham himself would surely have agreed with me; it's cricket not the heptathlon.

"But you're a professional sportsman, Pete. That's what you do for a living. Your body is the key piece of equipment that you use to do your job. You need to look after it. This is pretty simple stuff."

It's one thing learning all this theory at university; it's quite another dealing with the reality of being a professional cricket player in England. Most of your season isn't spent on the pitch: it's spent driving, navigating, checking into and staying in low-cost hotels, and passing the time when your side's batting. Most of the time it's dull beyond belief. And unless you have no interest in anything outside the game at all, you need an opportunity to let off steam; you need to have a bit of fun.

Our philosophy was that
any night out was better
than no night out.

9. THE BATTLE OF BUDMOUTH

Most of the games you play as a professional blur in the memory after a while. Obviously you remember taking five-fors, dismissing a really good batsman or scoring a fifty, but after a while it gets harder to remember what exactly happened in which game, and even the season in which it happened. But I can remember the hours that Col, Mike and me spent together on the road as though it was yesterday.

Mike was, without doubt, a very clever guy. But he had a very simple approach to life. "I just want to have some fun," he explained. "Here's the thing; as long as I'm playing professional sport, my father will leave me alone. But if I'm not playing sport he'll demand that I either become a lawyer or a banker. And that's no idle threat; he's got loads of contacts in the City. So as long as I'm driving around with you two idiots, I'm safe. I had a choice: professional sport or Sandhurst. I chose cricket because it involves less physical exercise. And, of course, there's less chance of getting shot."

"But is that the extent of your ambition in cricket, Mike?" I asked. "To avoid getting a *proper* job?" I wasn't sure if I really believed him. We'd already seen in the few games that he'd played with us that Mike was a very good off-spinner, far better than David Collister had ever been.

"I didn't say my ambition was to be a *bad* cricketer," he explained. "In fact I'll bet you that in every season I play at Wessex I'll never be lower than second in the club's wicket tally. You two, with your agricultural huff, puff and bluster, will be no match for my elegant and beguiling little twirlers. I'm not so sure about Herb though; he's a crafty little fucker."

Ignoring the various insults, I pressed him further. "But Mike, why aren't you looking to push on and fight for a Test place? If you end up taking a hatful of wickets for Wessex every year, surely England will come calling. *I'm* still focused on getting into the England set-up."

"Well my friend, maybe you just want it that bit more than me. But I know my own limitations. I was king of the hill at school, middle of the pack at university, and by the time I got to Surrey I couldn't even hold down a regular starting place. I know my place in the world of cricket. At Wessex, I'll be a key member of the side. At a bigger club, I won't. And if I ever do get called up by England, the chances of me hanging on to my place are almost non-existent."

"That's a pretty defeatist attitude, don't you think, Mike?"

"No Ledge, it's not. It's a healthy attitude. I'll tell you a story. A handful of years ago I got asked to go and do some net bowling for England, before an Oval Test. And I found myself bowling to David Gower. Of course, he won't remember this. But anyway, we were on one of those practice wickets out on the square that they have there, and this one was pretty worn. And I was thinking, 'I fancy my chances here. Around the wicket to a left-hander, with plenty of rough to work with, I reckon I can get him out.'"

"And did you?"

"Not even close. He had the professional courtesy to take a look at my first delivery. But after that he did whatever he liked. Frankly I was cannon fodder."

"So you thought, "'I couldn't get Gower out, so I'll give up.'"

"No, that's not it. No, what I realised was that I was pretty good at cricket, but that I was never going to make it to the very top. So, if I was going to play the game professionally, I was going to make pretty damn sure I had some fun along the way."

"And you had too much fun for Surrey's liking?"

"Apparently. Anyway, I'm beginning to bore myself. We're in London tonight with its cornucopia of nocturnal temptations. So, what shall we do?"

"I don't know," I replied. "Go out somewhere that's close enough to the hotel, so we can get back for eleven, I guess."

"You see Ledge, *that* is your problem. No ambition whatsoever old chap."

****

Despite our lack of consistent success on the pitch, I still have very fond memories of the seasons between 1987 and 1989. As a team we were struggling, never getting above sixteenth in the Championship, and lacking the firepower at the top of the order to do particularly well in the limited overs competitions. Dougie used to tell me around this time that Welland-Flanders would have to invest in the team if Wessex was ever going to compete with the bigger county sides. I think he'd even tried to fix a meeting with Welland-Flanders on a couple of occasions to talk about the potential for him to bring in some higher-profile players. But nothing came of it. In fact, it was either in 1988 or early 1989 that Welland-Flanders actually banned Dougie from Canberra Park. I was there when it happened, because Dougie was re-negotiating my contract for me at the time. He was saying that I was brilliant and still on course for an England call-up, while Welland-Flanders was pointing out that I was only third in the Wessex wicket-taking standings, behind Herb and Mike.

Then Dougie said something like this: "Listen, Sebastian, the players I represent are going to have to ask themselves if Wessex is a club with ambition; if Wessex is the club that is going to fully reward their talent. We're talking about Peter today, but if he can't get a deal commensurate with his ability, track-record and potential, perhaps I should be advising players like Braithwaite and Tomkins to consider other options outside of Wessex."

"Are you threatening me?" Welland-Flanders, who had only a moment before been quite calm, flew instantly into a rage. "I'm sick and tired of your tawdry little business practices. We're here to talk about Peter, and Peter alone. I've put a damned good offer on the table. I suggest you take it and get out. And Peter," he went on, addressing me directly. "This style of representation isn't doing you any favours. You're a good player, but don't go thinking that you're indispensable." He paused for a moment. "Actually Barrett, do you know what? I've simply had enough of looking at you. I really have. I don't ever want to see you at the club again. You can write to me if you ever need to get in contact. Good day."

Welland-Flanders was as good as his word. He told the groundsmen and ticketing staff that if ever they saw Dougie at Canberra Park again they were to escort him off the premises. Even with these occasional setbacks, playing cricket for Wessex during that period was still a pleasure. With Mike around, the season was something to look forward to. He was as good as his word: he was out to have fun, and it was very difficult to avoid having fun yourself if you hung around with Mike for any length of time. During the winters he worked as a ski instructor at a resort in the French Alps.

"You simply get a better class of totty over there," he explained one day from the back seat of the Sierra. "Don't get me wrong, I think that many of the girls we meet in places like the Aquarius, Barbarella's, Bogart's and that place in Chelmsford that I can never remember . . ."

"Uh-Dukes."

"That's right, Dukes. Anyway, the sort of English womanhood one finds in these places is perfectly charming: in an earthy sort of way, if you will. And as you both well know, I'm not above seeking occasional solace among such company. But those girls are far more suited to you sons of the soil."

"I've never been a farmer," I pointed out.

"But you know what I mean, surely? I've been bred and educated to appreciate a little more refinement. And one is rather more likely to encounter that refinement in Val-d'Isère than that place in Macclesfield."

"Uh-Harlequin's?"

"Exactly," Mike confirmed.

While Mike spent his winters seducing the sort of women he'd no doubt been to university with, I spent my time doing some work for Frank and looking for a new renovation project. Bethan and me had already paid off the mortgage on our flat, so we were in a pretty good position to raise finance ourselves without having to go back to Frank for any more loans. Bethan's job was going well and she was enjoying the teaching. She and Leslie spent the 1987 summer holidays walking in the Pyrenees. I was just thankful that she'd got a friend who enjoyed doing that sort of thing, because my idea of a break was lying beside a pool for a few days, not undertaking something not too dissimilar from a pre-season training programme.

I visited Danny a few times down in Port Bredy. Mainly I went down there to see if he'd got any interesting properties I could consider taking on, but it was good to catch up with him. We'd often go for lunch in a local café just round the corner from Davison's.

"I'm not sure this will come as any great surprise," he began one day, "but I'm fairly sure that Mum has moved in with Lionel. I was in Whetstock last week and I dropped by the house. I don't think she's actually living in Oxford Cottage at the moment. There was nothing in the kitchen cupboards and she'd turned off the fridge."

It may not have come as a surprise to Danny, but I had to admit that I hadn't seen it coming. Given that they already spent the whole working week together, I would have thought that Mum and Mr Hendricks would want a break from each other. I wasn't quite sure how I felt about it. Mum was, after all, still married. But as Danny pointed out, she couldn't live her life waiting for Dad to show up. It was five years since he'd disappeared, so the chances were that he wasn't coming back. It just felt a little bit weird to me, because I thought of Mr Hendricks as a sort of uncle, not my mum's new boyfriend.

Over time it became clear that Danny was right, but it wasn't a subject that we ever openly discussed with her. And we still don't. Whenever either of us goes over for Sunday lunch in Whetstock, Mum makes out that she's still living in Oxford Cottage, so we never get to set foot inside Mr Hendricks' place. But every time we go over there, Mum casually mentions that she's just invited "Lionel" to join us, as though it was a spur of the moment decision. Lionel would come down to Canberra Park a couple of times a season. And sometimes, over Sunday lunch, he'd even have a bit of a go at me for not taking enough wickets. I'd tell him it was a tough job, bowling to some of the best batsmen in the world. But then he'd always say that I shouldn't lose my focus. Honestly, I didn't mind getting lectured by Mr Hendricks; it was clear that he just wanted me to do well.

Towards the end of September in 1988 an ideal renovation property came onto the market. It was a semi-detached Victorian house in Somerton Street in Casterbridge, just a few yards from the old hospital where I was born. It was only two storeys, but I could see how it would make a couple of great flats. The location was perfect: just a couple of minutes' walk from the centre of Casterbridge. When I took Bethan around for a second viewing, she showed up with Leslie. I didn't mind, but when Leslie started telling me that I could *put the bathroom here*, *move the kitchen there* and all that sort of thing, I got a little bit irritated.

"Sorry Leslie, maybe I've missed something. Are you putting up half the money on this project?" I snapped.

"Calm down, Pete," Bethan cut in. "She's only trying to help. And I think she could be right about the ground-floor bathroom."

In the end, I did install the bathroom where Leslie had originally suggested. But I think what was actually riling me was the fact that just about every time I turned round, there was Leslie. Sometimes it felt as though she was actually living with us. It was good that Bethan had someone to go away with during the cricket season, but it would have been nice to see a little less of her during the rest of the year. I remember thinking that Leslie could do with getting a boyfriend. Not that I could think of anyone who might actually hit it off with her.

****

The summer of 1989 turned out to be a long, hot one. We actually started the season strongly, and initially there was an air of optimism about the dressing room. We beat Glamorgan at Canberra Park in our first Championship game of the season, and followed that up with a win at Northants. In that second game Alan Musgrove set up the victory with a very well put-together century. I don't think I could remember him ever batting so well. But after that, his game just mysteriously fell apart. Throughout June and July he didn't even make it into double figures again.

He started taking it out on Steve Braithwaite, in much the same way as he had with Phil Grey. On one occasion, Alan had been given out LBW on the third ball of a game, after Steve had called him through for a quick leg-bye on the previous delivery. When Steve was out, just before lunch, Alan was waiting for him in the dressing room.

"Admit it Steve, you just bottled it. You couldn't get off strike quick enough, could you?" Alan was warming up slowly.

Th-th-there w-was an easy r-r-run. S-s-so I c-called it."

"Either of us could have been gone there. You just haven't got any fucking bottle, have you Steve?"

"But y-y-you w-weren't run a-a-out, Alan. Y-you p-p-played around a-a s-straight one. The-the-there's err-only w-w-one p-person r-r-r-responsible for your w-wicket. And tha-tha-that's y-you."

It was a good speech. It would have been even better if he could have got through it a bit quicker, but it had the desired effect. While Braithwaite sounded permanently terrified, he had an inner confidence that Phil had lacked. Alan left him alone after that. Of course, Alan would try and slag off Steve to any other member of the team that would listen, but nobody was interested. Even Carl seemed to be keeping a little bit of a distance from his brother during that season. By now our victories seemed to have dried up along with Alan's runs, so as the summer just got hotter and hotter, tempers began to fray on a fairly regular basis. Even Herb had a right old go at me on one occasion. That was almost unheard off.

"Listen son, I can't bloody well do this on my own. We've got to create pressure. So it's no good me drying up an end, when you go and bowl filth like that at the other. That last spell was total rubbish, Ledge. Sometimes I reckon you're just wasting your time here."

I always felt bad whenever I let Herb down. That occasion was on July 1st at Headingley. It was the final day of a game and we'd allowed the Yorkshire tail-enders to bat us out of contention. But I think if anyone should have got the blame for my performance that morning, it should have been Col, not me. A few weeks earlier he'd wandered into the dressing room with a copy of *Melody Maker* and our fixture list.

"Uh-guys," he enthused. "We'll be able to see the Stone Roses during the Yorkshire game. Up for it?"

I'd never heard of the Stone Roses at that time, and I don't suppose that Mike had either. We probably both assumed that they'd be another of Col's dreary prog-rock outfits, but our general philosophy when touring was that any night out was better than no night out, so we agreed to go with him. When Mike and I found out that the gig was in Leeds Polytechnic, we both became positively enthusiastic. We'd be spending the night surrounded by beautiful young people and even more alluring bar prices.

When the band came on-stage, they were nothing like I'd expected. That's not to say that they were any better than I'd expected, it's just that they weren't the sort of band I'd have thought Col would get excited about. At the beginning of the set the singer was woefully out of tune, and in places it sounded like a complete mess. But once in a while they'd get a powerful funky groove going. And by the end of their set I felt that they were the most magical band I'd ever seen. I can't say for sure whether or not they'd actually improved that much over the course the gig, or whether it was simply that the tabs Col had given us in the bar beforehand had taken effect. I never became a regular user of ecstasy because it made me sweat like hell and played havoc with my physical coordination. But I couldn't deny that it could give you a lovely high.

After the gig finished we just wanted to stay out, so the three of us went on to the Warehouse. We all danced into the early hours of the morning, and Col gave it absolutely everything. I'd never seen him so into anything before. It was as though he was beginning to find himself at last. He'd spent all those years smoking weed and listening to *Atom Heart Mother* and all those other desperately dull Floyd records, and yet here he was, transformed into a god of the dance floor. It was as though he'd gone from one end of the musical spectrum to the other overnight, missing out all of the steps in between.

Col changed his look that summer. Really he just got his hair cut, but it made a startling difference to his appearance. He showed up at Canberra Park a couple of weeks after the Stone Roses gig with a grade-1 or grade-2. His visual transformation was just as fast and as radical as his musical one had been: he'd gone straight from his scarecrow-hippy look to a crew-cut in a single visit to the barber's. Actually, it may have been his *first* visit to the barber's. It turned out that he'd got these sky-blue eyes and prominent cheekbones. It wasn't just me that noticed the change in him. It must have been women too, because he started to get laid much more often. I can't say whether that was simply a consequence of spending more time in clubs where there *were* women, and spending less time in his living room with Floyd videos where there *weren't*, but whatever the reason his fortunes on that front changed dramatically.

I'd like to be able to say that the alterations he made to his repertoire of recreational drugs somehow had a positive impact on his bowling, but that wasn't the case. In fact, the changes to his lifestyle off the field made absolutely no difference to his performances on it whatsoever: sometimes he was brilliant and sometimes he was beyond terrible. But trying to predict which version of Col was going to show up at a cricket match was a mug's game.

That winter Col spent his time working for a sound installation company in London to learn about big club systems. So it came as no surprise after he quit the game that he took up sound engineering as a full-time career. He spent a number of years living out in Ibiza as an audio consultant to the big venues out there, and he's travelled the world installing systems. The man just loves his sounds, and he likes them huge.

Back at Canberra Park, by the end of August the heat had got to a number of the players and the atmosphere in the dressing room wasn't great. Our batsmen weren't scoring runs and us bowlers weren't taking wickets. Nothing we tried made any difference; as a team we were woeful. If we weren't going to finish bottom that year, it would only be because some other side was even worse. In the event Glamorgan did us that favour, but it was still a close-run thing.

The pressure was on when Kent came down to play us at Budmouth. They weren't having a great season themselves, and we saw their visit as an opportunity to pick up some crucial points, if not actually win the game. Tony Sinclair called the toss correctly and his decision to bat first was a no-brainer. It was a really hot day and there wasn't a cloud in the sky, so it would be hard work for Kent's bowlers. Alan Musgrove walked out to the middle with Steve Braithwaite. Alan's desperately poor run of form had continued right throughout August, so this represented his best opportunity to rescue something from the season.

That morning he had almost no footwork whatsoever, and the ball went past his bat on numerous occasions. But somehow he was still there at lunch-time. He'd only scored about twenty runs in the two hours he'd been out there, and almost half of those were edges through the slips. But in the final over before lunch he nailed a perfect cover-drive out of the middle of the bat: it was probably the best shot he'd played in weeks. Meanwhile, Braithwaite, Farrow and Bridges had all got out during the morning session, so after lunch Alan re-started his innings with Sinclair as his partner.

Gradually the runs began to flow more freely for Alan. Around halfway through the afternoon session he was able to raise his bat to acknowledge the applause for a hard-fought fifty. Now, with the bowlers flagging in the heat, and with the day-one pitch playing like a road, he had a real chance to go on and get a big score. At the other end Sinclair, Kelly and Mike had all come and gone, bringing Carl Musgrove to the crease. The brothers began to make good progress, with Alan moving steadily ahead into the eighties, and Carl latching on to anything loose and looking to be aggressive.

After our mini-collapse the atmosphere in the dressing room relaxed a bit and players went back to their crosswords, card games or newspapers. Mike – a *Times* reader – once told me that you could tell a lot about a person from the newspaper they read: for example he was always calling Bridges a *communist* because he took the *Guardian*. He dubbed Sebastian Welland-Flanders the *gentleman farmer* because he had the *Telegraph* delivered every day, and he said that Andy Farrow read the *Sun* because he genuinely was as *thick* as he looked. Personally I don't want any political bias from my paper, just the news. That's why I read the *Daily Mail*.

Shortly before tea our peace and calm was shattered by a series of calls from the middle of the ground.

"Yes!"

"No!"

"Keeper's!"

"FUCK! FUCK! FUCK!"

We looked out across the pitch. Both Musgroves were standing at the bowler's end of the wicket. Alan then began the long walk back to the pavilion. Next in, I grabbed my gear and made my way out to the middle. Passing Alan on the boundary edge I could see that he looked about ready to kill someone.

We reached the interval without further incident. "I'd better get ready to face the music," Carl said to me as we left the field. "Al isn't going to be a happy camper. But Ledge, I'm telling you, there was never a run there."

We arrived in the dressing room. The rest of the team, except for Alan, had already gone through to the dining area. I sat down to take off my kit.

Carl thought he'd get his point in first. "Sorry Al mate, but that was never a run."

"You fucking selfish fucking cunt Carl. My season's a fucking write-off, I finally get in, and you fucking well go and do that to me."

"Steady on mate, it's a run-out. It happens."

"If you'd just run, I'd still be batting."

"But there wasn't a run, was there?"

"You fucking cunt." Alan was, if anything, getting even more worked up. "I'm just sick of looking at you."

"What's this about, Al?" I'd never seen Carl look concerned about anything before, but the look of absolute hatred on his brother's face seemed to be unnerving him.

"What's this about? It's about you fucking my fucking career." Alan was beginning to adopt the stance of a bare-knuckle fighter. He was shaking with rage.

I think Carl panicked. "This isn't about Rachel, is it?"

"Rachel?" Alan, like me, was confused. "What the fuck has Rachel got to do with this?" It was an odd moment for that sort of confession. "Carl, you fucking piece of shit."

"Listen, Al . . ." began Carl, just as his brother delivered a thunderous right hook that landed squarely in the middle of his face. Alan had followed it up with a straight left, before Carl had any time to react.

There was blood everywhere: it was splattered over the dressing-room wall, and it was all over my face and my shirt. Carl's nose seemed to be hanging loosely from the space between his eyebrows. I was still trying to make sense of what had just happened when Carl pushed Alan back across the dressing room. He shoved him hard so that Alan staggered back and caught the side of his head against one of the clothes hooks on the wall. He yelped as blood started pouring down over his left ear. Carl took advantage as Alan was momentarily stunned and followed up with a massive straight blow down onto his brother's chin.

The noise in such a confined space was sickening. The sound of bones, flesh and teeth yielding to each blow seemed to be supernaturally loud. I was aware that I'd just frozen, stunned by the ferocity and the speed of the fight. Then there was a brief lull, with both twins gasping heavily, each looking for their next move. I took the opportunity to stand up.

"Guys, guys," I began. I hadn't exactly planned a speech, but I was going to say something about how we could all work this out.

I didn't have to worry about finding the right words though, because neither Alan nor Carl so much as even glanced in my direction. I took a step towards them, but if anything this just triggered the next phase of fighting. Carl landed a wicked blow into Alan's ribs and was rewarded by a sharp cracking sound. Alan groaned, but just came on wildly throwing punches at what remained of Carl's face. I was trying to see some way of getting myself between them, but if I'm perfectly honest I didn't relish the idea of playing the role of punch bag.

I had no idea how long it had been going on. Ten seconds? Thirty? I just needed some teammates to hear the commotion and come and help me. Then Carl lost his footing; he probably slipped in his own blood and suddenly he was down on the floor. But there was no reasoning with Alan; at that moment he was completely wild. He was just kicking his brother repeatedly, in the ribs, in the neck, in the groin, just wherever he could land a blow. I was trying to push Alan back, away from Carl, when Col and Justin Bridges came bursting through the dressing-room door. Together we were able to pull him away and sit him down on one of the locker benches.

I went back out to bat with Herb after tea (the scorecard simply records that C Musgrove retired hurt), and the opposition keeper said to me, "What the fuck happened to you at tea?"

I'd forgotten to change my shirt in the confusion, and it must have looked as though I'd just survived a car crash.

"Oh that," I replied. "Shaving cut. I'm very clumsy."

****

Neither Carl nor Alan ever played for Wessex again. And Rachel's marriage to Alan turned out to be a short one. I don't know if Welland-Flanders had shared a quiet word with his fellow county chief executives, but not a single club came in with an offer for either brother. For a while they both worked in different branches of Musgroves, but after the company went bust they went into business together, setting up a surf shop in Newquay. I guess that they just couldn't bear to be apart.

The biggest loser in the fallout from the whole fracas was probably Tony Sinclair. Welland-Flanders thought that he'd lost control of the dressing room, and that it was time to hand the captaincy on to someone else. Tony, by this time, was in his late thirties, and his contract expired at the end of the season. He wasn't offered an extension. He gave a farewell speech at our end-of-season gathering at the Black Horse over in Litton Bredy, and we all bid him well. Neither Musgrove showed up, which was probably for the best. As Mike pointed out, he was never a great captain, but he loved the game and he was a decent bloke.

I don't think it came as any surprise to anyone that Justin Bridges was named as skipper for the 1990 season. He was young, he was ambitious, and to the best of my knowledge, he was the only player at Wessex who'd ever read *The Art of Captaincy* by Mike Brearley. At Wessex we were about to enter the most successful period in the history of the club, and I was going to go on and play for England.

You know the sort of thing:
cross a river using only two rolls
of Andrex and a set of car keys.

10. FROM THE MIDDLE OF DARTMOOR TO THE FAR SIDE OF THE WORLD

I hadn't washed for three days. The elastic in my sweat-encrusted underpants was sharp like barbed wire, and it was cutting into the tops of my legs. It also felt as though my balls had been glued to the inside of my thighs. My arse itched incessantly. During the previous three days we'd experienced every type of rain that Dartmoor had to throw at us: the torrential kind that comes straight down, the usual stuff that hits you in the face at an angle of about forty-five degrees regardless of the direction you're walking in, and occasionally the full immersion soaking you get when the rain clouds themselves just sit there at ground level.

Wessex CC had a new captain, and we were getting our first experience of Justin Bridges' leadership. I'd taken a call from Mike a few weeks earlier, some time in March 1990.

"Ledge," Mike began. "Here's a funny thing. I've been made vice-captain of the team."

"You?" I replied. "No offence Mike, but I would have thought that you'd have been just about the last person Bridges would have wanted."

"Well quite. But he's a clever bastard though, isn't he?" I didn't immediately follow Mike's line of reasoning. "He said that he'd rather keep me close. So he wants me to travel with him to our away games and he wants you to look after Ronnie."

"Ronnie? Sorry, who's Ronnie?"

"Ah, you don't know," Mike went on. "Mark Corbett: a new batsman joining us from Devon."

"What's he like?" I asked.

"No idea, never met the fella. Anyway Bridges has a sort of three-point plan: first, he wants to break up the *cliques* as he calls them, because he thinks they're undermining team performance. That's why he doesn't want Col, you and me travelling together any more. Second, he thinks there's a drinking culture at the club that needs addressing. And third, he wants us to do a lot more team-building and training exercises."

"Are you beginning to wish you'd chosen the army now?"

"Well it's funny that you should say that Ledge, because I'm actually calling to tell you that we're starting the season with a couple of weeks' wilderness training on Dartmoor. You know the sort of thing: cross a river using only two rolls of Andrex and a set of car keys. And pray we don't get beaten up by 42 Commando who might be out there at the same time."

The first week hadn't been too bad. We were in a small complex, sleeping four to a room in small dorms: it was all very basic but it was comfortable. We spent our days learning survival skills, doing problem-solving exercises and testing ourselves on a nearby assault course. Come the second week, we were supposed to use all of the techniques we'd just been taught in order to complete an eighty-mile course and survive out there on the moor.

I'd been teamed up with Herb, Ronnie and a South African called Frank. Because I'd arrived half an hour late on the first day (I couldn't leave Casterbridge until I'd let the plumber into Somerton Street) I assumed that Frank was one of the course leaders. Just like them he had no sense of humour whatsoever and kept telling us that in order to survive we had to respect nature. It was only on the second day that someone told me he was actually a new member of our side.

Frank de Koch was from Bloemfontein. Although he'd played cricket for Orange Free State, he looked more like the sort of guy who'd spent a few years in the army and now worked on a nature reserve. He had a lot of khaki in his wardrobe.

Ronnie was no less enthusiastic than Frank to be joining our pre-season endurance programme. He was about my age, but this was the first time he had made the step-up to first-class cricket. He'd played the minor counties game for Devon over the previous few years as an amateur, and he'd earned his living travelling the county repairing telephone cables. By the time he arrived at Canberra Park it seemed as though he'd missed out on about five years' worth of conversation and was determined to catch up. His enthusiasm was plain to see, but I wouldn't have necessarily said that it was infectious.

Herb was clearly unhappy, but he was too much of a professional to actually say anything to Bridges. "I'm not sure what this has got to do with taking wickets," he mumbled to me as we found ourselves waist-deep in a fast-flowing stream, passing kit bags above our heads to our colleagues on the far bank. Other than that one brief moment of dissent, he endured the rest of our time on Dartmoor with a resigned look of world-weary acceptance.

I was sharing a tent with Herb, and it was the first time that I could say that he looked old to me. His forehead was lined and there was plenty of grey showing in his hair. I think he was sleeping better than me simply because he was exhausted. One morning towards the end of that second week I decided to go for a short walk on my own. Climbing out of the hollow where we'd made camp I saw a small town on the skyline, only a mile or so away. I didn't have a clue where I was, but the place looked big enough to have a café where I might, at the very least, be able to get a decent breakfast.

I was in luck: there was a café, and it was open. I ordered a full English breakfast and then made my way out to the back of the building where a couple of portacabins had been converted into toilets. I ran a bowl of lukewarm water and washed as best as I could. I felt as though I was in heaven.

Shortly after I got back inside the café my breakfast arrived. And shortly after that Col arrived and pulled up a chair at my table.

"Uh. Ledge. My lot, they're still asleep." He was with Bridges, Steve Braithwaite and Laurie Kelly. "What's breakfast like?"

"I don't think I've ever tasted anything better in my life," I replied.

Col went to order some breakfast, and then disappeared out the back to wash. When he came back I asked him where we were.

"Uh-this is Princetown. The big building at the other end of the town is Dartmoor prison."

"That makes sense. You wouldn't want the inmates getting too comfortable in their surroundings. Do you miss it round here?" I asked Col.

"Uh no. Not really." Col thought for a moment or two. "Do you think this is a taste of life under Justin's captaincy?"

I'd been too busy over the previous few days peeling my bollocks off the inside of my legs and scratching my arse to really give it much thought, but after everything that Mike had told me on the phone, I realised that things were going to change over the next couple of seasons.

We now had a lot of team meetings. We'd spend hours talking about how we were going to get a certain player out, how we were going to bat against a particular bowler, or what we thought we could do individually to improve our own game. We also started doing significantly more core fitness work: we'd do weights to build muscle strength and spend hours doing endurance exercises. I'd often go home moaning about it to Bethan, but she just said that it was good that the club was finally getting wise to modern training methods.

There were changes on the pitch too. Bridges moved Andy Farrow out of the slip cordon. Frank now stood at first slip. I don't think Bridges necessarily thought that Frank would hold on to more catches than Andy Farrow, rather that he'd get better performances out of Laurie Kelly. Unlike Farrow, Frank didn't find anything Kelly said funny. At first Kelly re-doubled his efforts, but soon he realised he was simply wasting his best material on him.

Bridges started fielding at mid-off. Initially I thought that this was to display some solidarity with those of us who had to run the hard yards in the outfield; he'd previously spent most of his time somewhere in the slip cordon. But soon I began to realise the truth of the matter. He wanted to be able to talk to his bowlers between every delivery that they bowled. He wanted control.

At the beginning of the season, he said to me that I was going to be the *engine house* of the Wessex attack. He was going to use Col and Frank in short bursts, but that it was going to be my job to run in all day. Mike would bowl his off-spin when the pitch offered some turn and then another new signing, Chris Forrester, would take wickets with his leg-spin.

So, starting that year, my role in the side changed. Bridges used to say to me, "Ledge, you've just got to stop them scoring and then the wickets will follow."

I'd sometimes ask him why none of the other seamers were being asked to share my workload. If they were bowling twelve or fifteen overs a day, I'd be bowling twenty or twenty-five.

"Ledge, you're the only one good enough to do it," he'd tell me. "Herb can't lead from the front any more, you've got to do it for him." Bridges had a point: by 1990 time was beginning to catch up with Herb. He could still bowl a probing spell with the new ball, but increasingly he needed periods of rest.

If nobody else was good enough or fit enough to do it, I didn't mind putting in a shift for the team, but what really did start to get on my nerves was that Bridges would have advice for me before every ball I bowled. At first it was just a running commentary: *that's right, he can't cut you from there, nice bit of shape on that last one, the big shot's coming, it's coming Ledge.* But then he started to tell me exactly what he wanted me to bowl every delivery.

"OK Ledge, let's go a bit fuller this time. Let's get him driving."

"Right, let's just dry him up on that fourth-stump line. Nothing short. I don't want to see anything through mid-wicket."

After a while it just felt as though I was his bowling machine. He'd do all the thinking and planning, but I was the unfortunate sod who had to run in all day and actually get the ball down there.

I might not have warmed to his methods, but we were beginning to win more matches under Bridges. In 1990 Wessex finished twelfth in the Championship, which was a considerable improvement over previous seasons. But I didn't see much of Mike or Col off the field that year. A combination of the new training regime, and the huge number of overs that I was bowling, meant that by the end of a day's play just about all I wanted to do was have a pint in the bar and go to bed.

Ronnie was a lovely bloke, but we didn't have that much fun on the road together. In fact, I found his enthusiasm for the game exhausting. He'd got his break very late, so he wanted to make the most of every moment of his new career.

He was first out to the training sessions and last off the field at the end of them. And he wanted to know everything about all the bowlers that he was going to be facing at every ground we travelled to. I didn't mind talking about Malcolm Marshall or Curtly Ambrose for a while; after all, it was quite good fun to put the fear of God in him. But when it came to discussing the merits of other players on the circuit, Ronnie could begin to test my patience.

I actually preferred it when Ronnie got talking about the other things in his life outside of cricket, because then I could just nod along. I wouldn't have to say too much. Ronnie was married to Nicola and they'd got two young children called James and Jessica. He could talk about his family for hours, but he'd also got quite a lot to say about utility bills. And mortgage rates. And loft insulation.

It wasn't until the 1992 season that I discovered that he loved Simply Red. So whenever we travelled together I'd put *Stars* on the car's CD player. Often we could just sit there, quietly enjoying the tunes until at least as far as "She's Got it Bad", before Ronnie wanted to start talking about bowlers again.

"Hey Pete, how does Martin Bicknell bowl his slower ball?"

"I don't know. Slower than his quicker one?"

Before the 1991 season started, Bill Davison retired and sold his business to Danny. Danny told me that it was a really tough decision for him and Angela to make. On the one hand, it was the ideal agency for Danny to buy: he'd worked there for six years and knew the business and the area very well. On the other, the property market was in the doldrums and Danny and Angela would be mortgaged to the hilt in order to raise the finance. Bill had apparently offered Danny the business at a decent price because he wanted to see it transferred into safe hands, but it was still a big sum of money. I felt proud of Danny for taking the plunge.

I remember the 1991 season at Wessex with mixed emotions. It was certainly one for the record books, because Wessex finished third in the Championship; the best result (at the time of writing) the club has ever achieved. Essex, with both Graham Gooch and Nasser Hussain in the batting line-up, won it that season, beating Warwickshire into second place. I'm not sure that we were ever in serious contention for the title, but there was certainly a buzz around the club that year.

But it was also my first season without Col in the side. He didn't find the decision to swap cricket for a life as an audio engineer in Ibiza particularly difficult. Mike was still around, but whatever fun he was having, he was being sure to have far away from the gaze of Justin Bridges. I'd occasionally go around to his house in Divinity Street for a few drinks after a home game, but those nights never got out of control like they would have done before.

Bridges made some further revisions to our bowling strategy that year. Or rather he had Gus Jackman revise the pitch that we were bowling on. Frank de Koch was to carry on charging in quickly for very short bursts, while Herb's opening spells with the new ball were to become shorter and shorter. Then the two spinners and me would take over. With this reliance on spin, Bridges needed turning wickets. So he turned to Gus to get them. The groundsman did what he was told and started preparing pitches with no more grass on them than was needed to hold the surface of the wicket together. The Canberra Park wicket that season had more in common with Eden Gardens in Kolkata than Headingley. On a couple of occasions the Test and County Cricket Board considered docking us points for a poor surface, but we just about got away with it. While it was a spinner's paradise, it offered almost no assistance for the seam bowler whatsoever. So I just had to get on with it. I was economical and I took some wickets, but it was a thankless task. By the end of the season I was absolutely knackered.

At least I didn't have Bridges in my ear when I was batting, so I always set out to have some fun. I scored a few rapid-fire half-centuries that year, and I hit more sixes than anyone else in the side. It was a welcome release to be able to express myself on the pitch, rather than just follow Bridges' instructions to the last letter. But by this point in my career I was beginning to wonder if I'd actually gone about as far as I could in the game. My job in the side under Bridges was simply to create pressure. I was beginning to feel like the unsung hero. So it seemed increasingly unlikely that I was ever going to get a shot at an England place. It's very rare that international seam bowlers don't open with the new ball for their club sides.

The next year, 1992, wasn't a great season: not for me and not for the club. It was the one period of my career in which I was blighted by injuries. I pulled a hamstring during our first fixture and was out for two months. And when I returned to the side at the beginning of July I picked up a side-strain almost immediately. So I only ended up playing the last four or five weeks of the season. Meanwhile, other sides in the league were now wise to Bridges' tactics down at Canberra Park, so they'd pack their own side with spinners. Wessex slid back down to ninth in the standings at the end of the year.

We knew that Bridges was lobbying Welland-Flanders for money to bring new players in, but we'd also heard that the club's finances weren't looking too good. It was rumoured that Forrester and de Koch were on more money than the rest of us. At the same time the side was ageing: Andy Farrow, Laurie Kelly and Herb were all coming to the end of their careers. The club could either accept that it had to go through the slow process of re-building from within, or throw money at the problem and sign more players from outside the club. Somehow I couldn't imagine that Sebastian Welland-Flanders would agree to increase the wage bill any further.

At the end of the 1992 season I had the strangest conversation with Justin Bridges. Throughout most of it I couldn't work out if he was trying to give me a motivational lecture or somehow get involved in the property business.

"How do you think it went this season?" Bridges began. We were sat in the members' room one afternoon in early September.

"Well it was tough, but this last month I've felt fit and strong again," I replied. I actually thought that I'd paid the price for him bowling me into the ground the previous year.

He took me by surprise with his next question. "Do you still have ambitions in the game?"

"Of course," I replied. "I haven't given up on playing for England. I've got to believe it could still happen."

"Well, it *could*. I suppose it *could* happen for any of us." The way he said *could* was clearly meant to indicate that flying pigs were more likely. He changed the subject. "I hear you're into property."

"I've done a couple of refurbishment projects. Made a little money from it." I found myself answering the question, but I didn't know where he was going with this. "I spent some time working for my brother's estate agency when I was injured this year."

"Is that where you see your future?" he asked with genuine enthusiasm.

"I haven't thought that far ahead to be honest. I may well be doing something in that line when my time in the game is up."

Then his tone changed a little. "It sounds to me as though you get more out of your property interests than you do from cricket." It was only at this point that I realised that this was his way of lifting me up for the next season. He continued, "You've been low on energy in the dressing room for the last couple of years, Peter."

"So would you if you'd bowled as many overs as me," I replied. "Especially on *that* track." I was pointing down towards the square below us.

"Well, take some time to think about it, Peter. Think about what's best for you."

He'd lost me again. Think about *what*? Bridges was undoubtedly a clever bloke, but he was never the most inspiring leader I ever played under.

****

On the first Saturday in April 1993 Bethan and me had just retuned from our morning run when the phone rang. By then we'd already been living in Durnover Green for some time. Funded by the sale of the Somerton Street flats and a couple of other renovation projects, we'd been able to make a cash purchase of a beautiful Georgian town house, just a short walk from the centre of Casterbridge.

"It's Rachel from Sebastian Welland-Flanders' office," said the former Mrs Alan Musgrove at the other end of the line.

Why would she be calling at eight-thirty on a Saturday morning? My contract still had a year to run, so it was unlikely to be anything to do with that. Or perhaps Justin Bridges had come up with some horrific pre-season team-building exercise that he couldn't face telling us about himself: potholing in Cumbria or something like that.

"Hello," I replied cautiously. "It's Peter here. What's up Rachel?"

"Well, I've just taken a call from Barbara at the TCCB," she began.

This was beginning to make more sense. The TCCB was no doubt about to do a full investigation into the stripped, crumbling wickets that Bridges had been getting Gus Jackman to prepare. I began to start calculating whether it was in my best interest to say that they were unsporting, or whether just to toe the club line.

"Barbara works for Ted Dexter," Rachel continued.

Blimey, I thought to myself, this has gone right to the top. Dexter had been the driving force behind the move to four-day Championship games for the upcoming season. But clearly four-day games weren't likely to work very well on Canberra Park wickets designed to crack up and fall apart on the second morning of the game.

"They want to know if you're available to fly to New Zealand next week."

"I suppose so," I replied, somewhat confused. "Can I ask why?"

"Well, Barbara said that they thought you'd demonstrated real character and skill last season, and they'd like you to join up with the Test squad."

This was so much to take in. So many thoughts started rushing through my mind. I didn't even know that the England team were out in New Zealand. I'm ashamed to admit that I'd stopped following their progress that winter after the disastrous Indian series. So I knew nothing about their equally unsuccessful trip to Sri Lanka, and I had absolutely no idea that the Kiwis had just racked up 580 against them in Auckland. But I felt a sense of elation and vindication. I always knew that I had what it takes to play at the very highest level, but I'd long sensed that even some of the people closest to me had their doubts. Even Bethan used to tell me to focus on Wessex. And I never thought Mike really took me seriously when I talked about playing Test match cricket.

I'd actually arranged to meet a couple of local estate agents in Casterbridge on the Monday morning to get a property valued. I'd have to ask Bethan to call them on Monday to postpone the appointments.

"Absolutely Rachel. I'm sure that will be fine." Listening to myself, I sounded as though I was just accepting a last-minute invitation to a dinner party.

"Good. Now we need to go through your travel itinerary." I just wanted to get off the phone and start the celebrations, but Rachel wanted to stay on the line and work through the practicalities of actually getting me there. "Right Peter, are you listening?" I assured her that I was. "First you need to come down to Canberra Park with your passport this morning. The second Test starts on Friday, but they want you there as soon as possible. Realistically I can get you on a flight first thing Monday morning, so you'll arrive on the Wednesday. Because of the timescales involved I'll book your flights, but the TCCB will arrange for a car to take you to Heathrow, and another to pick you up from Dunedin airport when you arrive?"

"Dun where?" I asked.

"Dunedin. It's on the South Island. You'll be flying business class, because you'll need to be as fresh as possible when you get there." I'd never flown business class before, but I certainly liked the sound of it. I made a mental note to call Dougie and tell him later that day. "You should take your usual match-day kit with you, and if you're called on to play, they'll issue you with England branded whites when you get there. You don't have any additional sponsorship on your bat other than the usual manufacturer's logo do you?"

"Errr . . . no," I replied.

But it wasn't my kit sponsorship that was bothering me. *If you're called on to play*, those were the words that were troubling me. In my initial excitement it hadn't occurred to me that I *wouldn't* play. Why would they fly me all that way just to carry the drinks? But the more I thought about it, most likely I was going as cover for someone else in the squad. If it was possible to feel both excited and deflated at the same time, that's how I felt.

"You've been called up to the Test squad?" enquired Bethan as I put down the phone. I nodded, grinning like a madman no doubt. "Blimey!" she went on. "Honestly, I didn't think that was still a possibility. But well done, you. That's fantastic."

"It's beyond fantastic," I remember saying. "I've been working towards this for more than twenty years."

"Now, you won't thank me for saying this," began Bethan, in that very wise teacher's tone she'd mastered. "But you've got to be realistic. You'll probably just join up with the squad while they take a look at you. Prepare well, impress them, and then you can see where it leads from there."

Of course Bethan was right, but after I'd driven down to Canberra Park to drop off my passport with Rachel and pump her for every last bit of information she might have gathered from Barbara, I had to spend the rest of the day ringing everyone I knew to tell them about my call-up.

I wanted to speak to Col in Ibiza, but I looked at the time and realised that he'd either still be out from the night before or fast asleep. So I rang Mike. "God, they pack these games in, don't they?" He sounded more surprised about the scheduling than my call-up. "Well look, don't get down on yourself if you don't get to play, just enjoy the trip. And try the wine. The new pinot noirs from Otago are sublime."

"I'm going to New Zealand," I corrected him.

"You're going to the Otago *region* in New Zealand you fuckwit." I might have just got into the England Test squad, but it obviously wasn't going to have any impact on the way Mike spoke to me. The last thing he said to me before hanging up was, "Don't forget Ledge, it's going to be cool down there."

When I hung up, I was thinking to myself: *cool*? It's going to be *fantastic*.

Five days later, as I followed my driver out of the airport terminal in Dunedin and across the tarmac towards his car, I finally realised what Mike had meant. He didn't mean *cool* as in groovy, he meant *cool* as in *not warm*. Only he wasn't quite right: it wasn't *cool* it was *bloody freezing*. I'll admit to a certain level of naiveté on my part: I'd assumed that I was going somewhere with holiday weather. They grow wine – so there's sunshine. It's not that far from Australia – where it's hot. I got on my flight at Heathrow dressed in a pair of shorts, a t-shirt, a light cotton jacket, and a pair of flip-flops. And despite the chill I was wearing the same ensemble at the other end of my journey. Because the rest of my clothes and all of my kit were apparently somewhere in South East Asia.

I didn't realise it when I'd set off, but the series in New Zealand had been tightly shoe-horned into the cricket calendar; no doubt to boost the coffers of the two countries' respective governing boards. Usually, the New Zealand cricket season finishes on the last weekend in March, so this two-Test series was extending things by a fortnight. The Kiwis had enjoyed a pretty good summer at home: they'd held a decent Australian team to a one-all draw in a three-match rubber. By the time I arrived in Dunedin, their summer had given way to autumn. It hardly felt like cricket weather at all. While I was waiting for my connection in Sydney I saw a newspaper report which described how torrential rain had rescued England in the Auckland Test. Apparently we'd made 157 for 8 in reply to their 580 when it started raining. And then it didn't stop raining for two and a half days.

My journey hadn't started too well. I didn't get much sleep over the weekend, so I wasn't feeling that great when the driver hit his horn outside our house at five o'clock on the Monday morning. Bethan wished me luck and I dragged my kit bag outside, where I saw a red Ford Escort estate parked up. There was a hand-written sign in the passenger window that read: "Legrond".

The lack of sleep had made me irritable, and I snapped at the guy, "Fuck's sake, it's *Legend*. That's not so hard, is it?"

"All right mate, calm down" he replied. "That's just what my controller told me."

I began to feel a little bit guilty about having a pop at the driver. So once we'd joined the M27, I thought I'd make my peace by asking him if he minded putting on my cassette copy of *Screamadelica*. He nodded that it was OK, so I passed him the tape. I couldn't help but smile when that Stonesy guitar riff started up at the beginning of "Movin' On Up". I remember thinking, "Now *this* is feel-good music." I think I must have fallen into a deep, almost spiritual sleep, because I woke up just as we were approaching Heathrow with the chorus still going round and round my head. It was a bit of a result really, because there's a fair bit of filler on the rest of the album.

I slept fitfully during the rest of the trip, so in addition to feeling somewhat underdressed by the time I finally got to Dunedin airport, I also felt rather light-headed. Fortunately my driver was already waiting for me in arrivals. He was holding up a placard that read: "Peter Legrawn, England Cricket Team". But by this point in the journey I was too tired to say anything about it. The driver asked me where my luggage was. He had the good sense not to find the answer amusing.

It's about twenty miles from the airport to the Carisbrook stadium in Dunedin. After passing a few miles of open farmland I fell asleep. The next thing I knew we were in the car park outside the venue. Carisbrook is nothing like a traditional English cricket ground. It was built as a rugby stadium and it looks like one: a large concrete one. As a cricket venue I found it hard to love. I wasn't the only one; a few years later the Kiwis started playing their Dunedin fixtures on the University Oval instead.

After explaining to the security guard who I was, I went through the main entrance to the stadium and found my way out onto the pitch. Temporary nets had been erected at both ends of the ground, and I recognised a number of England players away to my left. I made my way around the perimeter of the pitch to go and introduce myself. Suddenly I was conscious of feeling like an outsider.

Although there were batsmen in both England nets, the bowlers didn't appear to be in much of a hurry to bowl at them. I caught the eye of one of the seamers loitering at the beginning of his run-up. It was common knowledge around the county circuit that he was largely held together by any number of metal plates. He recognised me. And he was more than happy to stop and chat rather than to have to force another delivery out of his creaking body.

"It's Pete Legend, isn't it?" he asked. I nodded. "What on earth brings you out here?"

"I've been asked to join up with the squad," I replied.

"Oh, I had no idea. Well, nobody tells me anything anyway. It's great you're here because we could use another net bowler. The boss and the gaffer are over there" – he was pointing to a gaggle of people at the far end of the nets – "so you'd better go and introduce yourself."

I couldn't say this this brief conversation had exactly inspired me with any more confidence in the England set-up. They'd called me up at the eleventh hour, they couldn't find a taxi firm who could spell my name, and they hadn't even told a fellow seam bowler that I was joining the tour. And to add insult to injury, he thought I was just here as a training resource.

It felt weird going up to the main group because I knew them but I didn't *know* them. The coaches and the players all went by nicknames like Dwarf, Goat, Yogi and Huey, but I didn't feel that I could use them myself, so I wasn't sure what to call them. I've been out for a drink in the same bar as Ian Botham on several occasions down the years, and even though I'd like to think that we share a mutual professional respect, I don't know him well enough to just go up and say, "Hi Beefy, how's it going?" It just wouldn't feel quite right.

"Peter Legend," I said to the coach, offering my hand.

"Yes. Legend. Wessex!" he replied, as though he was answering a quiz question. "Yes, yes. Gave my middle order a torrid time with a spell from the Dinsdale end a couple of years ago." I knew that the coach had only just taken over the England job and that he was talking about his former county side.

"Well, unfortunately none of my luggage made it here, so I'm going to need to borrow some kit. For boots, I'm a size 10." I realised that it didn't look very professional on my part, but I thought it was best to explain the situation immediately.

"Borrow some kit?"

I filled him in on some more of the detail. "The airline lost my entire coffin. Whites, boots, gloves, bats, the whole lot." I didn't think that this should be too difficult a concept to grasp.

"Erm . . ." he replied, as though he was going to say something. But he didn't get any further. I was thinking that I was the one who was supposed to be jet-lagged, but it was the coach who was sounding completely dazed.

"Boss, Boss," his assistant butted in. "I think I know what's happened. Can I have a quick word?" He ushered the coach a few yards away and the pair of them spent a couple of minutes talking in hushed tones. Both of them glanced over to look at me occasionally.

The pair of them then walked back over to where they'd left me standing. The coach spoke first. "Pete, I am *so* sorry. That was no way to welcome you. It's been mayhem here over the last few days. Goochie never even got to join us in Auckland, and we'd been hoping that Gatt might make this leg of the tour, but he's been advised to stay at home. I just completely lost track of who's coming and going for a moment."

"Well that's a relief," I replied. "I thought I'd arrived in the wrong country for a moment there."

"Ah, very good, very funny," said the assistant. "Look, we're all finding our way here at the moment. We all need to get used to the new faces. Now, we're going to take a break for lunch in a few moments, so why don't you join us. And then we can see what we've got in the dressing room for you to wear."

There was a strange atmosphere around the team as the players ate lunch. With hindsight, I don't think that many of the squad were sure of either their place or their role in the side. There were a number of guys out there with less than a handful of caps to their name. None of the middle-order batsmen looked comfortable in their own skin. All of the bowlers who were sat around the table had copped some stick in the press recently for either being too wayward, too injury prone or just not having the technique or bottle for Test match cricket. Whenever there was laughter it always sounded a little forced. This didn't look like a team that was ready to start winning matches.

After lunch, the assistant coach grabbed me by the shoulder as he left the dining area and told me to head down to the dressing room in ten minutes' time, so he could sort me out with some kit. I spent those ten minutes staring out of the window, high above the pitch, wondering what it would be like to walk out there for England in this huge stadium. Something told me that I was no closer to finding out than if I'd been thousands of miles away in Casterbridge.

When I thought that ten minutes must have gone by, I followed the signs down to the away dressing room. I could hear voices inside, so I knocked and then cautiously pushed the door ajar. I caught a glimpse of the skipper, another batsman, the coach and the assistant.

One of the players yelled, "Not now!" I retreated from the room.

There was a solitary chair in the corridor. With absolutely nothing better to do I just sat down and waited for the assistant to call me when they were done. The conversation on the other side of the door went on for some time, and it gradually began to get more heated. I caught certain phrases, but most of the time I couldn't work out who had said what exactly.

"It's just bloody amateur time out here, isn't it?"

"No I won't fucking well calm down. It's just one cock-up after another."

I soon realised that it was the players who were getting increasing vocal. I guessed that the coach and his assistant were trying to placate them, but they were speaking more quietly, so I couldn't pick up on anything that they said. Then one of the players' contributions came through loud and clear. I assumed it must have been the skipper.

"I told you what I wanted, and it wasn't county trundler. Give me strength! He's not even a very good county trundler."

I was incensed. I'd just flown halfway around the world and lost my luggage, only to be professionally slandered by a key member of the national side. I was thinking to myself, "County trundler? County fucking trundler?" I'd concede that I'd lost a bit of zip over the last couple of years, but that was simply because Bridges had bowled me into the ground. I'd been a loyal servant to my club, done exactly what the captain had asked of me, and then this guy, who hadn't even had the courtesy to introduce himself, slags me off. If either of those players in that dressing room were re-writing the record books for England, then maybe, just maybe, they might have earned the right to have a pop. I reckoned that these guys needed to take a really good look at themselves.

As I sat there fuming, the door opened and the two players, followed by the coach, stormed off down the corridor. After a couple of moments the assistant emerged from the dressing room.

"Right Peter, you can come in. Let's see what we can find for . . ."

I didn't let him finish. I was livid. "What the fuck? What the fuck?" I realised that I'd started without much sense of what I was actually going to say. "You bring me all this way, just for that cunt to say that I'm shit. What's wrong with you fucking people?" Obviously I realise that this was no way to address a member of any team's coaching staff: younger readers particularly should be clear that this was just a momentary aberration on my part. However, at that precise moment, I do believe that there were mitigating circumstances.

"Listen, Peter . . ."

"No I won't fucking listen. What . . . Where's . . ." The combination of jetlag and fury was making it difficult for me to form sentences. "Yes, that's it. Where's the fucking professional courtesy?"

"So you think he's wrong, then?" The question took me by surprise.

"What? No. Yes. Of course I think he's fucking wrong."

"Well, then it's your job to show him that he's wrong."

"Is this how you treat all your fucking bowlers?"

"Not all of them. But sometimes the skip thinks an angry bowler is a better bowler."

"Well I'm certainly fucking angry," I said. Although by this point I was beginning to feel more confused than anything else.

"I tell you what, Peter," he continued. "Let's find you some clothes. Then you can take the mini-bus back to the hotel. Take the rest of the day off. Come back to the ground tomorrow and channel that anger in the nets. It's your job to demonstrate that you belong here."

The team hotel was only a few minutes drive from the stadium. I'd expected it to be something really quite impressive, but it looked more like the sort of motel you'd see in an American road movie. But on the plus side, the room I was given was large and clean, and because of my late arrival I didn't have to share it with anyone else. I wasn't really expecting to be able to sleep. But when I lay down on the bed, more in hope than expectation of dozing off, I must have gone out like a light.

We started off with some general fitness work on the outfield the next morning, and we followed that with a range of fielding drills. Then we worked on our individual skills in the nets. The assistant, who was an ex-bowler himself, gave me a certain amount of encouragement and would tell me when he thought I was getting a nice shape on my deliveries. Just before lunch I found myself bowling to the skipper.

"Listen mate," he called down the net, "I just want some decent wheels from you. And I don't mind if you over-step a couple of yards."

As a seam bowler that's just about as insulting as it gets: when a batsman tells you that you're nothing like quick enough to trouble him down the full length of the pitch. Well, there was no way I was giving him the satisfaction of shortening the wicket; there was professional pride at stake. So, I just followed the assistant's advice from the previous day and channelled my anger down all twenty-two yards of that net. I found pace in my body that I hadn't tapped since the '89 season. I beat him on the outside edge a few times and left him groping for the ball. Then he didn't look so fucking clever.

Later on in the afternoon it became quite clear to me that I wasn't going to be playing. The coach and his assistant, at different times, had gathered together those individuals who were going to get the nod for a number of tactical discussions. I was never invited to join one of these conversations. I got the message. The team contained a pair of out and out seam bowlers, a pair of all-rounders, a pair of wicket-keepers (which seemed to be the accepted wisdom at the time), a solitary orthodox spinner and some batsmen. Needless to say, none of those batsmen averaged forty or more in Test cricket.

Back in the hotel that night I felt a fool. I felt foolish that I'd ever believed that I could be part of this England team. And I felt that the rest of the squad were laughing at me. I'd flown all this way just to give them some net practice. And to cap it all I had to sit there all evening wearing all this Tetley Bitter branded England kit, because I didn't have any of my own clothes to change into. I must have looked like a travelling fan wearing all the replica gear, who'd somehow managed to book himself into the team's hotel.

The whole squad travelled down to the stadium the following morning. There were fans milling around outside as we arrived, there were groups of journalists hanging around together, and the New Zealand broadcast teams were preparing for the day ahead. I wish I could have at least felt excited to be part of it, but I just felt so hollow inside. In an hour or so the teams would be announced, the captains would go out to make the toss, and then I'd have four or five days to contemplate my lot as a *county trundler*.

We'd been out on the pitch running through the fielding drills for about thirty minutes when suddenly a big, cold gust of wind bullied its way across the ground. I noticed that at the other end of the stadium the Kiwis had started jogging back to towards the dressing rooms. The first drops of rain started falling. They were the size of marbles. A dozen or so of the stadium ground staff were wheeling out the covers to protect the wicket in the middle of the pitch. As the drops turned into a downpour we sprinted for the shelter of the players' tunnel. If that weather front had blown in just thirty minutes later, the captains would have named their teams and then tossed up. The day's play would still have been washed out, but my story would have turned out very differently.

. . . you'll be needing this.

11. THE DEFENCE OF DUNEDIN

Like any professional English cricketer I've spent my fair share of days cooped up in dressing rooms during rain delays – the humidity somehow amplifies the odours of decaying rubber and stale sweat. Condensation forms on whatever windows you might have, so you can't even see out. Of course, when you're with your mates you make the best of it: you play cards, you tell stories, and you rediscover old favourites from top-shelf magazines to pass the time. But out there in Dunedin I didn't have any mates in the dressing room, and I knew that the clock in there would feel like it was going backwards.

When it was clear that there wasn't going to be any play before lunch, I took myself for a walk around the stadium. I slowly made my way from bay to bay until I was on the far side of the pitch. Water was pooling on the roof above the stands and then falling down in numerous rivulets onto the concrete steps below. Bar a few incredibly optimistic England fans, the stands were otherwise deserted. I just sat there on my own. Play was finally abandoned for the day at about four o'clock. My return flight was in five days. It couldn't come soon enough.

That night I got asked if I wanted to join a number of players at the Curry Pot. I thought it would be good to at least see some of Dunedin, but I didn't think I'd be great company, so I thanked them for the offer but decided to stay in the hotel.

When I joined the squad for breakfast the following morning it was complete mayhem. Apparently three of the guys on the team sheet were now a rather disturbing shade of green. It was both all-rounders and one of the batsmen. Another of the players who'd been at the Curry Pot had figured out, by process of elimination, that the culprit must have been the shrimp biryani.

Over the next couple of hours the coach and the skipper appeared to try and work out every single permutation of the team that would prevent them from having to select me. There was even some talk about playing a third wicket-keeper.

We travelled down to the stadium. The weather had improved dramatically. It wasn't exactly warm, but overhead there was a cloudless blue sky. We were going to get in a full day's play, and whoever won the toss would almost certainly choose to bat. I warmed up with the rest of the squad and I took part in the usual fielding drills, but I was left with the impression that the skipper would rather send the team doctor in to bat at number three than select me to bolster our depleted bowling line-up.

At about twenty-five past ten, just five minutes before the skipper was due to go out for the toss, he walked up to me with the coach and the assistant.

"Legend, you're playing, don't let us down," he said flatly. "And Legend, you'll be needing this." He thrust something into my hand and strode purposely off towards the middle of the pitch.

I don't know if those are the traditional words a captain usually says to a player receiving his first England cap. I looked down at the blue fabric in my hand and stared at the three white lions. He was right though: I did *need* this. I needed this to prove to myself, and anyone who had ever doubted me, that I was good enough to make it all the way to the top. Finally I was Peter Legend of Wessex and England.

My elation lasted a good while into the first session. The skipper had lost the toss and the Kiwis, understandably, had chosen to bat. I hardly expected to open the bowling, but I thought I'd at least get an over or two before lunch. The skipper saw it differently and primarily used me as a specialist fine leg; this meant that I had to jog the entire length of the rectangular field between every over. We took an early wicket with the new ball. An extra man was brought into the slips and for a brief period the team demonstrated some real energy in the field. But it soon became clear that the Kiwi batsmen were settling in for a long stay at the crease.

No wickets fell in the afternoon session. I thought that after the drinks break I'd go through my warm-up exercises, just to remind the skipper that he did have another bowling option on the field. He bowled his spinner unchanged from one end and rotated his two main seamers at the other. When it looked as though they were both flagging, and that he'd finally have to bring me on, he invited various batsmen to bowl their part-time off-spin or medium pace.

The Kiwis finished the day with just over 300 runs on the board and only three wickets down. I'd bowled the penultimate over of the day. It was a maiden, so that was at least something to be positive about. The skipper and the coach kept us at the ground for a team meeting. They wanted to see more energy the following morning, they wanted us to break through the opposition's middle order quickly, and they wanted to see us batting in the early afternoon. It wasn't exactly Churchillian, but at least they were trying to stir the team a bit. There weren't many smiles around the dinner table in the hotel that night.

The following day started much like the previous one. The Kiwis were cautious in the first session, looking to get through it without losing any more wickets. This time I got to bowl immediately after the first drinks break. I thought the skipper was finally bringing me on for an extended spell, but it just happened that he wanted to give the spinner a go from the other end of the pitch, so he only needed a solitary over from me.

I bowled four more overs during the afternoon session. By this time the Kiwis were looking to get on with it, and they lost a couple of wickets trying to push the rate along. At tea they were at 450 for five. The other two seamers looked as though they'd just run back-to-back marathons and even the spinner was beginning to get a bit mouthy about his workload.

By the evening session the skipper had given up any thoughts of trying to dismiss the opposition and was just trying to slow their scoring rate. He had me bowl a tight off-stump line on a full length with one of our keepers up to the stumps. I wasn't to give them any opportunity to cut or pull to the short boundaries, and with the keeper up they were going to have to take risks if they wanted to come down the pitch to drive straight. I'd done this sort of a job countless times for Bridges over the past three years, so I knew exactly what was required. I finished with figures of 2 for 48, after an extended spell in the evening session. I had mixed feelings when I took my first wicket: a bit of seam movement away and a neat little grab from the keeper. I just wanted to stand in the middle of the strip and roar. I wanted to shout at the skipper, "See! That's how fucking good I am!" But given the context of the match situation I just kept a lid on it. Even so, it gave me a lift. Every time I walked back to my mark after that I just kept reciting in my head, *Peter Legend, Wessex and England, Peter Legend, Wessex and England.* The team may have tried to do everything possible to undermine me, but my quality still shone through. Not long after, I bagged another, as a right-hander got over-confident and tried to work a straight one through mid-wicket. Perhaps if I'd been brought on earlier the Kiwis wouldn't have been able to declare at 612-8.

The mood in the dressing room didn't exactly improve that evening. All we could do now was play for the draw, by batting out the final two days. In theory this shouldn't have been too difficult a task: the Kiwis had shown that there was nothing to fear in the wicket, so with the proviso that we went about the task sensibly and avoided the follow-on, we'd be safe. But looking at our batting line-up didn't exactly inspire me with confidence: there was a certain bravado among a few of the players, but I couldn't say for sure if they genuinely believed that they were going to go out there and save the game. Losing becomes a habit, and this England team had become all too practised at it.

Shortly after tea on the following day I was padded up and waiting to go out to bat. I'd been told I'd be batting at number ten, one place in the order behind a genuine number eleven, and one place in front of a complete rabbit. Our batting performance hadn't been great. Players were getting in, scoring twenty or so runs, and then getting out. They didn't know whether to just occupy the crease, or whether to try and play their natural game and get on with reducing the run deficit. There wasn't a collapse as such, but by tea we were seven wickets down with only a couple of hundred runs on the board. When the next wicket fell, I'd be walking out to bat in a Test match for the first time in my life. I'd never been too particular about my batting kit. I once saw Andy Farrow replace the grip on his handle fifteen times in a row until he finally thought that it felt right in his hands. I really don't understand that. But as I sat there, wearing someone else's gloves and helmet, holding a bat that I'd only ever used for ten minutes in the nets earlier that morning, everything felt strange. It was disconcerting. It was a bit like when you hire a car on the Continent. Sure, you still know how to drive, but you're conscious that everything feels different.

Watching the game from the players' balcony after tea it felt as though the next wicket could fall with any ball. I don't know how long I was sitting there. It somehow felt like hours, but it was probably only a handful of minutes. I was aware that my palms were sweating and that my throat was dry. Suddenly there was a raucous appeal from the Kiwis. The entire team had gone up for it and they all seemed to be pleading with the umpire. After an agonising delay the umpire's finger went up – I could hear the whoops of celebration from the opposition – and suddenly it was my turn to make my way out to the middle.

Everything felt so alien to me; from the kit I was wearing to the walk through the bowels of the stadium towards the pitch. As I emerged into the light, I started to jog down the final flight of stairs, past the fans in the lower tier of the stand and on towards the playing area. Just before I took the final couple of steps that would carry me over the boundary rope, I felt a hand pat me on the back of the shoulder. A voice said, "Good luck, son." I instinctively turned to look at the guy. I couldn't have glanced at him for more than a fraction of a second, but as I continued on my way out to the middle I couldn't shake the image of his searching blue eyes from my mind.

As was to be expected, there was a certain amount of chatter coming from the Kiwi fielders. They were going for the kill with just about the whole team in close catching positions, so it was hard to make out who was saying what.

I think it was the keeper who just kept repeating, "Nine, ten, jack boys. Here we go."

There was a bit of a delay while the skipper fiddled around with the field, bringing even more men right up close around me. The chatter was by now constant, but to be honest the only thing I could really focus on was the face of the guy in the stands.

And I think that's pretty much what I was still seeing when the bowler charged in and sent my off-stump cart-wheeling down the ground. I didn't see the ball at all. I just sort of prodded forward with the bat down a line where I thought it might be and hoped for the best. With the noise of the celebrating Kiwis ringing in my ears I made the long, slow walk back to the dressing room. I'd spent the entire day thinking that our batting line-up lacked the mental strength to do their job, and now I'd just gone out and got a first-baller myself. I could feel the humiliation in every bone of my body. I wanted to get off the pitch as fast as I could, but at the same time I didn't want to arrive back in the dressing room any sooner than I had to. I stared right down at the ground as I made my way back across the field.

I only took my eyes off the ground once during that long walk of shame: when the same guy in the stand who had wished me luck earlier, again patted me on the shoulder and said, "Bad luck, son."

I wasn't sure if this part of the stand was a members' area or not, but frankly I no longer cared about club rules and etiquette. As I walked past I turned to him and said, "Just fuck off, Dad."

The next hour or so in the dressing room was without a doubt the most depressing period of time I've ever spent in a cricket ground. Our rabbit at number eleven only lasted for a few minutes, so we were following-on soon enough. The openers were back in their gear and preparing to try and negotiate the remainder of the evening session. It was obvious that they weren't exactly looking forward to the challenge. But all I could think about was Dad and the complete balls-up I'd made of my first innings. Why, after all these years, did he pick *that* moment to show up? It wasn't as though he hadn't played the game himself. He knew that you need a clear mind to bat. It was almost as though he had wanted me to fail. Before I'd gone out to bat that day I didn't even know if he was still alive; but now I was thinking to myself that it would have been better if he wasn't.

Then immediately I started to feel guilty about wishing him dead. He was still, after all, my dad. But what sort of dad reappears after ten years, just as you're going out to play your first ever innings in a Test match? My head was whirring with these conflicting thoughts. One moment I wanted to be left alone to think things over and the next I wanted to go down into the stands and punch his lights out.

Then I heard the coach say, "Anyone want to volunteer for night-watchman?"

Without thinking for a single moment I just replied, "I'm up for it." Anything had got to be preferable to sitting in that dressing room feeling like this. I'd far rather be doing something than just sitting there torturing myself. Even if that something meant going out and getting sledged constantly by the opposition and risking the ultimate humiliation of losing my wicket twice in a single session.

Nobody else said a word. So, for the second time in less than an hour I found myself making the lonely journey out to the middle of the pitch. I had managed to get myself into a mood of grim determination. The coach bet me a tenner as I left the dressing room that I couldn't survive until the close of play. I didn't really need the additional motivation, but at least he was trying to help.

As I reached the middle one of the Kiwis said to me, "I hope you don't plan on hanging around any longer than you did last time."

In the heat of the moment, I just barked, "Fuck off, Skippy." Of course I knew that they didn't have kangaroos in New Zealand, but it was just the first thing that came into my head.

"Fella thinks he's in Australia," the guy told the rest of the team. "Let's see if he knows where his stumps are."

For the rest of my time at the crease that evening, and throughout the following morning I had to listen to endless kangaroo-themed sledging.

"What's that Skippy? You're going to play around a straight one?"

"Hey Skippy, are you ever going to show us where the middle of that bat is?"

Actually, I think it helped me concentrate. The more chatter there was around me, the easier I found it to focus. The ball was still new, so it was swinging around. I played and missed on a few occasions, but at least I was seeing it clearly, and I was getting right in behind anything that was straight. We lost another wicket in the final over of the day, so the match situation was simple: we had to bat out the entire final day with eight wickets in hand. The Kiwis certainly didn't think we were going to do it, and I'm not sure there were too many in our dressing room who genuinely thought we had much of a chance either.

Regardless of how badly the team was doing, I was feeling a bit better about myself by the time I walked off the pitch that night. I'd done my job as the night-watchman successfully, I'd won a tenner and I'd gone some way to making up for my earlier golden duck. I saw Dad in the stands and shouted to him to meet me by the main gate in an hour. So, later that evening we walked into the Carisbrook Hotel and I ordered a couple of Steinlagers. A neon sign in the window advertised *vacancies*, but the place itself looked more like a cross between an English pub and the jail in a Western film than somewhere you might actually want to check into for the night.

As we sat down in a quiet corner I could feel all those conflicting thoughts returning. Part of me still wanted to throttle him, but another part of me was pleased to see him after all this time. "Well, this is unexpected," I said.

"We've been busy. This was the first chance I've had to get down here."

"Sorry, who's *we*?" I enquired.

"Oh, the university admissions department. I had to work the weekend."

I wasn't really concerned that he hadn't made it to the ground until day four of the match; I was more interested in where he'd been for the last decade. "But we've heard nothing from you, Dad. You could have written or something. You could have let Mum know you were still alive."

"I don't think she'd have wanted to hear from me." I wasn't so sure, but he went on. "I reckon that my leaving was probably the best thing that could have ever happened to her. She moved in with Hendricks, right?"

I was wondering how he could have guessed that. "Well, not exactly," I replied, "but sort of. Anyway, how on earth did you end up here?"

"That's a long story Pete. Anyway, it's water under the bridge."

"That's as maybe Dad, but I think you owe Mum, Danny and me some sort of explanation."

"Look, I just fell out with a couple of guys. It happens. They said to me that I should leave Wessex, and I figured that was probably the best thing to do. I was in London for a short while, and then someone told me that I'd be able to emigrate here."

"You fell out with a couple of guys? Couldn't you go to the police?"

"It was complicated. You know, you get involved with people, when maybe you shouldn't, and things can turn nasty."

"Was this something to do with the encyclopaedia sales?"

"The what?" he replied blankly. "Oh those. No. Not really. Well a little bit I guess. Yeah, maybe like some sort of turf war I suppose. Look, things just got too difficult for me in Wessex, and that's it. Now tell me, how's your brother?"

"He's good. He owns his own estate agent business, down in Port Bredy."

Over the next couple of hours I answered Dad's questions about Wessex and bought him a couple more beers. But I was left with a sense that I hadn't really learned anything about him whatsoever.

"Is there anyone in your life over here?" I finally got to ask him, as we got up from the table. I really had to be on my way back to the team hotel.

"Not as such, no," he replied. "But this is a university town, it's full of interesting people passing through. I'm not lonely, if that's what you mean." I think he sort of winked at me, as if to say that I shouldn't worry about a lack of visitors to his bedroom, but I couldn't be sure. In that moment I found him a little unnerving.

"Do you think you'll ever come back to Wessex?" It seemed like the polite thing to ask. But by this point I was thinking that the rest of us could get along just fine without him.

"No, I don't think that would be a good idea," he answered.

I felt relieved and I didn't spend any time trying to persuade him to change his mind. It may have been disloyal to admit it, but I thought that Mum was probably far better off with Mr Hendricks than Dad. I decided to walk back to the team hotel that night. It gave me some time to reflect on everything that had happened during the course of the day. Plus I'd given Dad the last few dollars that I had on me, so that he could get a taxi back to his place somewhere north of the city. As far as I know he didn't show up on the final day of the game.

****

It took me a while to get to sleep that night. The whole trip had been a disaster. I had lost my luggage. The coach had needed to be reminded that I'd been asked to join the squad. The skipper had only bowled me as a last resort. Dad had shown up out the blue and fleeced me for the last dollar in my pocket. And I'd got out to the very first ball I faced in Test cricket. Eventually I must have tired of all those negative thoughts and I dozed off.

I woke up on Tuesday 13th April feeling much better. Somehow I was thinking far more clearly. My father had always been a disappointment. And it turned out that he was still a disappointment. There was nothing I could do about that. I'd discovered that the England set-up was a complete shambles. But it was a shambles before I arrived, and no doubt it would still be a shambles after I left. Again, there was nothing I could do about that. Suddenly everything seemed so simple. All I had to do was bat. There was absolutely nothing else I needed to think about. I didn't need to worry about scoring runs. I didn't need to worry about having the skipper in my ear: he'd got out the previous evening so he wouldn't be walking out to the middle with me. For the first time in days I actually felt good about myself. If we somehow saved the game it would be a miracle, so I didn't feel under any pressure whatsoever. Whether I lasted one ball or batted for hours, I was looking forward to it.

It was a close-run thing, but I didn't have to bat *all* day. The umpires offered us the light just after five o'clock as dark clouds rolled in over the city. My stay at the crease had lasted almost six hours. I had resisted every temptation to play my natural high-tempo scoring game, and I'd simply set out to frustrate the Kiwis ball after ball. I finished the game 38 not out. I'd taken singles every now and again, simply to rotate the strike and move the field around a bit, but I didn't play a single aggressive stroke in the entire innings. Professional sportsmen sometimes talk about being in *the zone* or in *the bubble*: well I just felt completely in command of my game that day. Nothing the Kiwis could throw at me or say to me made any difference: I just felt good. Of course I had some nerves when I first walked out in the morning session, but as soon as I felt the first delivery fall dead to ground, right out the middle of my bat, I realised that I had nothing to fear.

I don't actually remember too much about the day itself. The coach carried on betting me a tenner at the beginning of each session that I couldn't survive it, so I ended up taking £40 off him by the end of the match. Wickets fell fairly regularly at the other end throughout the day, but I reckoned that my sole responsibility was to look after myself. If the rest of the team couldn't hold up the other end between them, then we deserved to lose. My mind was completely uncluttered.

I was aware of some tension in the dressing room at teatime. By then we were six wickets down, but we also knew that the weather was closing in. I don't think, at the beginning of the day, there was any real belief that the Test could be saved, so initially the mood was pretty relaxed. It always is when there's nothing to lose. But as the draw became a real possibility, the nail biting started: no doubt there was more advice being given to the incoming batsmen, there were more players sat unmoving on the balcony. But I was just living in the moment. I just kept batting. The Kiwis gave up calling me Skippy some time in the morning session on that final day, and a little while after that they stopped sledging me at all. It wasn't working, and it wasn't going to work.

When play was abandoned for the day we were eight wickets down: the Kiwis were just two decent balls from winning the match. As I walked off the pitch I could see the dejection on the faces of the opposition: they'd thrown everything they had at us that day and they'd come up just short. The England fans in the ground were celebrating as though we'd just won the Ashes. I could see some of our players pumping their fists on the balcony. Sometimes, when you've been outplayed for days, grabbing a draw feels as good as a win.

But if I'm honest, that day I wasn't playing for England, or for the rest of my teammates, I was simply playing for myself. A number of the Kiwis shook my hand as we left the field: some grudgingly, some with genuine warmth and respect. At that moment I thought I could have gone on batting for another six hours, but as soon as I sat down in the dressing room a wave of exhaustion hit me. Hour after hour of intense mental concentration had taken its toll; I was absolutely shattered.

The rest of the squad were booked on a flight out of Dunedin early the next morning, but I wasn't due to leave until late in the afternoon so I had a few hours to myself. With time to kill I walked up to take a look at the city centre. I saw a wine shop and, remembering my conversation with Mike, went in to ask about the local pinot noir. I bought three bottles: one for Mike, one to share with Bethan and one for myself. I'd got my CD Walkman and two albums in my hand luggage, so I spent the next few hours in my hotel room listening to Nirvana's *Nevermind* and *Pills 'n' Thrills and Bellyaches* by The Happy Mondays, while slowly working my way through a bottle of Gibbstone Valley. Maybe if I'd known that I'd never play for England ever again, I wouldn't have felt as good as I did that afternoon.

I know, as well as any professional, that a player's statistics don't tell the whole story. But I think it's worth considering my figures in the Dunedin Test: two wickets at an average of 24, and a batting average of 38. Ian Botham, regarded as the best all-rounder that England has ever produced, finished his international career with a bowling average of 28 and a batting average of 34. Botham could have walked into any Test side in the world, and yet my statistics were even better than his. I'd proved that I belonged at that level. I'd proved that I belonged on the big stage.

Later in 1993 the following players all pulled on the England shirt at some point during our summer to face the Australians: Mike Atherton, Martin Bicknell, Andrew Caddick, Dominic Cork, Philip DeFreitas, John Emburey, Neil Fairbrother, Neil Foster, Angus Fraser, Mike Gatting, Graham Gooch, Graeme Hick, Nasser Hussain, Mark Ilott, Paul Jarvis, Mark Lathwell, Chris Lewis, Devon Malcolm, Matthew Maynard, Martin McCague, Derek Pringle, Mark Ramprakash, Dermot Reeve, Robin Smith, Alec Stewart, Peter Such, Graham Thorpe, Phil Tufnell and Steve Watkin.

Of those *twenty-nine* players perhaps a handful are household names, but I think most readers would agree that the majority are not. *Twenty-nine* players and no mention of Peter Legend: a player with a proven international pedigree. I never heard from anyone in the England set-up ever again.

Sometimes I think that, in a way, I was perhaps a victim of my own success. If England had lost that series against New Zealand, it would have been part of a record-breaking run of failure: Pakistan, India, Sri Lanka, New Zealand and Australia. But the Dunedin Test often gets forgotten because we *didn't* lose it, because I batted for six hours to save it. I may never have played for England again, but the experience did change my life. I'd made a success of my cricket career and now I was going to prove myself in the world of business.

The only thing I know about
cricket is in *Northanger Abbey*.

12. WINNING IN WESSEX

I had no idea just how much my life was about to change when I finally made my way through the arrivals area of Heathrow airport. I quickly spotted the driver waiting for me. He was holding up a board that read "Legend". "Third time lucky, eh?" I said as we met, but he just stared at me blankly.

Looking back, I now realise that nothing can prepare you for finding yourself at the centre of a media storm. When I walked through our front door in Durnover Green, just for a moment I thought that something was seriously wrong. Dougie was sat at the bottom of our stairs talking to someone on the phone. There were post-it notes stuck all over the wall around him, and he was scrawling frantically in a diary. His call finished abruptly.

"Fuck me you're going to be busy, mate," he said, looking up.

"Hello Dougie," I replied. "Yes, it's good to be home. I had a good trip; thanks for asking."

It turned out that the phone had started ringing the previous night, and then it hadn't really stopped. Bethan reckoned that it was Dougie's job, not hers, to manage the media, so she'd asked him to come over and take the calls himself. It seemed like every news outlet in Wessex and beyond wanted a piece of me. BBC Radio Wessex, Wessex Sound – the commercial FM station – numerous local papers with reporters from Budmouth, Casterbridge, Shaston, Port Bredy and other places further down the coast; they all wanted to talk to me. Dougie had even taken calls from the nationals; apparently the cricket writer from *Today* was desperate to come down to do a piece.

"Bloody hell, Dougie," I said. "I can't do all of these. I just don't have the time. I can't just drop everything to talk to the press."

"I tell you what Pete, while I'm representing you, you'll fucking well find the time." He sounded a little bit annoyed. "I've spent the last twenty-four hours working my fucking backside off for you, and you are going to talk to all of these cunts. Each and every single fucking one of them."

"Sure, Dougie. But the cricket comes first. And don't forget I've got a property to shift as well. We can work our way though these over the next couple of weeks, can't we?"

"Fuck's sake. You don't get it do you?"

"Get what, Dougie?" I was tired from the flight, and while it was great that all these people wanted to speak to me, I just thought that maybe I'd have a quiet drink with Bethan, go to bed, and then take it easy for the rest of the weekend.

"Jesus! OK, I'll go slowly for the hard of thinking," said Dougie. "Here's the thing Pete, you're hot for these guys *today*. Your story is *now*. Not next week. Fuck, by then they won't have just forgotten your name, they'll have even fucking well forgotten that they ever called you in the first place. Next week some idiot from Port Bredy will swim the fucking Channel or something, or they'll find out that there's a gay midfielder at Budmouth, and you, mate, will be history."

"OK, I understand that Dougie," I explained. "But look, there's an Ashes summer coming up. That'll be the big story, if I do well in that."

"Yeah, well that'll be great. But let's not count our chickens, eh?"

"You don't think I'll play in the Ashes?" I pushed him.

"Am I a fucking England selector? No, I'm just the bloke whose job it is to capitalise on what we've got right here and now." Dougie paused to look at his watch. "And right now, at nine-thirty on Friday night, all of Wessex wants to talk to you. But the clock is ticking. Come Monday you might be no more than fish and chip wrapping. That's how fucking fast it'll happen."

Dougie showed me the weekend schedule. We were to spend most of the time in the bar of the Regency Hotel, on Budmouth's promenade. We'd conduct most of the press interviews there, but then we'd be travelling around to the radio stations for a number of live broadcasts.

"Right Pete, I don't want you being fucking precious about any of this. Any photo opportunity that they want, we're going to give it to them."

It was only just beginning to dawn on me how embarrassing it was all going to be: I'd have to stand on the promenade and pretend to hit cricket balls into the sea, watched by a bunch of Saturday shoppers and tourists. I would have much preferred doing all of the interviews and the photographs up at Canberra Park; but of course that wasn't an option.

"Dougie," I protested, "you're not going to make me pose on the promenade in full kit are you?" I knew that whatever shots ended up in the paper would also end up in our dressing room with alternative headlines. In the event I got off fairly lightly. A picture of me in full whites holding my Double-L Beef-Cake had been re-titled: "Ledge poses like a twat on the promenade after agent banned from ground."

"Listen mate, if they want you to wear a kilt and stick the bat up your fucking arse, then that's what you're going to do," he replied.

By the end of the weekend I was absolutely exhausted. I didn't realise just how tired you could get from simply talking. Sure, I knew that talking could get really boring; I'd learned that from Justin Bridges' endless tactical discussions. But I didn't realise just how tiring it is to answer question after question for hours on end. Over that weekend I think I must have shared every opinion that I've ever held. And over the course of the interviews I'd had to invent some new ones about subjects I'd never even thought about before. When did I first start playing? How did I feel when I took the call from England? How did it feel receiving my England cap? I was being asked the same questions over and over again. The sports journalists mainly stuck to the cricket but the radio stations, and some of the news journalists, asked me all this completely random stuff as well: y-fronts versus boxer shorts? Best tourist attractions in Wessex? How would I spend a million pounds? Was I cat person or a dog person? It just went on and on. During a short break between interviews I asked Dougie what the point of all this was.

"The point, seeing as you clearly need it fucking spelled out, is to make you famous." Dougie had spent most of the weekend telling me to smile more and be nice. "And once you're famous, then we can make some fucking money. It really isn't rocket science."

I thought I'd already gone and done the thing that was supposed to make me famous: I was the first ever Wessex player to win an England cap, and I'd pretty much single-handedly saved the game I'd played in. But Dougie said that wasn't enough: we needed to *get my face out there*. The game hadn't been shown in England, so nobody back home had actually been able to watch me play.

One place where my face was already out there was Canberra Park. A huge banner had been hung from the wall that separated the car park from the main road. There was a massive photo of me, taken from the 1992 team picture, and underneath it read: "Season tickets on sale now! Support England's Peter Legend and the Wessex team at Canberra Park this summer."

Where it used to just say "Wessex" on our schedule board outside the dressing room, someone had crossed it out and written "The Peter Legend All Stars". But Mike explained why the lads hadn't really ripped into me. Apparently, Sebastian Welland-Flanders had actually come down to the dressing room while I was away to tell the squad that the club was in serious financial difficulty. Bridges' captaincy had ushered in the most successful period in Wessex's history, but the financial cost was unsustainable. Finishing higher in the Championship had brought more people through the turnstiles, but not enough to offset the increase in the club's wage bill.

"The club is going to do everything that it can to generate some more revenue," Mike later explained to me. "And if that involves erecting an image of you, even one that's large enough to bring a blush to the face of the most egomaniacal dictator, then so be it. Desperate times and all that."

I struggled through my first week back in pre-season training. I had to fit meetings with estate agents around the club's schedule, and Dougie was still coming up with more interviews. By the end of the week I was finally looking forward to a couple of days off. But then the commercial opportunities that Dougie had been looking into happened very quickly.

Dougie had been doing some marketing consultancy work for World of Furniture Land. They owned a number of big out-of-town stores across the West Country. Some readers might remember the television ads that they used to run: they were just a series of still photographs of various products, with the price displayed prominently on the screen. A female voice-over artist would describe them: "This occasional leather sofa in classic chocolate brown offers exceptional value for money at only £299. This offer must end on Bank Holiday Monday." The advertisements would always finish with the shop name – World of Furniture Land – being sung to the tune of "Take That Look off Your Face", from the musical *Tell Me on a Sunday*.

"You are in the fucking money, sunshine," he shouted down the phone. "You can thank me any fucking time you like, but you are the new face of World of Furniture Land."

Much like when Gary Lineker first took over on *Match of the Day*, it was a case of learning presentation skills on the job. I had to make a number of adverts where I'd walk around one of the stores – usually the one outside Budmouth – describing individual pieces of furniture. The scripts were really good; the guys writing them would always somehow link the furniture back to cricket. A typical thirty-second spot might go something like this:

> *My name is Peter Legend of Wessex and England. I've been bowled over by the prices at World of Furniture Land, so I want to put their quality to the Test. Now, I know a sweet shot when I see one and I also know a great three-piece suite. And this black patent leather number is an absolute peach. And talking about a great delivery, at World of Furniture Land delivery is free on all orders over £200. So get down to World of Furniture Land and find out why they knock the competition for six!*

"You're as wooden as that table you're selling," Mike said to me when the first batch of adverts went on air. He was talking about one of the early ads I'd made for a *hat-trick deal*. There were usually one or two of those every month: customers would get a big discount if they took three items. In this case, a table, a set of matching chairs and a dessert trolley.

Fortunately I got better at the whole thing fairly quickly. Just doing the voice-overs for radio advertisements helped. Unlike the television shoots, there'd only be a handful of people in the recording studio so there was much less pressure. And after a while I got to know most of the lines off by heart, so I only had to learn small bits of the script each time. I'd always get to start with the same introduction and we'd always include something about the free delivery service.

It was around this time that Terry Le Saux from the *Echo* and me started performing "An Evening With Peter Legend". Terry would interview me about my career, I'd tell stories from my days on the road with Col and Mike and then we'd hold a Q&A with the audience. We took the show to hotels, sports clubs and even the Butlins in Minehead. It was a great little earner because the overheads were so low.

Not everything went quite so well. I finished the season without a bat sponsor. Dougie put it to the guys at Layton Landy that they should make a commemorative Legend Beef-Cake Special, which we'd license for a few grand. Rather than them taking our proposal seriously, our meeting descended into an ugly spat when they claimed that they'd been giving me more free bats over the years than was actually the case. Theirs was a disappointing attitude because I'd wanted to support a local manufacturer. Dougie decided it was best that I removed the Double-L branding from all of my bats for the remainder of the season.

May of 1993 went by in a flash. What with the World of Furniture Land campaign, "An Evening With Peter Legend" and of course my on-field commit-ments with Wessex, I didn't have a single moment to stop and think. I simply wasn't aware that time was passing so quickly. But before I knew it, the England squad for the first Test against the Australians had been announced. And I wasn't in it. I rang Sebastian Welland-Flanders to ask him if he could find out if there had been a mistake. But nobody from the TCCB ever called me. Nobody ever even called Welland-Flanders.

Things turn around very quickly in professional sport. At the beginning of the season I was full of optimism. The Wessex ticket sales drive had apparently gone very well: so much so that the club's immediate financial future was now assured. People wanted to see a Wessex player who'd proved himself at Test match level; attendance records were broken as people flocked to Canberra Park to watch me play. It felt as though I was about to embark on an exciting new phase of my career. But the announcement of that squad for the Old Trafford Test just killed my optimism stone dead.

That series is now largely remembered for Shane Warne's *ball of the century*, but for me it was all about the fickle nature of England's selection policies. If you look at that delivery on YouTube, you've got to ask questions about Gatting's stance. He's showing all three pegs to the bowler. I'm not saying that the ball itself wasn't any good, but if Gatt had just covered his stumps, it would have simply hit his pad and gone down in the scorebook as a dot. If he'd set himself up a bit better, it's just possible that the media would have then put England's selection policy under the microscope, rather than writing about that one single delivery for the next twenty years.

As the summer wore on, I was finding it increasingly difficult to motivate myself for county games. I'd played on the biggest stage in world cricket, and now I found myself turning out in front of a few hundred people on a windswept Wednesday in Hove. As a professional, of course, you should be able to perform to the maximum of your ability regardless of the match context. But it's not that simple. Even Viv Richards couldn't always replicate his international form for his county. The truth is that some us are just somehow wired to perform better when it really matters; we belong on the big stage.

While Wessex might have been having a good season financially, on the field we were struggling. Herb was, by now, very much into the twilight of his career. It was pretty obvious to everyone that this would be his last year at the club. I'm not sure that he'd have admitted it to himself, but he'd probably gone on too long already. He'd lost his zip; he was going for too many runs and he wasn't taking any wickets. It was sad to watch.

I'd swear that you could hear him rattling around the field like a student in rag week, such was the collection of bits of metal that he was carrying around to prise lumps out of the ball. Where previously his mastery of the seam bowler's dark arts had been subtle and skilful, now it was just plain crude. While Herb never got directly accused of ball tampering – usually everyone would agree that the thing had just hit something solid on a trip over the boundary – it was probably only his long-standing reputation that earned him some leniency from the officials.

Marcus Tomkins, the young keeper represented by Dougie, got a decent run in the side that year. Despite being a fitness fanatic, Laurie Kelly could do nothing about the lower back problems that he'd increasingly been suffering from. I'm surprised that his lower vertebrae hadn't already been reduced to dust, but Kelly was still able to turn out for a few of our one-day games. Tomkins may have even been the better keeper, but his appearances served as a constant reminder that the team I had played with for all those years was in the process of breaking up. Laurie Kelly had his critics – and I'm not sure that his outspoken attitudes would go down very well in the politically correct, public relations friendly world of cricket today – but he'd been behind the stumps for almost all of my professional career. It never occurred to me that I could ever miss him. But I did.

Andy Farrow missed him even more. Like Herb, Andy only had a year left on his contract, and it was now a few seasons since he'd topped the Wessex averages. By 1993, Steve Braithwaite had become the most important batsman at the club. Reputation lasts longer than both form and ability, so it usually takes a little while for you to notice that a player has passed his peak. For years, if ever we lost wickets at the top of the order, the sight of Andy walking out to the middle would give us confidence. We just didn't realise it at first, but by 1993 it was far more likely to be Steve, Ronnie or Bridges himself who scored the runs.

Bridges was now all over the media. He wrote "An Expert's View", a weekly column in the *Echo* about the Ashes that summer, and when we weren't playing he'd do radio commentary. Maybe he was all talked out, because at least he stopped giving me ball-by-ball instructions on the pitch.

Increasingly it was Mike who was holding things together: he'd become the club's most consistent wicket taker, he was scoring useful lower-order runs and he'd taken a particular interest in mentoring younger players from the development programme. It was clear to all of us that a number of those junior players would – ready or not – be making the step-up to the first team the following season. He didn't seem to be having much *fun* like the Mike of old, but I got the sense that he was somehow enjoying the challenge.

"Well, in case you haven't noticed, Ledge, we're up shit creek," he explained to me when I asked him about his new-found professionalism. "Bridges seems more interested in writing about it than doing anything about it, so I'm just trying to muck in where I can."

****

One Friday that summer I got home from a game in Southampton. I was hoping that Bethan would be in, so that we could go out for a meal and talk about everything that had been going on. I hadn't seen too much of her since she'd got the head of department job at Casterbridge Secondary. Even before she'd officially started there seemed to be so many more things that she was expected to get involved with: there were more meetings with the headmaster, more meetings with other teachers, more meetings with parents, more meetings with local sports clubs and so on. We'd didn't see that much of each other during the cricket season, but now it didn't look as though we were going to see too much of each other during the rest of the year either.

She was at home when I got in that night. But so was Leslie. The floor was covered with essays and I had to shift a pile of travel brochures off the sofa to find somewhere to sit.

"So Leslie, you're doing your marking over here now?" I asked.

"Yeah, it's my fourth year's final piece of work this term. *Much Ado About Nothing*," Leslie answered.

"Well, there's quite a lot of it across my living room."

"Mmmmm, sorry about that," she replied, "but we're going to be watching *Howard's End* later on video."

I considered making a knob gag, but then thought better of it. I might have got a laugh out of Bethan if Leslie hadn't been there.

Instead I just said, "Great." That meant more period drama. These days I can just about sit through a period drama on the television without falling asleep. But it's something that you have to train yourself to do, like eating sprouts or filling in a tax return. I still don't really understand the appeal of watching a bunch of people sitting with their knees unnaturally close together, drinking tea and getting easily offended by each other.

"You know that Leslie doesn't have a television, Pete." Bethan was sticking up for her mate.

"Well it seems to me that she does," I replied, pointing at the set in the corner of our living room. "That one."

Leslie could tell that I wasn't best impressed, so I think she felt that she had to make some conversation. It's the only time that I can ever remember talking about cricket with her.

"I hear you did really well for England earlier this year." When Leslie said this I wasn't sure if it was simply a statement of fact or a question.

"Erm . . . yes. I spent all of the last day at the crease to earn a draw."

"So, you didn't win?" Leslie sounded a little confused.

"No, the Kiwis had batted us out of the game. By the final day we were only playing for the draw."

"Oh." Leslie sounded both confused and disappointed. "Did you have a replay then?"

"No, it doesn't work like that. It's Test match cricket."

"Actually, I don't know that much about cricket," Leslie offered. "The only thing I know is in *Northanger Abbey*."

"Where?" I asked. I was assuming it must be a club in the Lancashire leagues.

"'She was fond of all boy's plays, and greatly preferred cricket not merely to dolls, but to the more heroic enjoyments of infancy, nursing a dormouse, feeding a canary-bird, or watering a rose-bush'," Leslie recited.

"Eh?"

"You know what?" Leslie sounded very pleased with herself. "I can't usually quote chunks of texts, but it was on the syllabus this year. It just shows how Austen was prepared to have her heroines challenge traditional gender stereotypes."

Maybe I should have felt a little embarrassed that I hadn't recognised the title of a famous book, but mainly I was annoyed that even when we were supposed to be talking about cricket it still all came back to period drama.

"*That's* what you know about cricket?" I asked.

"There isn't some law that says everyone's got to be interested in it, Pete."

Bethan was playing the role of peacemaker.

I started on a brief speech. "But it's part of our history, it's part of our culture. Cricket is . . ." But then, looking at Leslie, I realised it was hopeless. "So, you two, where are you going on holiday this year?"

****

In August Bethan and Leslie travelled to Italy: they spent a couple of weeks walking around the lakes and then moved on to Florence. Back in England our ever-changing Test side lost the Ashes with two games still to play. England appeared to be operating some sort of revolving-door selection strategy, which even included the captaincy. At times it felt as though I was the only eligible professional not to have been given a call-up. However, at Wessex our season gradually began to improve. We put together a short winning run in the Championship, which at one point briefly got us into the top half of the table. All things considered, finishing twelfth at the end of the season wasn't too bad a result at all.

Unfortunately, my new career as the face of World of Furniture Land ended as suddenly as it had begun that August. I was arriving back from Northampton with Ronnie, fully expecting to be shooting a kitchen commercial that night, when I saw Dougie's car parked up outside our place in Durnover Green. At the time he was driving a bright orange Toyota MR2. His relationship with Camara had fallen apart, so he'd no doubt decided that he needed some sexy wheels. I said goodbye to Ronnie as he hauled his coffin from my car over to his own, and then I went and rapped on Dougie's window. He was dozing in the driving seat.

"Jesus. Shit. Fucking hell, Pete," he said, waking irritably. "And when the fuck are you going to get a fucking mobile phone? I've been sat here for more than an hour."

"Yeah sure, I'll get a phone just to make your life a little bit easier," I told him as he climbed out of the Toyota. "Bethan thinks that they're really expensive and that I don't need one." To be fair to Bethan, back in 1993 most people thought like that. But back in 1993 people also used to spend a lot more time sitting around waiting for other people to show up somewhere or other. Dougie followed me inside the house.

"Look, there's been some sort of misunderstanding with the guys at World of Furniture Land," he began.

"What, a mix-up on dates?" I asked. I was actually thinking it was fine by me because I could use an evening off. I'd bowled for most of the morning session that day, and in truth I hadn't really been looking forward to spending half the night working.

"No. Not that sort of misunderstanding," Dougie corrected me. "Look, as of today I'm no longer doing any work for World of Furniture Land . . ."

"Shit!" I exclaimed.

"And as of this evening, neither are you."

"Fuck." I really hadn't seen this coming. "Isn't the campaign working? I thought they were pleased with how it's going."

"No it's not that. Actually, it's the best fucking campaign they've ever had." Dougie sounded bitter. "But the fuckers over there would rather bite their fucking noses off to spite their own stupid fucking faces."

"Dougie, I don't follow."

"What it is Pete, is this . . ." He paused for a moment. "They're saying that I didn't tell them that I represented you, which is total fucking bollocks, of course. So by their reckoning, they're paying me twice: once for my consultancy work and then again as your agent."

"But you told them about that up front, didn't you?"

"Of course I fucking did," confirmed Dougie. "But it's only now that they've decided it's a problem."

"So where do we stand with the money?" I thought I might as well ask him, even though this didn't seem like a great moment to do so. I was owed a sizeable sum of cash for the work I'd already done, but I was yet to actually see any of it.

"Oh, don't worry about that. I'd already authorised the payment to an offshore account, so everything we're owed up until the end of last month is sorted. I'll get you your money soon enough."

"Well, that's not the end of the world then, is it?" The money I'd already earned was several times what I could expect to see from Wessex in a season. Sure, it was disappointing that it hadn't lasted longer, but all in all it hadn't exactly been a disaster.

"But they're questioning my fucking integrity, Pete. And in my business all I have is my reputation. And those fuckers are trying to fucking trash it."

****

Like Dougie, I was having my own career troubles. I was wondering if county cricket was still enough for me. Within the space of a few weeks I'd experienced the elation of being finally recognised as an international player and the despair that came with the realisation that I wasn't going to play for England again. I guess you're always happy with what you've got, be it a bike, a car, a house or a girl-friend, until you try something better. And when I played for England, I tried something better. Perhaps if I'd come unstuck at that level, then I could have happily accepted that I belonged playing the county game. But that's not what happened; I didn't just do well, I excelled. Wessex Cricket Club hadn't changed that year, but I had. Finally, I was able to at least consider the idea that there could be life after cricket. And as soon as I began thinking like that it also occurred to me that I didn't want to hang on until the bitter end like David Collister or Herb.

And then one evening, when Bethan was still away with Leslie, the phone rang, setting in train a course of events that would change my life forever.

"Pete, it's Danny. I'm not going to beat around the bush. I'm in the shit and I need your help."

I hadn't seen much of Danny that summer. He'd been busy. Angela had given birth to their first child, Dylan, the previous year and by all accounts he was proving quite a handful. On top of that, one of the smaller local estate agents in Casterbridge had approached Danny to find out if he was interested in buying the business. Lyall's was a fairly small operation specialising in properties at the lower end of the market. Actually it didn't specialise as such, rather it just wasn't the sort of place that owners of the town's bigger properties would even consider when it came to selling. The office wasn't in a great location and it looked a bit shabby. Nonetheless it had a reasonable turnover.

Danny had wrestled with the pros and cons of buying the business. The Port Bredy office was going well, but the housing market was far from flying in 1993, so he was still carrying significant amounts of debt. Davison's was able to compete for a pretty broad range of business, right up to the premium segment, so Lyall's wasn't a great fit with his existing business. But John Lyall was now in his mid-sixties and desperate to retire, so the asking price was very reasonable. Danny, with one eye on the future, wanted a foothold in Casterbridge. If he could just manage the cash flow over the next couple of years he'd be well placed for the future. Danny and Angela eventually decided to go for it on the basis that only a perfect storm of unlikely events could get them into any real trouble.

The perfect storm of events which got Danny and Angela into real trouble included the discovery of dry rot in their house, the failure of their central-heating system, the engine seizure in Danny's mid-eighties Granada and the collapse of two housing chains, in which Davison's lost three commissions. Danny had already raised every single penny that he could from the banks and the building societies, he was using his credit card to buy food, and he had no means of paying his staff at the end of the month. He was set to lose everything. And if that wasn't enough, they'd just found out that Angela was expecting their second child.

"How much do you need?" I asked.

He replied with a large number. Most of our savings were held in joint accounts that Bethan looked after. I thought to myself that his timing was terrible, what with her being away in Italy.

"Listen Danny, I want to help but I'm going to need to speak to Dougie first." I then explained to him that I was yet to see any of the money from my work for World of Furniture Land and that I didn't know how long it would take to get at it.

"I think I've got perhaps a week, Pete," Danny said. "I hate to have to ask this of you, but I really don't know who else I can turn to."

I managed to get hold of Dougie later that night. He was spending his evenings cruising around Budmouth harbourside in the MR2, hoping to impress someone and get lucky. He didn't sound as though he'd cheered up much since we'd last spoken, but he agreed to come around to my place the following evening to meet Danny.

I hadn't mentioned to Danny that Dougie would be joining us. I don't know if that was somehow intentional on my part or whether I'd simply forgotten to tell him. I heard Danny ring the doorbell and I went to let him in.

"What the fuck is *he* doing here?" Danny said this under his breath, pointing to the unmistakable Toyota that was parked across the road from the house.

Great start, I thought to myself. But I said to Danny, "Well, *he* is the one with the money right now."

"I could have lived without you bringing Dougie into all of this."

Danny followed me through to the kitchen, where Dougie was sat at the table.

"Sol with lime?" I offered Danny.

"No thanks, I'm fine. Hello Dougie." Danny was at least making an effort to sound a little less hostile.

I wasn't quite sure how to begin the discussion. I knew how much money Danny wanted. And I knew that, on paper at least, I could more than cover the amount. But what I didn't know was how long it would take Dougie to access it, what with it being in a Guernsey bank account.

"So, where to begin?" I started. "Danny, can you just tell Dougie how much money you need, and by when?"

"Sure. Well I need, all told, twenty thousand. And I need it by the 25th. Staff wages, our mortgage and the rental on the offices are all due at pretty much the same time."

I winced. I'd never lived like this; juggling all these outgoings to such fine margins.

"The businesses are in good shape," Danny continued. "I've got a decent portfolio of stock in both Port Bredy and here in Casterbridge, and I've got seven properties all told under offer. So, I've drawn up a repayment plan. Basically, I'm asking for a three-month payment holiday, and then I'd repay you Pete, in twenty monthly instalments."

This sounded reasonable to me. I didn't have any immediate need for the cash, and if I wanted to start another renovation project, I could still draw on the remainder of the World of Furniture Land funds or the balance in our joint account. I was maybe just a little annoyed that Danny hadn't said anything about interest. It had seemed fair enough that I'd paid Frank interest when we'd borrowed money from him, so I thought it was reasonable that I should earn some when I lent money in turn.

"Regarding interest," Danny continued, quickly putting my mind at rest. "At the moment variable-rate mortgages are coming in at around the 7 per cent mark, so I've worked on the basis of paying you 8 per cent. I've gone for twenty equal payments on the schedule for the sake of simplicity."

Danny handed me the sheet of paper. It didn't contain any surprises. It made sense to me.

"Can I see that?" asked Dougie.

"So," I said, looking at Dougie. "How soon can we get the money to Danny?"

"Well, let's hold our horses for a moment, shall we?" Dougie paused for a moment to ensure that he had our attention. "And maybe we should all stop and consider whether this is a fair deal for Pete?"

"Yes, it's a fair deal," Danny hissed at Dougie. "But even if it isn't, it's his money we're talking about, not yours. So I don't really see what it's got to do with you. The only question is . . ."

"I'll tell you what it's got to do with me, Danny," Dougie butted in. "What it's got to do with me is that I've looked after Pete all of his working life. And Pete hasn't done too badly out of that arrangement at all, as you can see." Dougie made a brief gesture to draw our attention to the house we were sat in.

"Listen mate," Danny interjected. "Pete's done very well. That's great. And well done you for helping him get there." If that was supposed be a compliment, it didn't sound much like one. "But I'm here because he's my brother. This is a family matter, and as far as I see it, we're only asking you how long it's going to take to actually get hold of Pete's funds."

"Of course he's your brother." Dougie sounded calm and composed. "But families fall out over money all the time. Obviously Pete wants to help you, but you're in danger of treating him like a mug."

"How the . . ." Danny stopped himself and started again, making a deliberate effort to keep calm. "How on earth am I treating Pete like a mug?"

"Well, you're asking Pete for money because you've run out of other options. The bank won't lend to you for a reason. And then you have the nerve to try and look like the big guy, by offering Pete a point over the standard mortgage rate."

"Fuck's sake, pal." Danny's patience snapped. "Can you get the sodding money here or can't you?"

I decided to take the heat out of the situation. "Hey guys, calm down," I barked to get their attention. "Now Dougie, I don't understand. Why do you think Danny is treating me like a mug?"

"Well, this is just about the riskiest loan in business that you could possibly make."

"Oh Jesus, here we go," snarled Danny.

"If it all goes belly up, the building society gets the house. The bank is near the front in the queue of creditors. But Pete, if you lend Danny money, you'll be right at the back of that queue."

"Of course I'm going to pay him back, he's my brother." Danny was trying to be calm.

"Of course you *want* to pay him back, but let's face it, the real issue is whether you *can* pay him back. You're not being honest with Pete about the risks, and that's why you're treating him like a mug."

"Pete," Danny said to me, "I'm not trying to treat you like a mug."

"Listen." Dougie was pointing at me. "The business is under-capitalised." That was the first time I'd heard the expression. "You lend Danny this money and maybe he survives until Christmas, or maybe he doesn't. What you have to understand Pete is that this isn't a loan, it's a punt."

"Pete," Danny interrupted. "The underlying business is healthy."

"Underlying business?" Dougie asked sarcastically. "If you don't get this cash there is no business. As I said, it's a punt."

"Look," Danny said, "the situation I'm in is unprecedented, it's unique; all these things happening to me at the same time. Nobody could have predicted this."

"And nobody can predict what will go wrong next time." Dougie looked at me as he said this.

Danny got up to leave. "I didn't want to have to come here, Pete. I've got a child, I've got another one on the way and I'm about to lose my house and my business. And he" – Danny glanced at Dougie – "just takes the opportunity to treat me like a piece of shit."

"I want to help Danny," I said to Dougie.

"Do you want to *really* help him?" asked Dougie.

"Yes," I replied. Danny was still standing behind his chair at the table.

"Well, here's what I think is a sensible plan," Dougie began.

When he finished, Danny said, "You have got to be out of your fucking mind. No fucking way. You total fucking cunt Barrett, fuck you." And with that he walked out and slammed the door.

****

Later that month I got home from a game at Canberra Park to find that Bethan was back. There were a couple of decent-looking bottles of Chianti on the kitchen table.

We hugged and then I took a step back and asked, "Noticed anything different about me?"

"No," she replied, after staring at me for a couple of moments with a quizzical look on her face. "Should I?"

"I'm an estate agent!" I announced.

"Really? I thought that you were a cricket player," she replied.

"I am. Still a cricket player, that is," I confirmed.

"Well perhaps you'd like to explain to me what you're going on about. And perhaps you'd like to do so over one of these?" Bethan nodded towards the Chianti bottles.

I thought that Dougie had made some very good points on the night we discussed the loan; points I wouldn't have thought of myself at the time. Basically he was saying that Danny was over-extended, and that even the slightest loss of, or delay to, his commissions could push him back into bankruptcy. If I lent Danny the twenty grand there was still no guarantee that the business would survive because he still had no cash reserves or any access to further credit. So Dougie suggested to Danny that I actually put thirty grand into the business. With a healthy balance sheet, Danny wouldn't have to put all of his energy into day-to-day survival, and he'd actually have the time to think about growth.

However, if I was going to put such a large figure into the business, Dougie argued that I should rightly be rewarded properly. It was, after all, a considerable sum of money that I'd be investing. He thought that a fair figure was 51 per cent of the business. Danny pointed out that thirty grand was a fraction of the sum that he'd paid for Davison's and Lyall's. And he pointed out that Dougie was *fucking well taking the piss.*

Dougie's argument was that the business was as good as bust, so that whatever Danny had previously invested in it was irrelevant. He also pointed out that a hundred per cent of his business without my investment was worth, in his expression, *the square root of fuck-all.* Dougie went on to say that, in the long term, he'd love to be involved in the business in a consultancy capacity. And we could talk about how that might work after the deal had been completed.

Danny called me up the following night and we had another difficult conversation. I said to him, "Danny, can you tell me that Dougie is wrong and that I'd be making you a risk-free loan?"

Danny replied, "You know I can't do that. Look, I'm asking you for a favour, that's all."

He was asking me for a twenty-grand favour. That might not seem like a huge amount today, but back then it sounded like a fair bit of cash to me. I told him that I'd think about it overnight. To be honest I just didn't know what to do. It seemed to me that Dougie had made all the better arguments, but of course at the end of the day Danny was my brother.

In the event I didn't need to make a decision. Danny and Angela talked about it some more and she persuaded him that it was better to own just under half of a well-capitalised business than all of a bankrupt one. Later that day Dougie transferred the funds into my account and Danny and me met at Riley and Sharpe to make the whole thing legal.

"Blimey," Bethan said when I'd got to the end of the story. "You drove a bloody hard bargain there, didn't you?"

"In all honesty Bethan, I don't know what was fair," I replied. "Dougie initially reckoned that I should be looking at 70 per cent. Obviously Danny didn't want to give up any of the business at all."

"I think if I'd been here I'd have said to just lend Danny the money. He's worked so hard to try and make a success of it."

"Well you weren't here, were you?" I said this with some irritation. "You were swanning around Europe somewhere with your girlfriend."

"My what?" said Bethan with a start.

"Your girlfriend," I replied.

"Why are you calling her that?" asked Bethan suspiciously.

"Because she's a *girl*. Because she's your *friend*." It surely wasn't that hard to understand.

"Oh, right. I see," said Bethan, scanning my face for any deeper meaning. I had no idea what she was hoping to find.

"Listen," I said in as conciliatory a tone as I could muster. I really didn't want to start a fight. "You were away with *Leslie* and I had to make a decision on my own. So that's what I did. But now you're here, you tell me I got it wrong."

"Look, sorry," said Bethan. "I was only saying I might have seen it differently, that's all. But as you rightly say, I wasn't here. Anyway," she said more brightly, "what do you make of this wine? Delicious isn't it?"

****

With a reasonably strong finish to the season, most of us at Wessex could look back on the year with some level of satisfaction. Our collection of ageing professionals and understudies from the development programme hadn't actually done too badly at all. I was named player of the season for the second time in my career. I think that there were other players that may have made it a close-run thing: Steve Braithwaite with his runs, for example, or Mike with his all-round contribution to the team. Nonetheless, it was good to have my efforts recognised, even if my end-of-season averages didn't read quite as well as some of my stats from previous years. About half of the team, myself included, were out of contract at the end of the summer, so a number of us would be waiting anxiously on news from the club. What very slight concerns I might have had about my own contract disappeared when I was named man of the season: the club was hardly likely to let me go.

We had a quiet evening at the Black Horse that year. Most of us knew that Herb and Andy were unlikely to be offered new contracts, but at the time there hadn't been any word from the club. So we couldn't make it a big farewell party, but neither could we really talk about looking forward to the next summer. Justin Bridges said a few words and congratulated various players for their contribution over the course of the season. Mike also said a few words about some of the younger players at the club, picking out some of their performances to talk about. He went on to say that with these players around, the future for Wessex CC looked really promising. But despite Mike's best efforts, it wasn't a particularly uplifting or memorable occasion. In fact, at one point there was so little conversation that Ronnie got out a pile of photographs of his children's school sports day. He'd won the parents' egg-and-spoon race by some distance apparently.

I took a call from Rachel towards the end of September that year, and she asked me if I could come over to Canberra Park for a meeting with Welland-Flanders and Justin Bridges. By that time I was already getting quite involved in Lyall's, so I asked her if it was urgent and whether we couldn't put it off until the New Year. She phoned me back to say that was fine, and that she'd be in touch to make an appointment nearer the time. Later that autumn I heard from Mike that Herb and Andy had, as expected, been let go. It certainly wasn't a surprise, and from a purely cricketing point of view, it was the right thing for the club to do. But they had been at Wessex throughout my entire professional career; the pair of them seemed like part of the furniture at Canberra Park. It was hard for me to imagine the team without them. It was also hard to imagine what both of them might do outside cricket. I knew that those educated players like Mike and Justin Bridges would do just fine after they retired from the game, but with Herb and Andy I couldn't be so sure.

By Christmas of that year I was beginning to wonder if it might be time for me to hang my boots up as well. I'd spent the previous three months shadowing Colin, who ran the Lyall's office. I absolutely loved it. I got as big a kick out of us winning an instruction or seeing a sale go through as I did from just about anything I'd ever done on a cricket pitch. That November, we sold a three-bed ex-council house. It was the first property that I'd seen all the way through the process: I was there for the valuation; I was there when the buyer viewed it and I was there when the sale finally went through. Very quickly I realised that this was what I wanted to do with the rest of my life. I told Danny that I was considering retiring from the game to focus on the business, and initially he tried to talk me out of it.

"Listen Pete," he said to me. "You can get involved in the business any time you like, but surely you don't want to walk away from cricket just yet. Very few people get the opportunity to play professional sport; you're easily good for another two or three years in the game. You're too young to quit just yet."

I understood where he was coming from. But I wasn't sure that I wanted to be the old pro in a young team. Plus I found the business exciting: you talked to people, you made stuff happen and if you did it well, then you saw the money come in. Frankly, nobody really cared if Wessex finished twelfth, fourteenth or sixteenth in the Championship. But if Colin and me went out and didn't win an instruction, we really did care. We'd talk about what had gone wrong and what we'd do differently next time. I loved it. I felt that what I was doing actually mattered. So, by the time Rachel called in February to schedule an appointment with Sebastian Welland-Flanders I'd already made up my mind. I was going to work in the estate agency full time.

Walking away from the game when I did was probably one of the best deci-sions that I ever made. I went out at the top, at the peak of my powers. Not many players can say that. And in the years that followed we built a highly successful business. Of course, it wasn't always plain sailing. Danny and me had a number of arguments over the years. Danny has always been a great estate agent, but he does have a tendency to get too focused on the day-to-day running of the business; sometimes he lacks that bigger vision you need to take it to the next level. For example, over the years he never really understood the value that Dougie was able to offer. I'd insisted, right from our early days, that we retain Dougie as a permanent consultant to the business. I thought Dougie was invaluable whenever Danny and me got bogged down over an issue.

"We're only paying him because he's your mate, Pete," Danny said to me at one of our Monday morning meetings. "We could be spending that money on marketing."

"Danny, he doesn't need to be in the office all the time to come up with good ideas," I replied.

"*All the time?*" Danny shouted at me. "He's NEVER in the bloody office."

"The re-branding project was Dougie's idea," I reminded Danny.

"No it was not, Pete." Danny could get very heated in these meetings. "I'd always known that we needed to re-brand the offices, it was just an issue of cost and timing. Unfortunately, from bitter personal experience, I know what it feels like to screw up your cash flow."

It seemed to me that whenever Dougie came up with a good idea, Danny would claim that he'd had it first. During my first year in the business we were still operating as Davison's in Port Bredy and Lyall's in Casterbridge. Dougie suggested that we should re-brand both offices so that we just had one busi-ness name. It would be especially important, he argued, if we were looking to expand the business to a number of branches across the region. When Danny finally agreed that the timing was right in early 1996, I didn't realise that the process of re-branding itself would lead to so much further friction between us.

We argued about the name for some weeks before eventually agreeing on Legend Estate Services. However, it was when I came up with the idea for our logo – the top of a set of stumps with the bails jumping clear in the centre to form a triangular roofline – that the real arguments began.

"We're in the business of selling and letting our clients' property, not cel-ebrating your cricket career." Danny wasn't happy.

"But I like it. I think it's good." I wasn't afraid to push my point.

"Of course you like it. You like it because it's all about *you*. Peter Legend the cricket player. You're just saying: *look at me – I played for England.*

Our clients don't care Pete, they really don't."

"Look," I said. "It's not my fault that you're jealous. It's stopping you from seeing a good idea."

"I am not jealous, Pete. You played one bloody Test match and blocked out a knackered, disinterested mediocre attack for a day. Big fucking deal. And that's something worth bloody celebrating, is it?" When Danny was in the wrong sometimes he could just lash out.

"I'm sorry you didn't have the bottle to back up your talent Danny, I really am." I didn't want to have to bring this up, but I thought that he was forcing me into it. "But we can't walk away from a good idea just because it hurts your feelings."

"Fuck off Pete, just fuck off." Danny had now completely lost it. "It's not about my *feelings*, it's about the fact that it's an appalling idea. Our logo shouldn't look like it's a printing error on some Lord's merchandising."

It was a shame that Danny wouldn't budge on this issue, because I had no option but to remind him that he was only a minority shareholder in the business. Today, the *broken stumps roofline*, as I call it, is a distinctive sight on our office exteriors, our sale boards, our website and our literature. It's also a great way to start up a conversation with a prospective client; it gives us an opportunity to tell them something about our story. Estate agency is, after all, a people business.

Despite these occasional disagreements, we steadily built up our network of offices over the years. When the lease expired on our original Casterbridge office we moved to a larger, better located site, near our key competitors in the high street. In 1999 we first opened in Budmouth; and today it's our busiest office. By then we'd also opened branches in Emminster and Sherton Abbas. Legend Estate Services is now recognised as a major player in the Wessex residential property market, even winning the Wessex Sound Regional Business of the Year award in 2006, the only estate agency ever to have done so.

Back when I was playing cricket I didn't realise that I had what it takes to be commercially successful. That said, I know my own limitations: I need good people around me who are able to concentrate on the detail. But what I bring to the business is a passion for property, great people skills and, most importantly of all, a will to win. So if you're a Wessex homeowner looking to sell or let your property, at Legend Estate Services we will work damned hard to gain your instruction and get the best possible price for you. That's just what we do. My name is above the door and I am immensely proud of that fact.

It looked like a wedding cake,
rather than a traditional church
with a classic steeple.

13. THE PORT BREDY CHURCH REUNION

One afternoon in late March 2011 I was sat at my desk in the Legend Estate Services head office, above our Budmouth branch. My phone rang. It was Valerie the receptionist, calling up from the ground floor.

"Hi Peter, I've got a David Collister on the line," Valerie announced. "He says that it's a personal call."

"Blimey, there's a name I haven't heard for some time. Can you put him through, Val? Thanks."

"David, how on earth are you?"

"I'm fine Peter, I'm fine."

"Wow. I drove past Litton Bredy the other day, and I was remembering all those stories you used to tell about Herb."

"I can't believe you still remember any of them," David replied. "Anyway, look, actually the reason I'm calling is about Herb."

"Is he OK?"

"Herb's fine," David started. "But his wife died yesterday."

"Oh." I didn't know what to say. "That's sad news."

"Yes it is. But in some ways it's a relief; she's been ill for some time now." I felt a pang of guilt that I hadn't kept in touch with Herb. "Look, the funeral is next Tuesday in Port Bredy. Are you able to come?"

"Of course," I replied.

"It's obviously been very tough on Herb, so I've been ringing around the old team to see who can make it," David explained. "Mike and Justin are in the country at the moment so they'll be coming, along with any others I can rustle up."

I jotted down the details in my diary and entered David's number into my iPhone. After I'd hung up I found that I couldn't really concentrate, so I grabbed my jacket and walked down to the Costa Coffee to get myself a medium skinny cappuccino. Then I walked through to the beach front and just stared out to sea. In all honesty, the last few years had been difficult and, for whatever reason, the news about Herb's wife had suddenly made *me* feel lonely. As I leant against the railing, staring out at the grey sea beneath a grey sky, I felt a tear roll down my cheek. I really needed to get a grip.

"This is ridiculous," I thought to myself. "You've never even met Herb's wife. Look, you're going to go along and support Herb. Plus it'll be good to see some of the old guys again. And more importantly, Ledge, you've got to pull yourself together and sell some bloody houses. Come on!"

****

It was four or five months since Bethan had moved out of Durnover Green. At the time it felt very sudden, but things hadn't been great between us for a while. Something changed when Philippa Docherty first showed up a few years earlier. After I finished my playing career Bethan and Leslie had continued to go on trips together during the school holidays. It suited me just fine if they'd done something like walked the length of Hadrian's Wall or gone and climbed Mount Kilimanjaro, because then there was a better chance that Bethan would be knackered and we could then both just go and chill out together somewhere warm beside a pool.

Leslie had been promoted to head of English at the school. She certainly didn't let that success go to her wardrobe in any way. She continued to wear massive cheap-looking glasses and what I presume were second-hand jumpers from charity shops. I think she must have eventually realised that her old donkey jacket was making her look like a tramp, but as luck would have it, she found something equally unfashionable from North Face as a replacement. She still looked as though she was cutting her own hair. She did, however, buy a lovely period property on the other side of the County Gardens from our first renovation project in Duchy Road. I don't know if she's bought herself a television more recently, but I do know that as late as 2009 she was still using mine as her primary set.

Leslie was keen to make something of the garden at her new place. For the first few months after she moved in she'd regularly invite Bethan over at the weekends to help her with weeding and planting and all that sort of thing. Unfortunately, it turned out that neither of them seemed to be blessed with green fingers, so Leslie auditioned any number of local professional gardeners.

As I understand it, she went through numerous local horticulturists and landscapers until she met Philippa. Philippa was, according to Leslie, the first person to really understand what she was looking for. She was also the first of Leslie's gardeners to come round to our place in Durnover Green. She arrived with Leslie and the box set of *North and South*. (This was the BBC production featuring Richard Armitage, and not the American Civil War drama of the same name starring Patrick Swayzee.) I can't remember the specifics, but a posh girl from the South of England ends up in an industrial town in the north where she falls in love with Armitage, but for one reason and another it takes them several episodes to get it on.

During the first DVD I was struggling and I needed a break. Even a walk as far as the kitchen fridge and back would be better than nothing. "Anyone want a beer?" I asked.

Bethan and Leslie shook their heads, but Philippa got up and said, "Sure. I'll come with you." I think she must have been as bored as I was.

Philippa had lived in and around Casterbridge all of her life. In 2005 she must have been in her mid-twenties. She had various Celtic tattoos on her arms, she wore her dark hair short and messy (but in a way which suggested she'd given it some thought), and in addition to a number of piercings in both ears she also had a nose ring. I thought that she was more handsome than good-looking.

"Well Pete, this is a bit odd isn't it?" she asked.

"I suppose I've got used to it," I replied, grabbing a couple of bottles of Peroni from the fridge. "But, as long as I've known her, Leslie has refused to get her own television."

"Not that," said Philippa. "I meant the three of us being here. It's a bit strange don't you think?"

"I hadn't given it any thought," I answered. It suddenly occurred to me that the pair of them might well have taught Philippa. "Were you in either of Bethan or Leslie's classes?"

"I always skipped sport, always had a sick note. That sounds a bit funny now that I'm outdoors every day doing manual work for a living." Philippa smiled at the memory. "I was in one of Leslie's classes for literature, but I never read the books. So I just kept my head down."

"I tried that approach too. Didn't always work."

"But anyway," Philippa began again. "How long has it been like this?"

I was about to ask her what she meant when Bethan stuck her head around the kitchen door.

"Changed my mind, I *will* have one of those." She took the Peroni out of my hand. "Right you two, are you going to join us for the next episode? Or am I interrupting something?"

It turned out that it was highly unlikely that Bethan could have interrupted anything. But I didn't figure that out for another couple of years. Philippa started joining Bethan and Leslie on their summer trips. I didn't think that was particularly unusual at first; although I did wonder if Philippa wouldn't have had more fun spending time with people of her own age. But then the sort of trips they'd go on began to change. They began swapping their usual trekking and climbing expeditions for long city breaks. I can't remember all of the places that they went throughout that period, but I know that they spent time in Berlin and Barcelona, in addition to visiting Montreal, San Francisco and even Portland, Oregon.

Personally I would have preferred it if they'd crossed the Andes, trekked through the Kalahari Desert or had a crack at scaling K2, because it would have meant that my two weeks at an upmarket beach resort somewhere in the Mediterranean would be all the more enjoyable. But increasingly when Bethan got back from her city trips with Leslie and Philippa she'd be irritable and she'd have energy to burn. So, rather than just lying under an umbrella, listening to music and having a waiter refill my glass from time to time, I'd have to spend days sweating my arse off in the sun following Bethan around the ruins of an aqueduct or something similar.

It turned out that the Portland trip was the last one that the three of them ever made together. I reckoned that they must have had some sort of bust-up out there, because Leslie was around at our place less often after that. The ten days we spent on Malta, just after Bethan got back from that trip, weren't great either. We were staying in the Radisson Blu Resort and Spa. It could have been marvellous: the weather was fantastic and the location was perfect for a relaxing break. However, Bethan spent the entire time forcing me to walk miles in the baking heat to go and see various piles of stones across the island. At one point I remember her saying that we could never talk about anything interesting because I didn't know anything about anything interesting.

"You don't read any books. You've never been to an art gallery. And I think the last time we went to the cinema together was when you bullied me into watching *Saving Private Ryan*. I'm bored Pete, I'm bored!"

The following year, in August 2008, Leslie and Philippa went to Sydney. But Bethan chose to stay at home. It felt like the end of an era. Sometime later that year Bethan and me were eating dinner in silence. This had become a regular occurrence, but it some ways it was preferable to irritable conversation.

"Philippa has moved in with Leslie," she said suddenly.

"Oh, right." That didn't strike me as earth-shattering news. "Well, what's she got, three or four bedrooms? I guess it makes sense if they're both happy about it."

"Pete, they'll just be using the one bedroom."

"Bloody hell," was all I could say. Now it began to make some sense. I couldn't understand why Philippa had been hanging out with the pair of them, but now it was becoming clear. "Here in Casterbridge? Wow!"

"Right here in Casterbridge, Pete. Lesbians, they get everywhere, you know." Bethan was quickly getting back into sarcasm mode.

"Sure, I know that," I said. "But I don't know that I've ever met any."

"Well congratulations are in order. Now you've definitely met at least two."

"Did *you* know? About Leslie being gay I mean?" A lot of things about Leslie were beginning to make more sense to me now.

"Of course I bloody knew," Bethan replied tersely.

"Umm, has she always been gay, or is this kind of a new thing?" I had the sense that whatever I asked it was going to prove a dumb question.

"Yeah it's a new thing, Pete. She just thought she'd try it last week, and it turned out that she liked it." Bethan gave me a withering look as she said this.

"OK, OK," I said, trying to take a little bit of the heat out of the situation. "I was just wondering – that's all."

"Look, she had a couple of boyfriends when she was younger," Bethan explained in a slightly less aggressive tone. "They didn't work out and she began to realise that she was gay."

"And it didn't bother you?" I asked. Again, as soon as I'd said it, I realised that it was yet another dumb question.

"No. Should it have done, Pete? She was my best friend."

"*Was?*" I stressed the word. "Are you no longer friends?"

"It's difficult. Philippa's so young. She's young enough to be my daughter, and we don't really have anything to say to each other. But Leslie adores her, so everything's changed." Bethan said this with some sadness.

I could tell that she was very down about the whole thing. The lesbian thing was weird; I hadn't seen that coming. I just thought that Leslie had appalling dress sense and was difficult to talk to. I tried to imagine if I could have been close friends with someone who I knew was gay – but not actually knowing any homosexuals made this really difficult. I only really knew anything about them at all from the television. I like watching Stephen Fry and Graham Norton, but they're not exactly the sort of people you're likely to meet in the world of professional sport.

Bethan might have been less depressed about it all if she hadn't begun to be disillusioned with work around the same time. For whole chunks of the year she'd spend more time talking about the upcoming Ofsted inspection than about the sports and the kids. It was a shame, because Bethan had loved the job when she first got it, but over the years it seemed to have worn her down.

I can't really offer any excuses for it, but in 2010 I made a bad situation worse. The previous year we'd acquired an independent agency in Shaston, the beautiful market town in north Wessex. I was spending several days a week up there helping to integrate the branch into the rest of our network, familiarising myself with the town and its housing stock, and generally developing the business. Rather than drive back to Casterbridge after a long day, I would often spend either the Wednesday or Thursday night up there so that I was ready and fresh for the next day.

During my time in Shaston I met a lady who conducted a considerable amount of conveyancing work around the area. To my regret, one thing led to another and we found ourselves having drinks in the bar of the Duke's Arms one evening. And from there it was only a flight or two of stairs to my room. Bethan and me were going through a difficult time at home – which I realise doesn't make my actions any more excusable. But I'm not the first man to have shown weakness in the face of temptation, and no doubt I will not be the last. Perhaps Bethan might have been a little more understanding if she had not found out about it in the way that she did. I'd written a short email to the lady in question.

> *Hi there, XXXX*
> *I still can't stop thinking about last Weds.*
> *A very special night. Possibly unbeatable.*
> *But I'm certainly willing to give it a try.*
> *Lounge bar of the Duke's Arms at 8?*
> *Dinner followed by anything you desire.*
> *Love,*
> *Peter*

Unfortunately I'd clicked *reply* to a note from Bethan about picking up some liquid drain cleaner for the shower. I got this reply.

> *Pete,*
> *Bethan here. Remember me? Your wife?*
> *You're a dickhead. And a moron.*
> *I'm moving into Bridestock.*
> *Love,*
> *Bethan*

Frank had sold the caravan park a couple of years earlier, and he and Moira had bought a small town house in the centre of Port Bredy. Now that Frank no longer needed to live close to the business, there was no reason to keep the house in Bridestock. At the time of our email exchange it was on the market through our Port Bredy branch. I'd said to Frank that we'd take it on a sole agency deal for 1 per cent. I reckoned that he'd be looking for a good deal, not charity.

Bethan picked up the keys and told Danny to pull the property off the market. By the time I got back from Shaston, she'd grabbed some of her clothes and had moved out of Durnover Green. She didn't answer my calls or reply to any of my mails or texts. I considered going around to see Frank and Moira to ask them if they could get Bethan to talk to me, but that would have involved telling them about the thing in Shaston. We should have been celebrating our thirtieth anniversary at the time. Mum had sent us a card. It arrived shortly after Bethan had left. I put it out on the kitchen table for a few weeks. It served as a reminder of just how stupid I'd been.

****

Not long after Bethan moved out, Danny sold his stake in Legend Estate Services. Overall, we'd been incredibly successful. Like all business owners, Danny and me had our disagreements over the years. They could be about trivial things, like a small detail on the layout of our homepage; or they could be over big things, such as us not seeing eye to eye on a senior appointment, or whether or not to acquire a new office. It didn't help that Danny's relationship with Dougie had become increasingly fractious over the years. It wasn't professional, it was personal.

"Seriously Pete, I wonder," Danny asked me when we were both at the Budmouth branch one evening. "Where the hell does his money actually come from? I know he fleeces us for a fistful of cash every month, but where does he get the rest of it?"

"You know as well as I do that he's got numerous interests." Frankly I was bored having to go through all this again. "He's still in music, he's representing a number of Wessex players, there's his other consultancy work, and he's also an investor now."

"Frankly Pete, that's got to be bollocks." Any mention of Dougie would get Danny ranting and raving in no time. "He manages a couple of pub bands, four junior players who, between them, haven't got a pot to piss in, and he hasn't had any marketing work since trashing his reputation over that thing with the furniture shop."

"Why don't you spend a little more time thinking about how we can make a success of our business and a little less time worrying about him?" I suggested.

"Please! Spare me the sanctimonious bullshit, Pete." I'd got to admit that Danny did come out with some pretty good stuff during these arguments occasionally.

"He's got that penthouse overlooking Jurassic Beach, he's driving a 911 and he dresses exclusively in Boss. He's living like a millionaire, but he can't be making more than a handful of grand a month."

"Danny, he's helped us grow the business. Dougie's always been there when we've needed him. Can't you see that?"

"We've built this business *in spite* of him, not *because* of him." Danny couldn't be persuaded. "In fact we'd have done it sooner if you hadn't been so quick to shower him with our cash every month."

"Oh, that old chestnut again. I wouldn't pay him if I didn't think he wasn't adding value." It was an important point and I had to set Danny right on it. "And you wouldn't be in business at all if it weren't for my money and Dougie's business nous."

"Un-fucking-believable. Shall I tell you what happened? What actually happened?" Danny was shouting now. "What happened was that I over-extended myself once. Just once. And I got properly burned. It just so happened that you'd fluked your way into some cash and were able to help me out. For that I'm grateful, OK? But that little scrote of a mate of yours . . ." I raised my hand asking Danny to stop, but he continued. "That feral little excuse for a human being saw the opportunity to line his pockets at my expense for the rest of his life."

Meanwhile Dougie had just carried on being Dougie. It was certainly true that his cars had got more expensive and that he'd traded up his home a few times over the years, but he was still involved in the same sorts of businesses. He'd been fortunate that Sebastian Welland-Flanders had retired to a French Mediterranean coastal village to spend his final years yachting, so the ban from Canberra Park was lifted. That had certainly made it easier for him to forge relationships with new players. He was briefly married for a second time in 1999. I didn't go to the ceremony because it was held at very short notice in Las Vegas. As I understand it, he'd signed a prenuptial agreement beforehand, so at least he didn't get wiped out again financially. He'd learned a valuable lesson from his marriage to Belinda.

Things came to a head between Danny and Dougie in September 2010. Dougie had called the pair of us to a meeting to discuss a business venture that he was proposing.

"Of all the costs we face at Legend Estate Services, which do we think represents the worst value for money?" Dougie was sat opposite Danny and me, across our boardroom table. Valerie had set up the room with a selection of tea, coffee, Diet Cokes and two-finger Kit Kats. One of the few benefits of Bethan having moved out was guilt-free snacking. "The worst value for money?" Dougie prompted us again.

"Am I looking at him?" asked Danny.

"I'll ignore that, Danny," said Dougie. "I'll tell you what offers the worst value for money. This does."

Dougie turned up an A4-sized white board with the rightmove.co.uk logo on it.

"No shit, Sherlock," Danny mumbled.

"We spend several hundred quid, per branch, every week of the fucking year with this lot. And every year these fuckers just squeeze us that bit harder, asking for more and more money. And what do we do?" Dougie paused for a moment. "We only go and fucking pay them, that's what we do."

"We pay them, Dougie," Danny said, "because, for better or worse, they are by some margin our most important source of buyers."

"Well, what if I told you that we didn't have to pay them?" Dougie asked. "And what if I told you, we can not only stop paying them, but we can also generate a whole new revenue stream as well?'

"Sounds interesting," I said.

"Well, here's the answer." Dougie turned over a second white board. On it, in a simple black font, was printed: yournexthome.co.uk.

"Never heard of them," said Danny.

"Well that's because the brand hasn't been launched yet," said Dougie with a smile. "What we're going to do is set up a serious alternative to rightmove. Not only are we going to own our own website to attract buyers, but we're going to charge our competitors to use it too."

"Have you any idea how much it's going to cost to start up this website and market it?" Danny asked. "That's going to require a serious injection of cash."

"I'm not a fucking idiot, Danny. I know that." Dougie gathered himself before he went on. "So, here's the plan. You sell a 40 per cent stake in Legend Estate Services to raise the development capital and the three of us become equal partners in yournexthome.co.uk. The only thing I'd ask, as the founder, is that I hold the controlling 1 per cent stake."

"I take it all back, Dougie. You're a funny guy." Danny smiled. Briefly. "But just so I'm clear, me and little brother here," he was pointing at me, "put in a handful of hundred grand, while you register a domain name for about thirty quid. Actually, I'm being harsh, I forgot the price of your two boards from prontaprint." Danny then clapped both of his hands to the top of his head as though he was having a revelation. "I'm being naïve again, aren't I? You went and got Valerie to print those boards, didn't you? So actually I've paid for those myself."

"Yes Danny, I've registered the domain name. But what I'm bringing to the table is the big idea. That's where my value lies. What do you think, Pete?" Dougie was looking at me.

"I love the ambition, Dougie," I replied. "But can you break down the costs involved? I've no idea what level of investment is required to bring a website to market."

"Jesus Christ," exclaimed Danny. "I can't believe we're even having this conversation. This is the final straw, so I'm going to make it really simple for all three of us. This afternoon I'm going to contact our auditors, I'm going to get the company valued, and I'm going to sell my stake. Pete, as you may recall you have first refusal on it. And Dougie, if I ever see you in my life again, it'll be too soon."

And with that he got up and left the room.

I'd spent almost twenty years of my life building the business, so there was no way I was going to let any outsider buy Danny's share of Legend Estate Services. However, the majority of my savings were tied up in joint accounts managed by Bethan, so I had no choice but to go to the bank to raise the necessary finance. Things moved very quickly after Danny's decision to sell, and by the end of February the following year I was the sole owner of the entire business. Although the interest rate on the financing wasn't excessive, it was nonetheless an additional cost that the business had to bear. And after agonising about it for a few days, I told Dougie that I'd have no choice but to dispense with his services as a consultant for the foreseeable future. I'm not going to pretend that he was very happy about it, but at the time I didn't have much choice.

The last funeral I'd attended was Laurie Kelly's. He'd become a postman since retiring from cricket, but had maintained his punishing fitness routine. He'd dropped dead one afternoon while training for a triathlon. Only Andy Farrow and me from the club had attended the service. I remember the vicar saying that not everybody always agreed with Laurie and that some of his views were *challenging*. That was the word he used: *challenging*. Presumably, what he was getting at was that Kelly was an outspoken racist. I remember thinking, "Either say it, or shut the fuck up." Either way, it hardly seemed to matter any longer.

Andy, understandably, took it very badly. Kelly was his best friend in the game and they'd stayed pretty close since retiring. However, Andy didn't share Laurie's enthusiasm for endurance sports. In fact he'd become a barman in the Black Horse at Litton Bredy. And it didn't look as though he'd drunk that much less than he'd served since he'd been working there. He was considerably overweight and his face was red with any number of broken veins. He cut a very sad figure that day. It was hard to imagine him as the close fielder with the lightning reflexes, or as the batsman who could scamper the tightest of singles. That day, Andy certainly looked more like a veteran barman than one of the best cricketers that Wessex has ever produced. As the vicar droned on, I found myself wondering how someone so obsessed by neatness and cleanliness had found himself working in a traditional old boozer. I could only imagine that the Black Horse must have the cleanest glasses in the entire county.

****

It sounds dreadful to say this, but I was actually looking forward to Mrs Brunton's funeral. I was missing Bethan and I was finding work particularly stressful at the time. Every day I was fielding countless calls from offices all around the network about marketing, invoicing, pricing, staffing and so on. Everybody seemed to want something from me, but I didn't have anyone to turn to for support. I'd heard that Danny was spending his time in Hampshire looking for a business to buy, and of course Dougie wouldn't speak to me on a point of principle. The funeral would give me a chance to turn off my phone and get away from work for a few hours. I'd have the opportunity to catch up with some old faces and to offer my condolences to Herb.

There was going to be the church service, followed by the burial on the far side of the town. Then there would be drinks in the Admiral Rodney, back in the centre of Port Bredy. I arrived outside the churchyard in the early afternoon, with half an hour to spare before the service began. The church was up a short steep slope from the road so that it looked out over the surrounding buildings. It was one of those nineteenth-century structures that looked like a wedding cake, rather than a traditional church with a classic steeple. David Collister was already there, waiting at the end of the pathway by the road. I'm not sure that I'd have recognised him if I hadn't been looking out for him. His hair was completely white, and it seemed to be trying to escape from his head in the strong breeze.

"Peter, good to see you," he said as he shook my hand firmly. "This is my friend, Jeremy."

"Hullo," said Jeremy, offering his hand. He was a short, rotund man with a red face, who I would have guessed was around my age. He looked a jovial type, but not exactly in peak physical condition."

"Peter Legend," I said.

"Jeremy used to teach Latin at Sherton Abbas, but he now runs Bad Boy Bacchus in Somerset," explained David.

"Sorry, Bad what?"

"Bad Boy Bacchus," David repeated. "I'd say it's the best independent wine merchant this side of Bristol." I think Jeremy may have blushed a little.

"He doesn't need to say that," Jeremy said in a rather coy manner. "But do you know what? I'd like to think he's right."

"I've had the chance to follow Jeremy all over France since I retired from teaching," David enthused. "Bordeaux, Burgundy, the Loire, the Rhone. It's been fantastic."

"Well we both enjoy a vintage drop or two, don't we Davey?" There was a slightly disturbing twinkle in Jeremy's eye as he said this.

"I didn't know if they'd make it," said Collister, changing the subject. "But it's Alan and Carl."

It was too. Carl had filled out considerably, and, dressed in a dark suit for the funeral, he looked like an ageing security man to the stars. He must have been thinning on top because his head was shaved. Alan was carrying less weight and wearing more hair, yet somehow Carl seemed to have aged better. They were both very tanned. I found out later on that they were now running a sports bar in Spain called the Premiership, just along from Fuengirola. Alan had married for a second time, though once again it hadn't worked out. Nobody asked Carl if he'd had anything to do with the breakdown of the relationship on this occasion. I found myself thinking that perhaps they'd lost a little bit of that Musgrove self-confidence over the years. I couldn't imagine it had been a walk in the park trying to keep a big bar with big overheads running in Spain through the recession. But they were surprisingly good company, and even more surprisingly, they hadn't killed each other.

Tony Sinclair arrived next. His face was weather worn, but he looked well. After a spate of trying various jobs in the early nineties, he'd got a job as a gardener-cum-groundsman on a large estate on the Cornish side of the River Tamar. He planted stuff, chain-sawed other stuff and drove one of those diesel lawnmowers most days. "It's a great job," he said in the Admiral Rodney later that afternoon. "I get outdoors every day come rain or shine and I don't have to worry whether ten other blokes are still standing where I told them to."

Charles Hunter, the new chief executive at Wessex, was a larger-than-life character. He had made his money as a wholesaler of replacement tractor parts; his company is the market leader in Wessex. I don't think that David Collister would have needed to work that hard to persuade him to come to the funeral because he seemed to love talking to all of the retired players. The club hadn't become any more successful on the pitch under his stewardship, but he had by all accounts worked very hard to develop the ground and the facilities. For example, he'd ensured that the club had invested in floodlights for T20 games at Canberra Park. He may have looked like an old traditionalist, but Hunter seemed to be determined to drag the club into the twenty-first century. He couldn't stay long after the service, but we all agreed that it was good to see that he'd come down to pay his respects.

Mike Andrews got out of a silver Mercedes and walked over to join us. An attractive blonde woman was behind the wheel. I'd have guessed that she must have been fifteen years his junior. There were two kids in the back of the car.

"Is that your family?" I asked him. I hadn't seen Mike since 1994, when he'd quit the game and left Budmouth.

"Yep, that's Nat and the kids," Mike confirmed. "We're staying with Nat's parents in Bath for a few days. The kids are going to spend the afternoon down on Jurassic Beach, and then we'll drive back this evening. I expect that I'll be told that I'm stinking of booze, and of course I'll be desperate for a piss by the time we reach Taunton."

Mike had become a lawyer. "I ensure that rich people are rewarded for failure," he explained. "So I also try to keep less fortunate ones alive." Mike earned his money by working as an employment lawyer, mainly for football managers. "It's brilliant: half of them will be fired every two years, and of those, every single one of them will end up in a dispute with their clubs. They are the gift that just keeps giving." With football managers to pay his bills, Mike described how he devoted much of his time to working with an organisation that gives legal aid to prisoners around the world – particularly those who have been held without trial or who are facing the death penalty. He'd met Nat when they were both working through the night trying to win a reprieve for an inmate on Death Row in Texas.

If Mike looked well, then Justin Bridges looked even better. He looked fit and tanned, and there was an easy confidence about him. I want to say that he behaved as though he was a minor celebrity, but that could just be because I knew that he was a presenter on South African television. He'd gone down to Johannesburg one winter to do some schools coaching, and one thing had led to another and he'd ended up, after a stint as a commentator, as the anchor-man on their national cricket coverage.

He made a point of talking to me later in the pub. "Peter, it's a funny thing, but it was only when I re-read *One Summer* – after it had been published that is – that I thought that maybe I'd been too candid. But I'd like to think that I was as harsh on myself as on anyone else in the team. I trust there's no hard feelings."

"No sure, it's fine," I said. We didn't get to talk about it any further because Alan Musgrove then accosted him about something or other. Actually, I had no idea what Bridges was on about.

Sometime later, when I was talking to Mike, I asked him if he knew what *One Summer* was, and why Bridges thought he owed me an apology.

"You haven't read it?" Mike queried.

"No," I replied. "What is it?"

"*One Summer on the South Coast*," Mike said. "Typical sort of limp-wristed, whimsical title for one of those books about under-achievement in county cricket. I remember thinking that some of it was a bit close to the bone."

"You've read it?" I asked.

"Of course." Mike sounded almost surprised at the question. "Actually I didn't come out of it too badly to be honest. I thought most of the stuff he wrote about me was probably fair enough."

"What's it about exactly?" I was curious.

"Specifically, it's about our season in 1991, when we came third," Mike explained. "But really it's the tale of a talented captain who raised a rag-tag bunch of mediocre players to new heights. It's a sort of cricketing version of *The Dirty Dozen*."

"Does he talk about me in it?" I felt that I had to know.

"Yeah, you come up a fair bit," Mike said. "But it's very much Justin's perspective on things. I wouldn't take any of it to heart. After all, it's a long time ago and you've moved on since then, haven't you?

"You mean with my business?"

"Exactly," Mike confirmed.

"But what did he say about me in it?" I sensed that it couldn't be good. Otherwise why would Bridges have just offered me an apology?

"Oh, just stuff." Mike wasn't exactly being very forthcoming. "Look, you should think about writing your own book. You know, born on the wrong side of the tracks in Crapstock or wherever the hell it was."

"Whetstock," I corrected him.

"Whetstock, right. A tale of rags to riches," suggested Mike. "The Dick Whittington of Canberra Park."

"Just because he's on television somewhere doesn't mean that Bridges' opinion is worth any more than mine," I added. "And he didn't even get to play for England."

"Quite. I always got the impression that Justin would have wanted to be a captain at Middlesex, but he wasn't quite up to it," Mike said. "Poor fella couldn't match Brearley for leadership or Strauss with the bat. Anyway, the world's full of books by those gentlemen skippers. You should write your own and do it your way."

Before I knew it people were saying their goodbyes and beginning to drift away. I was meaning to ask Justin Bridges about his book again, but I found out that he'd already left. Apparently he was on a midnight flight out of Heathrow down to Cape Town, so he couldn't hang around. Mike had to leave next. Nat had called him from the car to say that she was waiting outside. He was going to spend another couple of nights in Bath, before going back to their home in Richmond. And shortly after that he was flying out to the Middle East to lobby on behalf of some political prisoners.

"Mike," I asked him just before he left, "what you're doing now, is it *fun*?"

"Fun? I'm not sure. But I do know something. It *matters*. It really does. And maybe that's even better. Listen, Ledge," Mike said as he made to leave, "good luck with your business, and think about telling your story. You never know, you might actually enjoy writing it."

Alan and Carl said their goodbyes a little while afterwards; they had to make their way over to Budmouth for a family meal. I promised to drop by the Premiership if I ever find myself down near Fuengirola.

After all of the effort that David had put in to getting everyone together I thought that he'd stay for most of the evening. But it turned out that Jeremy had a private wine tasting to run later that evening in Frome, so the two of them left shortly after six o'clock. An hour later those of us who were still in the Admiral Rodney had all pulled up our chairs around a single table. Apart from Herb, I didn't know any of the others. I think they must have been Port Bredy locals or members of the church congregation. I offered to buy a round of drinks, but everybody politely declined. I guess they were all in their sixties or seventies and had pretty much had enough for the day. Then Herb thanked everyone for coming and said that he'd got to get home. I'd hardly spoken to him all day, so I asked if I could walk back with him. I wasn't quite sure what I was going to say to him. I hadn't seen him for twenty years.

While we slowly wandered back across the town, the clouds in front of us briefly glowed orange as the evening sun fell away behind them. And just as the colour drained from the sky we turned right, back up the road in front of the silhouette of the church, and on towards Herb's house. Herb told me that he'd gone over to Canberra Park a couple of years earlier to watch a game of T20.

"That's not bloody cricket. I don't know what it is, but it isn't cricket." He seemed quite angry about it. "It's just marketing. There's no soul. But what do they know about cricket, eh? Those that don't play the bloody game?"

Personally, I love T20. I'm not sure I'd have wanted to bowl in it, but I like to see guys smashing sixes all around the park. But more than that I like to see the grounds full. I believe that the county game had to adapt or die, and I liked the way Charles Hunter was going about things at Wessex. Of course, I didn't say any of this to Herb that evening. We'd just buried his wife of forty years and I didn't think that either of us would have wanted to get stuck into a heated debate.

I was shocked when I first saw Herb in the church earlier that afternoon. I'd always thought of him as a wily determined craftsman, someone who was sharp and quick-witted. It obviously wasn't the best of days to judge him after all these years, but the old spark he used to have was gone. You might even have thought he could be a simpleton. He'd always been lithe, but now he was no more than skin and bone: the old suit that he was wearing hung off his body like the sail on a becalmed boat. When I was sat beside him in the Admiral Rodney I noticed that his shirt collar was filthy. I was wondering if he'd be able to look after himself.

We arrived at Herb's cottage. It was a two-up two-down, and just like Oxford Cottage where I'd grown up, you walked straight into the living room from the road. Herb asked me if I'd like a cup of tea, and we went inside. Even after Herb had turned on the light the room still seemed dark. Herb shuffled through into the kitchen at the back of the house. As I waited for him to return, I looked at the various photos that surrounded the front room. Apart from one of the Bruntons on their wedding day, most of the pictures were either shots of Herb bowling or old team photographs. I found one that must have been from the late eighties in which Herb was flanked by Col and me. But then I went back to the wedding photo: it had been taken in front of the church down the road, where the service had been held that afternoon. I looked at the couple with all their energy, vitality and optimism, and wondered how it could all have been reduced to *this*.

I'd been in houses like this before, and the memories came flooding back. The dirt-encrusted windowsills, the lank curtains, the peeling wallpaper, the Bakelite electrical switches on the walls and the smell: that inescapable mixture of cabbage, decomposition and old people. This could have been one of those houses in Whetstock where Danny and me sat in silence while Mum talked to pensioners about articles in *The Watchtower*.

Herb, after some time, emerged from the kitchen with two mugs of tea. I think that the milk was off, but I didn't say anything. I stayed for half an hour or so, and we talked. Or rather Herb talked and I listened. Herb hadn't really worked since retiring from the game. He'd had a couple of brief temporary jobs, but he hadn't been able to hang on to them. He confided to me that he wasn't *good with letters*, and that he'd struggled to find regular employment. It seemed that he'd spent the last twenty years living on benefits and the money his wife had earned as a dinner lady at the local school. Herb had given his whole life to cricket, but it didn't look as though cricket had given him much in return.

I'd been wanting to cry at various moments throughout the day, but I'd kept a grip on myself. I didn't even really know what it was that I wanted to cry about: the death of a woman I'd never even met, Herb's loss and loneliness, or perhaps it was something more selfish: maybe I just wanted to cry about the loss of my own marriage. But when I stepped out of Herb's house and into the dark street outside I couldn't hold it any longer and the tears just came pouring down my face. My abiding memory of the day was watching Herb in the cemetery. He was doing his damnedest to stay in control of himself. One of the women from the church congregation was holding his forearm to offer him support. I could see that every single thing that happened was forcing him to dig ever deeper to find the strength to get through it: the vicar's words, the lowering of the coffin into the ground and the sound of that first splash of dirt as it landed on the wood below. I couldn't bear to watch Herb any longer, and I stared down into the space in front of me. The scattering of soil had briefly left one word still legible on the brass plate. I kept my eyes focused on that single name: Myrtle.

****

Herb works for Legend Estate Services now. If you market your property through our Port Bredy branch it could well be Herb that takes the internal measurements and photos for our website. He also looks after all of our sale boards in the area, and he generally helps out around the branch. It took him a little while to get used to the digital camera and the electronic tape measures we use, but now he can do as good a job as anyone in the company. I told him that I'd only employ him if he allowed me to send a professional team of cleaners to do a thorough job on his house. His pride hasn't yet allowed me to pay someone to paint the exterior of the place – it's still the shabbiest-looking property in his terrace – but maybe one day I'll just send round a decorating team when I know he's out.

I know that I can't replace the life that he once had, but I couldn't bear to think of him wasting away on his own. Some of the guys in the branch have showed him how to use the launderette on the high street, and sometimes when they're passing his house they'll nip in to check that he's got food in the fridge. He's still basically a grumpy bastard, but I think he's a popular member of the team in Port Bredy. I hope he chooses to stay with us for some time.

I'll admit that running Legend Estate Services on my own has been tough: it's not so much a job as a way of life. I've been interviewing candidates for a general management position – someone to take some of the day-to-day responsibilities off my desk – but as yet I haven't found the right person. Regardless, I remain committed to providing property owners with the very best sales and letting service across Wessex.

I haven't spoken to Danny for some time. I read on the Estate Agent Today site that he'd bought a small two-branch operation near the New Forest. I regret that his leaving the company was so acrimonious and I hope that at some time in the future we'll be able to look back and laugh about the whole thing. It goes without saying that I wish Danny all the best in his new venture.

I'm yet to take Dougie back on as a consultant. With Danny no longer around I'm focused on the operational side of the business at the moment, but of course as soon as I need some more of his *blue-sky thinking*, as he calls it, it'll be great to get Dougie's input again. He occasionally buys me dinner and picks my brain about cricket these days: as an agent he values the perspective of an ex-pro such as myself. After the spot-fixing scandal involving Pakistan at Lord's in 2010, he came to talk to me about it so that he could ensure that none of his guys were exposed to anything like that. We both joked that Wessex players wouldn't be at any risk at all if it was all based around the overall match result – bookies and gamblers would have to believe that Wessex were more likely to win a game before they offered the team cash to lose it. I warned Dougie that numerous illegal bookmakers and shady characters involved in betting syndicates could be shadowing the Indian team around the country when they toured in 2011. He said that he'd definitely make sure that his players didn't get involved with any of them.

Dougie will sometimes moan to me that it's getting increasingly difficult to run a business in the UK: he thinks that's there's more red tape to negotiate than ever before. He says that it stifles creativity and entrepreneurialism. I'm not sure if that's true, but then I'm not the one who has endured, in Dougie's words, the *aggressive attention of the Inland Revenue* for the last few months. He's now confident that he's answered their questions satisfactorily and he can devote his energies to exciting new commercial projects.

Since I've been working on this book I've had some contact with Bethan. Mainly it's just been stuff regarding things to do with our savings accounts, paying the council tax and that sort of thing. But over time we've started swapping the odd personal message as well. I'm not sure she's ready to forgive me over the incident in Shaston yet, but she did write me a nice note recently. She was walking past our Port Bredy branch and had recognised Herb working in the office, so she mailed to say it was good that we'd taken him on. She's accepted an invitation from me to dinner. Some TV chef has opened a high-end restaurant in Emminster of all places, so I thought that I'd ask her if she wanted to try it with me. I spent a long time writing a short note: not too serious, not too casual.

When she replied later that day I could feel my heart racing and I was aware that my palms had gone all clammy. How crazy is that at my age? Her note simply said, "OK."

Wish me luck. Maybe my story isn't over just yet.

There was so much for the
traditionalist to dislike: the white ball,
the uniforms . . . the dancers . . .

14. THE HERB BRUNTON STAND

Dougie was arrested and charged with tax evasion in August 2012. He was subsequently tried at Casterbridge Crown Court in March of the following year. While I was waiting for the case to come to trial I took the opportunity to track down a copy of *One Summer on the South Coast* by Justin Bridges (Pitch Prose, 1995). I can only say that Bridges' apology might have been somewhat more meaningful if he hadn't waited seventeen years to deliver it. And that I'm disappointed that this toxic combination of character assassinations and factual inaccuracies has been festering on the shelves of libraries, and in the homes of genuine cricket fans, for all this time.

I eventually found a copy through the Oxfam online bookstore. That was no mean feat in itself: understandably, it had been out of print for some time. It goes without saying that I didn't recognise the Wessex team Bridges describes. Here he is on the bowlers that propelled him to his cherished third-place finish in the Championship.

Legend was an infuriating cricketer. While he wasn't blessed with a natural talent for the game, he was more than capable of putting in creditable performances from time to time. I had watched Legend work hard at his core skills in the early stages of his career, but since then he had taken to approaching the season in much the same way one might embark on a Club 18–30 holiday. In fact, I often wondered if he thought that his time at Wessex was simply a well-deserved break from the property renovation business he ran during the winter months. I don't know how much encouragement Legend needed to treat the season as some form of bacchanalian endurance programme, but in Andrews he had found the club rep from hell. Andrews was possibly the most naturally gifted player in the Wessex squad, but he had a boredom threshold that was positively subterranean. I always thought of him as a Puck-like character: not intrinsically malevo-lent, but more than capable of casting his mischievous spells over the other players. Beresford was his other key disciple. More of a human trebuchet than an actual bowler, Beresford's professional career surely owed more to nature's quasi-random distribution of physical attributes, rather than any strongly held ambition on his part to become a first-class cricketer. If Andrews suggested a night on Flaming Lamborghinis, then Legend would be the first to dive in and order a round, while Beresford would be the one who had to be carried out of the bar when they were finished. Legend might have achieved more in the game but for the dearth of competition for places at the club and the lack of leadership during those most crucial years of his career. One of my first tasks as captain was to try and build some sort of effective bowling unit out of these none-too-promising component parts.

When I read the book I experienced a range of emotions. At first I was baffled. Why would the captain of a team devote so much of his book to conducting a hatchet job on his former teammates? Then I felt angry. I can't say that it made comfortable reading to personally be the subject of such bitter criticism. And finally, I felt pity. I wondered what sort of lonely, insecure and two-faced individual would be reduced to writing such offensive lies about former colleagues.

It felt like a betrayal. For three years of my life he had told me every day that nobody else was strong enough, fit enough or good enough to do the job that I did day-in day-out for the team. And yet, as soon as he'd retired from the game he wrote a book that basically described me as a drunken British tourist running amok in Benidorm. But what is particularly insulting is the way that Bridges writes about players as though we were merely tools at his disposal. He uses the word *component*: it's as though he was assembling a washing machine rather than a team of individual professionals.

Despite me walking away from the game at the height of my powers to run Legend Estate Services, Bridges goes on to claim that I was about to be released by Wessex.

A combination of ambition and commercial naiveté on my part had put the club under significant financial pressure. I'd pushed Sebastian to bring in a couple of proven performers at some expense, but we still lacked the quality across the rest of the squad to consistently challenge for honours. We had a number of players at Wessex who still had at least another year on their contract, but who were no longer capable of putting in match-winning performances. Age had caught up with

Kelly, Brunton and Farrow; but in the case of Legend, I just didn't think his heart was in it any more. These were some of our bigger earners at the club, and until any of them left we couldn't bring in any new players. I tried suggesting to Legend at the end of the 1992 season that he might want to retire from the game and focus on his outside interests, but he declined to take the hint. By the time Legend did retire from the game at the end of the following season he was already out of contract. He must have realised that his time at Wessex was up because he kept putting off meeting Sebastian, who wanted to be able to explain to him face to face that the club wouldn't be offering him new terms.

As I explained in an earlier chapter, Bridges approached me at the end of the 1992 season to deliver what was, in my opinion, a very poor and confused motivational speech. I was a key member of the Wessex side, both in 1992 and 1993, so his recollections simply don't make any sense at all. By suggesting that Welland-Flanders would not have offered me a new contract for 1994 and beyond, Bridges brazenly ignores the fact that I was the club's player of the season.

He returns to the subject in a subsequent passage, in which his obvious bitterness gets the better of his grasp of the facts.

Legend's call-up to the England team must surely have been as big a surprise to Legend himself as to anyone else in the game. Even at the peak of his powers some five years earlier, a Test cap for Legend would have been unexpected. The rumour circulating around the press corps at the time was that the intention had been to call up Peter Le Grande to the squad, so that the management could take a closer look at him. Le Grande was a wrist-spinner, turning out for Oxford University. He had made a big impact in 1992 by taking a five-for in every match he'd played against county opposition. For a short while there was intense speculation that he could be England's Shane Warne. Legend, the informed gossip suggested, was simply the beneficiary of an administrative cock-up: the first ever Test player to have been selected on the basis of Chinese whispers. Whether Legend could have foreseen that he'd actually finish his career with a Test cap when he flew out to New Zealand, I can't say. He acquitted himself pretty well in the game by all accounts; blocking out an admittedly under-strength Kiwi attack for the best part of a day. Wessex seized the opportunity to capitalise on Legend's good fortune, and based a

*very successful ticket sales marketing strategy around him. Fittingly
perhaps, he finished his career as the player of the season, even if that
owed more to the members' acknowledgement of the club's precarious
financial position than to their appreciation of his somewhat lacklustre
final season on the pitch.*

Before reading *One Summer* I'd never even heard of Peter Le Grande. So I did
some research. He had indeed played a handful of games against county opposition
in 1992, and he played two further games the following season. But he didn't
add to his wicket tally. Perhaps he got the yips. But whatever happened, he never
joined a first-class county after leaving university and quite simply disappeared
from the game completely. To suggest that a rank amateur would be called up
to the England squad to bowl leg-breaks on a seaming New Zealand wicket
is quite simply preposterous. With my first-hand knowledge of the England
management set-up at the time, I'll concede that they were disorganised and
chaotic, but they were not insane. The idea that they would have considered
throwing a rookie into the cauldron of Test cricket is insulting both to myself
and to Le Grande.

At the time I didn't realise the extent of Bridges' jealousy towards me: I was
selected to play at the highest level, a distinction that Bridges himself is unable
to claim. To invent such a convoluted and unbelievable story, simply to belittle
my achievements, reflects poorly on Bridges' character, both as a former professional cricketer and as a man. I'll admit that reading *One Summer* made me
very angry for some time. But on reflection, I really just feel sorry for the author
of this spiteful sporting memoir (although I wonder if it shouldn't actually be
considered a work of fiction). I am sorry that the author didn't feel that his *own*
story would be of sufficient interest to readers, and I am particularly sorry that
he felt the need to drag others' reputations through the dirt.

****

In the 2012–13 financial year HM Revenue and Customs successfully prosecuted
over six hundred individuals. Douglas Terrence Barrett was one of them.

You may not have noticed, but over the last few years the papers have been
full of stories about plumbers who have been successfully prosecuted for tax
evasion. Most of the cases are almost identical: the plumber concerned had been
asking his clients for payment in cash, he hadn't declared the income and so he
hadn't paid the tax. Prior to Dougie's arrest I don't think that I'd really paid
attention to any of these stories. But afterwards I was seeing them everywhere.

Usually the coverage would finish with a paragraph like this:

The police are always interested in hearing from members of the public who have suspicions about people who appear to be living an expensive lifestyle with no obvious means of supporting it. Contact the police on . . . etc., etc.

Obviously Dougie wasn't a plumber, and I can't recall reading about any other music and sports agents being directly targeted, but I had to wonder if he wasn't brought to the attention of the police by a member of the public who'd read one of these stories. I remember Dougie telling me that he'd spent no more on cars and clothes than other people had spent on raising their kids. But he didn't see members of the public grassing each other up because they knew that their neighbours were sending their children to private school or taking them on nice holidays.

Shortly after his arrest Dougie asked me if I'd be willing to appear as a character witness, assuming that the case ever came to trial. Naturally I agreed, but I also suggested that he should get a couple of current players to appear alongside me. I made a call to Charles Hunter. I explained the situation and asked if he could put me in touch with a couple of the higher-profile players that Dougie represented. Charles said that he'd sound them out and get back to me. I first sensed that something was wrong when Charles called me a couple of days later, saying that none of the players thought that it was a good idea. Apparently they had been evasive when Charles asked them about it, but he couldn't be sure why.

I went from sensing that something was wrong, to knowing that something was wrong, when Legend Estate Services itself became part of the investigation. I hadn't paid Dougie for any consulting services for more than a year, so I was somewhat surprised to be asked to meet a police inspector and some people from HMRC. It turned out that they weren't just interested in Dougie's recent activity; they were looking for evidence of financial transactions going back years. We had always paid Dougie in cash. It never really bothered me; I just thought it was the way he liked to do business. Danny was always meticulous about getting a receipt from Dougie before he'd hand over any payment, so we had records dating back for a considerable period of time. Consequently, when the investigative team showed up, I became a witness for the prosecution. At that point I stopped work on the character statement I'd been preparing.

Dougie's apartment was raided right at the beginning of the investigation. It was stated in court that he had over forty thousand pounds in cash on the property, the majority of it hidden in different rooms in bundles of around five thousand each. The prosecution alleged that the money had been received from one Mr Manish Dasgupta of Wembley in northwest London. Dougie claimed that the cash was payment for several shipments of wine that had then been distributed to various independent retailers across the South East. But there was some confusion as to whether or not Mr Dasgupta had any interests in the wine wholesaling business. Regardless, it was clear to the court that Dougie had made no attempt to declare any of the cash as income. Nor had he declared any of the fees that he'd earned from Legend Estate Services over the years. And it transpired that he hadn't declared the earnings from his sports equipment wholesale business either. Up until the trial I was unaware that he was in the sports equipment wholesale business – nor that I'd featured in promotional materials down the years using various bits of LL kit.

In the raid it was discovered that Dougie's garage served as a storeroom for professional-quality cricket equipment. The inspectors found more than twenty factory-packaged Layton Landy grade-1 willow bats. Most of them were the latest 2013 models, but several dated back a few years. He even had a pristine-condition Beef-Cake which Nigel Layton, now the company's managing director, estimated would have been crafted around 1992. In total, the stock was estimated to have a current retail value of approximately seven thousand pounds.

My appearance in court was not an experience that I'd like to ever repeat. I had to give evidence against my friend of almost forty years while staring him in the face. The defence counsel then took the opportunity to imply that much of the cash *allegedly* paid by Legend Estate Services to Mr Barrett had actually ended up lining *my* pockets. I was bitterly disappointed that I had been required to appear for the prosecution, and I was incensed that, in so doing, I was forced to defend my own reputation.

Dougie stood accused of avoiding tax on several hundred thousand pounds of income, over a period stretching back more than a decade. The exact amounts, including the total sums paid by Legend Estate Services over that period, were included in the press coverage. Dougie was found guilty and handed a custodial sentence of two and a half years. Cynthia was the only person who came to the court to support him. Syd had passed away a few years earlier. Cynthia was too angry to even acknowledge me after I had taken the stand. Prior to announcing the sentence the judge made a lengthy closing speech. I can't remember exactly what he said, but it included lots of words like disingenuous, disgraced, discredited, dishonest, deceitful and disloyal. That last one struck me most: after all of those years I was left doubting the very foundations of my friendship with Dougie. Was he really *disloyal*? Hadn't he helped me earn money when I was starting out? Hadn't he helped me negotiate my contracts? Hadn't he helped me win sponsorship deals? And hadn't he helped me set myself up in business? Surely Dougie was anything but disloyal. I didn't want to think about it.

And neither did I want to believe that Dougie was guilty of tax evasion, but I had to admit that the evidence was persuasive. I also thought that his business relationship with Mr Dasgupta sounded very suspicious. As did the fact that none of Dougie's current players would stand by him. It would be all too easy to turn into a conspiracy theorist and start thinking that Dougie's relationship with an Indian businessmen and the refusal of his players to appear in court were somehow related. I'd like to think that they were not. The jury returned a unanimous verdict. I have no intention of adding my voice to the chorus of condemnation in the court itself and in the media. The majority of Dougie's assets were seized to pay back the money he owed. And on top of that he'll be marked by his conviction, and by his time inside, for the rest of his life. He was once successful, and now he is ruined. That surely is punishment enough.

****

"If you try and make me wear that, I'm bloody well going home." Herb sounded like he meant it.

We were sat in the top row of the brand new stand on the eastern side of the ground. I wanted him to try on one of the promotional helmets that they'd been giving away as people entered Canberra Park. Unlike the real thing worn by the players, they had *Wessex Smugglers* stencilled on the back.

"Look," I said. "The grille just unclips, so you can still drink your pint."

"I mean it, Peter."

It would have been fun to see Herb wearing it, but I was actually just relieved that he'd agreed to come to a T20 match at all. There was so much for the traditionalist to dislike: the white ball, the uniforms, the breakneck speed of the game, the dancers and the regular bursts of music. Personally I like the music, it's all part of the show. At Canberra Park the fielding teams run out to either Robbie Williams' "Let me entertain you", or "Ready to go" by Republica. The incoming Wessex batsmen walk out to the middle accompanied by a blast of AC/DC's "For those about to rock". In common with most other grounds, dismissed batsmen usually leave the field to the sound of "Another one bites the dust". However, the Wessex DJ sometimes swaps this for "Knocking on Heaven's Door" (always the Guns N' Roses version). And if the Smugglers hit a six, we're treated to a blast of "Rocket Man". I don't think that Herb even knows who Elton John is, let alone any of the other artists that get played at a Canberra Park T20 game. It probably all just sounds like noise to him. But it was important that he was there that night.

A few weeks earlier, shortly after Dougie's trial, I had attended a board meeting at Canberra Park. I'd read in the *Echo* that a new stand was being built in time for the beginning of the 2013 season, so I rang up Charles Hunter and suggested to him that it should be named after Herb. He said that he liked the idea, but that it wasn't a decision he could make alone. So he invited me come and to make the case. It was almost thirty years since I'd first set foot in the member's room of the pavilion. In some ways it was as though nothing had changed at all in that time; the décor must have been refreshed a few times over the years, but it still felt as though you were stepping into a Victorian gentlemen's club. It occurred to me just how much I must have changed over the years: the very idea of Sebastian Welland-Flanders allowing me to attend a board meeting would have been ludicrous.

I'd prepared myself for the meeting by putting in a call to Archie, the club's scorer, to make sure that I'd got all of my facts straight. I didn't want to make a mess of things on the night. There were three options tabled: the East Stand, the Taylor McBride Group Stand and the Herbert Brunton Stand. The member in favour of calling it the East Stand basically argued that it would be easier to find for older spectators and first-time visitors to Canberra Park. The member advocating the Taylor McBride Group Stand had to declare an interest that he did indeed also work for the accountancy firm in question, but that the revenue from his proposed five-year sponsorship deal would be substantial.

Then I stood up to speak. "Herbert Brunton made his debut for Wessex in August 1969. He played his final game for the club in July 1993. Only Bruce Forsyth has entertained more people for a longer period of time." I got the laugh I was hoping for. "In a career which spanned four decades, Herb took 847 first-class wickets for Wessex Cricket Club. Needless to say that is our club record. Herb was very unfortunate that England never recognised his talent and commitment to the game; it would be a travesty if his own club were to do the same. I believe that the new stand in Canberra Park should be named after Herbert Brunton."

We then discussed the three proposals for the best part of an hour, but I knew almost immediately after I'd finished speaking that the result was never in doubt. Canberra Park is not so large that people get lost in it very easily. And as one member pointed out, calling the new seating the East Stand only really helps if you're holding a compass or know that the main entrance to the ground is to the south. The Taylor McBride Group's sponsorship offer looked rather less generous once their various demands for complimentary hospitality services had been taken into account, so when it came to a show of hands I won a comfortable victory.

Charles Hunter then decided that the stand should be officially opened on the night of the season's first floodlit T20 match. Herb himself would no doubt have preferred it if the ceremony had taken place in front of about thirty-five people on the Tuesday morning of a Championship game. But as Hunter pointed out to Herb and me, if it wasn't for T20 then the club wouldn't have built the Herbert Brunton Stand in the first place. The ceremony itself would be very simple. Smugglin' Steve Dalton, the club's regular match-night announcer, would ask Herb a few questions in front of the new stand about his career before the game started. Then Herb would cut a huge purple sash that was wrapped around the lower tier of seats. I called Hunter back later on to make sure that Smugglin' Steve steered clear of any questions to do with T20.

I invited a number of people to join Herb and me in his stand that evening. The one person that I really wanted to be there was my new business partner. It was eighteen months since I'd arranged to meet Bethan for dinner in Emminster. It was an awkward evening. She was adamant that we weren't just going to sweep the Shaston incident under the carpet. I wasn't really sure what to say. You can only repeat the word *sorry* so many times, until it really ceases to mean anything at all. It was fortunate that the food was so good. It's actually quite difficult to get a proper row going when both of you have to keep breaking off to go, "Blimey, you have to try *this*."

The next time we met up, our conversation turned to work. I was admitting, as much to myself as to Bethan, just how difficult I was finding it to run Legend Estate Services without Danny. I didn't realise how much time would be taken up with the administration and people management. By then Bethan had already decided that she had faced her last Ofsted inspection, but she wasn't sure what to do next. As we talked, she asked me more questions about the business and made some good suggestions about how I could solve some of the more pressing issues I was facing. And after that, whenever we'd catch up, she'd ask me if we'd won the instruction on a property that I'd been talking about, or whether it looked as though an offer for a really big sale was still going through. In the end I don't quite know if it was her idea or mine, but when she left Casterbridge Secondary in the summer of 2012, she joined Legend Estate Services as my co-director.

So far it's worked out really well. Bethan is based in Budmouth and looks after all of our general management: the accounts, the financing, the marketing budget, the IT and all that sort of thing. I spend most of my time on the road. I try to get out to all of our branches at least once during the week, and I make sure I'm available to meet our vendors. It's my job to be the public face of the company. I'm not going to pretend that our life is now perfect; it's not. Bethan has moved back into Durnover Green and we take things one day at a time. We're currently trying to agree on a holiday for later in the year that is both *interesting* and *relaxing*. The best compromise I've found so far is a river cruise on the Rhine and the Moselle: every two days I'll have to get off the boat and go charging around a castle or a historic city, but in between times I'll be able to just sit by the bar and watch the scenery drift by. I'm hoping that Bethan will agree to this.

Frank and Moira joined us in the Herbert Brunton Stand that night. I've started going over to see them in Port Bredy with Bethan recently, but we haven't, as yet, discussed why I didn't come round for about eighteen months. It's as though we're all pretending that I popped out to get a carton of milk one day and it just took me a little longer than expected. On the one hand I'd like to clear the air and say that we had a few problems with our marriage and now we're trying to work them out, but on the other I'm not sure that I want to sit through another one of Frank's bollockings. Since retiring he's put much of his energy into writing comments on the *Telegraph* website. Moira says he must spend more time writing things on there than any of the journalists who are actually paid to do so. If you ever find yourself on the *Telegraph,* look out for FrankFromWessex. He describes his own commenting style as *robust and straightforward*, while Bethan says that he comes across as a *bit of a nut job.*

Mum made it down from Whetstock that night, with Mr Hendricks. They are still, according to her, just friends. Lionel had sold up the shop some ten years earlier and was enjoying retirement in a bungalow on the far side of the school playing field in Whetstock. I'm as sure as I can be that Mum lives with him there, but she still denies that there's ever been anything going on between them. I told her that I'd arrange for a taxi to take them both home to Whetstock. "Now Peter," she told me very deliberately. "Be sure to tell the driver that he's going to be dropping me off first at Oxford Cottage, and that he's then going to take Mr Hendricks on to his house in Barton Close." I'm not sure T20 was Mum's cup of tea, but Lionel certainly enjoyed it.

Herb and me weren't the only ex-professionals sitting in the Herbert Brunton Stand. I'd called Danny a couple of weeks earlier and asked him if he'd like to come along. I knew that he'd always remembered Herb fondly from his time at the club. I hadn't spoken to Danny for more than a year, so I felt a bit awkward when I rang him. It sounded as though his business was going well. We swapped notes on the differences between his new operation, Laine Hunter, and Legend Estate Services. At Laine Hunter, Danny told me, the transaction level per branch was lower, but the average sales price – because of the New Forest location – was significantly higher. "It makes for a lumpier income stream," he explained.

I brought up the subject of Dougie's trial. Danny resisted the opportunity to tell me that he'd always known that Dougie was trouble. He seemed more concerned that I might have had a tough time appearing for the prosecution. He laughed when I told him that Dougie might have been selling half of the bats that I was supposed to be getting as part of my sponsorship deal. "You could have just asked me," he said. "I always got four Double-L's a year. Of course, I used to go and see Eric Layton myself to choose them."

The evening went well. Smugglin' Steve asked Herb how many of his 847 wickets he could remember, who his first victim was, who he'd got out the most times and who was his most prized scalp. At first Herb was a bit nervous talking into the microphone, but after a few moments he got used to it, and perhaps he even enjoyed being back in the limelight after all these years. He then cut the purple ribbon and Charles Hunter announced that the Herbert Brunton Stand was open.

The Smugglers won the toss and batted. They did pretty well that night, scoring somewhere around 170. It was classic T20: there were loads of boundaries, there was lots of music to celebrate those boundaries, and there were all sorts of moves from the dancers, who spent the entire evening right in front of our stand. I don't think Frank, Moira, Mum and Lionel had seen anything like it at a cricket ground before. It was as though they were seeing colour television for the first time. During the innings break I asked Danny if he'd come to the bar with me to help carry the drinks back.

Standing in the queue, waiting to get served, I said to Danny, "Maybe I was born thirty years too soon."

"Yeah, T20 would have suited you," Danny laughed.

"So much has changed since we first played here," I replied. "It's almost unrecognisable."

We reached the front of the queue. On this side of the ground you could only get bitter or lager, so I just ordered six pints of each. I reckoned we could worry about who drank what when we got back to our seats. The catering staff set the pints in those handy cardboard handles that allow you to carry four drinks in each hand. I took two and Danny picked up the remaining one. Before we got back to the others in the stand I wanted to ask Danny something.

"After everything that's happened, are we still good? You and me?"

"We're good, Peter. We're good."

I paused. I wanted to give him a hug, but it would have been a bit of a performance to put down all the drinks first. I felt awkward for a moment.

"Really, we're good," Danny repeated, punching my shoulder with his free hand.

The PA around the ground sprang back into life. The Smugglers were on their way out onto the field to the sound of Republica's filthy guitar riff. I couldn't help but feel a little excited as Danny and me made our way back to the Herbert Brunton Stand. I was looking forward to the second innings.

My name is Peter Legend.

This was my story.